The Material Subject

The Material Subject emphasises how bodily and material cultures combine to make and transform subjects dynamically. The book is based on the French *Matière à Penser* (MaP) school of thought, which draws upon the ideas of Mauss, Schilder, Foucault and Bourdieu, among others, to enhance the anthropological study of embodiment, practices, techniques, materiality and power.

Through theoretical sophistication and empirical field research, case studies from Europe, Africa and Asia bring MaP's ideas into dialogue with other strands of material culture studies in the English-speaking world. These studies mediate different scales of engagement through a sensori-motor, affective and cognitive focus on practices of making and doing. Examples range from the precarity of professional divers in French public works to the gendered subjectivity of female carpet weavers in Morocco, from the ways Swiss watchmakers transmit craft knowledge to how Hindu devotees in India make efficacious use of altars, and from the enskilment of Paiwan indigenous people in Taiwan to the prestige of women's wild silk wrappers in Burkina Faso. The chapters are organised according to domains of practice, defined as 'matter of' work and technology, heritage, politics, religion and knowledge.

Scholars and students with an interest in material culture will gain valuable access to global research, rooted in a specific intellectual tradition.

Urmila Mohan is an anthropologist and curator of material culture and religion who researches textiles, practices and aesthetics in India and Indonesia. She is an Honorary Research Fellow in the Department of Anthropology, University College London, UK.

Laurence Douny specialises in the anthropology and history of materials, techniques and design with a focus on West African wild silks. She is a Research Associate at the cluster 'Matters of Activity. Image Space Materials' at the Humboldt University in Berlin, Germany.

'This important book brings French and Anglo anthropological traditions of studying the body in practice, material culture and subjectivity into fruitful dialogue with one another. Informed by Mauss, Foucault and seminal ideas of key *Matière à Penser* scholars, the editors and contributing authors offer fresh and inspiring perspectives on the ways that bodies and objects "move together in the material world."'

Trevor Marchand, *Emeritus Professor of Social Anthropology, SOAS*

'A landmark contribution to the cross-disciplinary study of material culture. *The Material Subject* delivers a timely and original introduction to the influential French *Matière à Penser* School for anglophone readers. Urmila Mohan and Laurence Douny have crafted an essential addition to the bookshelves of every scholar of material culture.'

Dan Hicks, *Professor of Contemporary Archaeology, University of Oxford*

'Urmila Mohan and Laurence Douny have assembled a remarkable collection of essays that present to anglophone audiences the important legacy of the work of the *Matière à Penser* group, insightfully exploring subjectivation as a material process. This impressive book promises to enrich the study of material culture in a host of fields.'

David Morgan, *Professor of Religious Studies, Duke University*

The Material Subject
Rethinking Bodies and Objects in Motion

**Edited by Urmila Mohan
and Laurence Douny**

LONDON AND NEW YORK

First published 2021
by Routledge
2 Park Square, Milton Park, Abingdon, Oxon OX14 4RN

and by Routledge
52 Vanderbilt Avenue, New York, NY 10017

Routledge is an imprint of the Taylor & Francis Group, an informa business

© 2021 selection and editorial matter, Urmila Mohan and Laurence Douny; individual chapters, the contributors

The right of Urmila Mohan and Laurence Douny to be identified as the authors of the editorial material, and of the authors for their individual chapters, has been asserted in accordance with sections 77 and 78 of the Copyright, Designs and Patents Act 1988.

All rights reserved. No part of this book may be reprinted or reproduced or utilised in any form or by any electronic, mechanical, or other means, now known or hereafter invented, including photocopying and recording, or in any information storage or retrieval system, without permission in writing from the publishers.

Cover image: Metamorphosis, 2019. Woven sculpture by Claire Le Pape.

Trademark notice: Product or corporate names may be trademarks or registered trademarks, and are used only for identification and explanation without intent to infringe.

British Library Cataloguing-in-Publication Data
A catalogue record for this book is available from the British Library

Library of Congress Cataloging-in-Publication Data
Names: Mohan, Urmila, editor. | Douny, Laurence, editor.
Title: The material subject : Rethinking Bodies and Objects in Motion / [edited by] Urmila Mohan and Laurence Douny.
Description: Abingdon, Oxon ; New York, NY : Routledge, 2021. | Includes bibliographical references and index.
Identifiers: LCCN 2020022923 (print) | LCCN 2020022924 (ebook) | ISBN 9781350077362 (hardback) | ISBN 9781003086031 (ebook)
Subjects: LCSH: Material culture--Philosophy. | Material culture--Research. | Matiere à penser (Group)
Classification: LCC GN406 .M3727 2020 (print) | LCC GN406 (ebook) | DDC 306--dc23
LC record available at https://lccn.loc.gov/2020022923
LC ebook record available at https://lccn.loc.gov/2020022924

ISBN: 978-1-350-07736-2 (hbk)
ISBN: 978-1-003-08603-1 (ebk)

Typeset in Times NR MT Pro
by KnowledgeWorks Global Ltd.

For our families

Contents

List of figures	ix
Notes on contributors	xi
Acknowledgements	xv
Foreword by Jean-Pierre Warnier	xvii

Introduction   1

1 Subjects, their bodies and their objects   3
LAURENCE DOUNY AND URMILA MOHAN

Matter of work and technology   31

2 Making do and wanting: The professional diver's predicament   33
CÉLINE ROSSELIN-BAREILLE

3 'Management' and its refuse   47
AGNÈS JEANJEAN

4 Clothing choices and questioning the incorporation of *habitus*   61
MARIE-PIERRE JULIEN

Matter of heritage   75

5 Museum objects in motion: Colonial leftovers and French cultural politics   77
MÉLANIE ROUSTAN

viii *Contents*

6 **The material shaping of women's subjectivities: Wild-silk textiles of the Marka-Dafing as a cultural heritage** 93
LAURENCE DOUNY

Matter of politics 105

7 **Politics matters: *Matière à Politique*** 107
JEAN-PIERRE WARNIER

8 **Chronicles of a moral war: Ascetic subjectivation and formation of the Javanese state** 121
ROMAIN BERTRAND

Matter of religion 135

9 **Opening and closing gestures: Weaving rituals that give and sustain life** 137
MYRIEM NAJI

10 **Devotion on the home altar as 'efficacious intimacy' in a Hindu group** 151
URMILA MOHAN

Matter of knowledge 167

11 **Anthropology of knowledge transmission beyond dichotomies: Learning and subjectivation among watchmakers in Switzerland** 169
HERVÉ MUNZ

12 **The enskilled subject: Two paths to becoming a skilled person among the Paiwan indigenous people of Taiwan** 185
GEOFFREY GOWLLAND

13 **Afterword: Matter(s) of material culture** 199
NATHAN SCHLANGER

Index 213

List of figures

1.1 Diagram of MaP's focus on the subject and subjectification process, illustrating how it draws from the ideas of Foucault, Mauss and Bourdieu, among others, as well as the specific manner in which the bodily and material are combined. 5
2.1 A suit to be patched up. Arles, France, July 2011. 36
2.2 A diver with his dish-washing gloves. Arles, France, August 2011. 38
2.3 Materials on hand (neoprene) for improvised solutions. The 'thing' with the correct dimensions to protect the barge from the metal. Arles, France, August 2011. 41
3.1 Workshop kitchen for spa technicians. South of France, 2015. 53
3.2 Workshop with tools and store of supplies. South of France, 2015. 55
3.3 Spoon and rope fashioned into an alarm for the machine that sorts bath robes. South of France, 2015. 56
4.1 Luc shows how he puts on his jeans with difficulty. Strasbourg, France, 2012. 64
4.2 Diva in New York Yankees cap (face blurred for privacy). Haut-Rhin, France, 2011. 66
5.1 African artefact and Parisian visitor at the *Musée du Quai Branly*. Paris, 2009. 81
5.2 France and New Zealand's officials and Māori representatives during the restitution ceremony of *Toi Moko*. Paris, 2012. 86
5.3 The former colonial museum during its occupation by immigrant strikers. Paris, 2011. 88
6.1 West African wild silk cocoon used in weaving Marka-Dafing women's wrappers called *tuntun*. The stripes of wild silk show as light brown. 94
6.2 Women wearing wild silk wrappers and matching headscarves while dancing in line at a Djanjoba in Safané in 2011. 100
7.1 Territorialisation through the *ngang fo* ritual drawing the limits of the kingdom. Mankon, 2009. 111
7.2 Giving out life substances. Here, raffia wine is dispensed from the royal cup. Mankon, 2009. 112

x *List of figures*

7.3 A 'bushfaller' seated on a motorbike, back to the kingdom with the resources of the global market. Mankon, 2009. 114

8.1 K.G.P.A.A. Hamengkoe Nagara I, son of Sultan of Jogjakarta Hamengkoe Boewana VIII (r. 1931–1939), 1895, dressed in batik wrapper with *parang rusak barong* motif reserved for royalty. 127

9.1 Weaver working on a *hmal* in the 'inside' of *astta*, with her little brother looking through the iron upright. Ayt Ubial village, 2002. 138

9.2 Shed/countershed with rod lifted and lowered during the making of the hood of an *akhnif* cloak. Ayt Waghrda village, 2003. 141

9.3 Weavers working on a carpet commission. Taznakht, 2005. 142

9.4 Weaver working on the latest carpet trend. Ayt Ubial village, 2011. 146

10.1 Radha-Krishna deities 'asleep' in a box next to Snehalata's altar. Mayapur, January 2013. 156

10.2 Padma's shelf converted into a bedroom for Prabhupada. Mayapur, 2012. 159

10.3 Padma making a shirt pattern for Haladini's home deity. Mayapur, 2012. 161

11.1 A junior watchmaker named Richard introduces me to the documents (functioning figures, graphics and charts, descriptions of tasks and instructions for procedures) he uses while attempting to time a mechanical watch. Geneva, 2013. 174

11.2 Trainees acquiring 'by themselves' visual expertise at the workshop of a vocational training school in the Swiss Jura region, 2012. 176

11.3 Trainees working silently at their benches at the workshop of a vocational training school in the Swiss Jura region, 2012. 179

12.1 House combining slate with brick-and-mortar wall and concrete columns. The dilapidated appearance is the result of the torrential rains that accompanied typhoon Morakot in 2009. Paridrayan, 2013. 189

12.2 Building a grave with bricks and mortar. The floor will later be partially covered with concrete. Paridrayan, 2013. 191

12.3 Slate carving near the village of Paridrayan, representing the 100-pacer snake, considered the 'friend' of the Paiwan people, 2013. 194

Notes on contributors

Romain Bertrand is a Senior Researcher at Fondation Nationale des Sciences Politiques in Paris. He earned his PhD in political science in 2000. His dissertation explored the ways members of the Javanese aristocracy entered politics in colonial Indonesia between 1880 and 1930. He has published extensively on the colonial encounter, especially in South-East Asia in an attempt at developing a symmetrical approach avoiding a Eurocentric bias. He teaches at Sciences Po Paris and has been a visiting professor in New York, Shanghai and Cornell.

Laurence Douny is a Research Fellow at The Humboldt University in Berlin, where she is working on West African silks as part of the 'weaving cluster' of the 'Matter of Activity: Image – Space – Material' program. Douny earned her PhD from University College London (2007) and has been working since 2001 on West African material cultures, more specifically on the anthropology and history of weaving techniques, materials and design. She is the author of *Living in a Landscape of Scarcity: Materiality and Cosmology in West Africa* (2014) and currently working on her book *Elusive Materials: The Hidden Silk Road of West Africa*.

Geoffrey Gowlland is an Honorary Research Fellow at the Museum of Cultural History, University of Oslo. His current research addresses indigenous people, activism, cultural revitalisation and material culture practices in Taiwan. In previous research, he has explored the meanings of craft production in China's turn to capitalism and global discourses on heritage, and practice-based learning and work ethics among Taiwanese ceramics producers. His monograph *Reinventing Craft in China: The Contemporary Politics of Yixing Zisha Ceramics* was published by Sean Kingston in 2017.

Agnès Jeanjean is Professor of Anthropology, Université Côte d'Azur, Laboratoire d'anthropologie et de psychologie cognitives et sociales. After several years of research on dirty works, sewer workers and urban waste disposal, she proposed an anthropology of societies by their remains. Through contemporary transformations of waste treatment,

xii *Notes on contributors*

she studies the effects of new management on knowledge, subjectification and transmission. Publications online: 'Peindre la voix, écrire le déchet', *Techniques & Culture*, 65–66 (2016); with S. Le Lay and O. Roueff, 'Où va homo detritus', *Mouvements*, 87 (2016); 'Le Management du résidu', *Ethnologie Française*, 153 (2015).

Marie-Pierre Julien is a Lecturer of Anthropology and Sociology, University of Lorraine, Nancy, as well as a founding member of the MaP group. Her research concerns the anthropology of material culture, bodies, age and food practices. Along with Céline Rosselin, she coauthored *La Culture Matérielle* (La Découverte, 2005) and coedited *Le Sujet Contre les Objets ... Tout Contre* (CTHS, 2009). Regarding food practices, she coedited with Nicoletta Diasio, *Anthropology of Family Food Practices, Constraints, Adjustments and Innovations* (Peter Lang, 2018). About bodies, she coedited with Ingrid Voléry, *From Measuring Rods to DNA Sequencing: Assessing the Human* (2020, Palgrave-Springer).

Urmila Mohan is an Honorary Research Fellow at the Department of Anthropology, University College London (UCL) where she earned her doctorate in 2015. She has also taught courses on anthropology and history as an adjunct faculty at New York University. Mohan is the founder of *The Jugaad Project* (thejugaadproject.pub), a working group and publication that supports innovation and diversity in material culture and religion studies. She has a background in art and design and researches textiles, practices and aesthetics in India and Indonesia. Her publications include: *Clothing as Devotion in Contemporary Hinduism* (2019); *Fabricating Power with Balinese Textiles* (2018); and coedited with Jean-Pierre Warnier, a special issue on religious subjectivation (*Journal of Material Culture*, 2017).

Hervé Munz is a Lecturer in Anthropology, Department of Geography and Environment, Geneva School of Social Sciences, as well as Scientific Coordinator, University of Geneva, of a project on politics of scale and intangible cultural heritage. His PhD in anthropology, University of Neuchâtel (2015), dealt with the transmission of know-how and heritage-making in the Swiss watch industry. His postdoctoral fellowship (2016) with the Swiss National Science Foundation covered the transfer of technical knowledge on Swiss watch servicing in Greater China. He authored *La Transmission en Jeu: Apprendre, Pratiquer, Patrimonialiser L'horlogerie en Suisse* (2016) and coauthored *Politiques de la Tradition. Le Patrimoine Culturel Immatériel* (2018).

Myriem Naji is an Honorary Research Fellow, University College London (UCL), where she earned her PhD in anthropology (2008). In 2011, she curated an exhibition at the Brunei Gallery, London, on Amazigh weavers. She has also researched organic agriculture in the South of France, publishing 'Creativity and Tradition: Keeping Craft Alive

Among Moroccan Carpet Weavers and French Organic Farmers', in the edited volume *Critical Craft: Technology, Globalization, and Capitalism* (2016). Her articles have been published in *Textile: The Journal of Cloth and Culture* (2019), *Anthropology & Education Quarterly* (2012) and *Journal of Material Culture* (2009).

Céline Rosselin-Bareille is Senior Lecturer, University of Orléans, and researcher at the Centre d'Etudes des Techniques, des Connaissances et des Pratiques, Paris. As MaP's founding member, she focuses on material culture and the consequences of object incorporation on the construction of subjects and power relations in work situations. Part of a multidisciplinary dialogue involving bio-psycho-social dimensions, she has published on sensorial experiences, incorporation and expertise. With Marie-Pierre Julien, she coauthored *La Culture Matérielle* (2005) and coedited *Les Sujets Contre les Objets… Tout Contre* (2009). She edited *Matières à Former in Socio-anthropologie* (2017), an issue dedicated to the meeting of subject and object in materialities.

Mélanie Roustan is an anthropologist at the National Museum of Natural History in Paris. As a Lecturer, she teaches in the Museum's Masters in Museology. She researches material culture, heritage and territories in the PALOC laboratory. She currently studies the uses of indigeneity in museums and zoological gardens as places of encounter between natural and cultural heritages. She authored *Sous l'emprise des objets? Culture matérielle et autonomie* (2007), coauthored *Voyage au Musée du quai Branly* (2012) with Octave Debary and coedited *La recherche dans les institutions patrimoniales. Sources matérielles et ressources numériques* (2016), with Anne Monjaret.

Nathan Schlanger is Professor of Archaeology at the Ecole Nationale des Chartes in Paris. He has worked at the Institut National d'histoire de l'art, the Ecole du Louvre and the Institut National de Recherches Archéologiques Preventives. Besides an interest in archaeological heritage management at an international scale, his research focusses on the history of archaeology and anthropology in European and colonial settings, and on technology and material culture studies. Recent publications include *European Archaeology Abroad* (ed. 2013), *Marcel Mauss. Techniques, Technology and Civilisation* (2006 and 2012) and *André Leroi-Gourhan on Technology. Material Civilization, Operational Behavior and the Evolution of Technicity* (2021).

Jean-Pierre Warnier is Honorary Professor/Research Fellow at Centre d'Etudes Africaines, Paris. After earning his PhD in Anthropology (1975, University of Pennsylvania) he taught anthropology in Nigeria, Cameroon, and, since 1985, at University Paris-Descartes. He has researched the economic and political history of the Cameroon Grassfields and studied bodily and material cultures as technologies of

xiv *Notes on contributors*

kingship and power. His publications include *The Pot-King. The Body and Technologies of Power* (2007); 'Technology as Efficacious Action on Objects... and Subjects', *Journal of Material Culture* (2009); and with Urmila Mohan, 'Marching the Devotional Subject: The Bodily-and-Material Cultures of Religion', *Journal of Material Culture* (2017).

Acknowledgements

I am greatly honoured to have the opportunity to edit this book with my colleague Dr. Laurence Douny, and, thereby, share the accomplishments of *Matière à Penser* (MaP) with a wider audience. Indeed, the scholarship in this volume reflects many years of hard work, and sustained thought and discussion by MaP's core members and global associates. I am most grateful for the collaboration of Dr. Marie-Pierre Julien, Dr. Céline Rosselin-Bareille, Prof. Agnès Jeanjean, Asst. Prof. Mélanie Roustan, Dr. Geoffrey Gowlland, Dr. Hervé Munz, Dr. Myriem Naji and Dr. Romain Bertrand. A special thanks to Prof. Nathan Schlanger for authoring an insightful Afterword for this volume, as well as for his support of this project.

My deepest gratitude to Professor Jean-Pierre Warnier, a most generous teacher and mentor. With decades of distinguished research and service to the profession, Prof. Warnier is a model for the way he has been able to combine rigorous scholarship and teaching with collegiality. To describe the impetus behind this book, I must also acknowledge the start of my association with Prof. Warnier (via a reference from Dr. Douny), and a May 2014 symposium, *The Bodily AND Material Cultures of Religious Subjectivation,* at the Department of Anthropology, University College London (UCL). This event was a platform to explore a *Matière à Religion* approach and was funded by UCL Anthropology and the *Journal of Material Culture*. It was organised by UCL Anthropology with the Interdisciplinary Research Group (GDRI) 'Anthropology and Art History' at the Musée du Quai Branly. I am most grateful to Professor Susanne Küchler, Professor in the Department of Anthropology, and former Head of Department (2010-2019), UCL, and keynote speaker, Professor David Morgan, Professor of Religious Studies and Professor of Art, Art History and Visual Studies, Duke University, for their support, as well as the enthusiastic participants who greatly enriched this event with their presentations and discussion. More recently, thanks to Dr. Marie-Pierre Julien and Dr. Céline Rosselin-Bareille, I participated in the 2017 international seminar, *Corps et Culture Matérielle* at MSH Paris Nord, and was able to meet and interact with MaP's other members and associates.

The scope of this book was greatly enriched by the discerning comments of anonymous reviewers. A special debt is owed to current and former xvi *Acknowledgements*

members of Bloomsbury's publication team who helped make this book a reality, especially the Commissioning Editors, Miriam Cantwell and Lucy Carroll, and Editorial Assistant, Lily McMahon. Subsequently, this publication was acquired by Routledge where I would like to thank Katherine Ong, Editor, Anthropology; Megan Hiatt, Senior Production Editor; and Kangan Gupta, Editorial Assistant. At KnowledgeWorks Global Ltd., Rajiv Kumar was the Project Manager who efficiently supervised the production process. Our manuscript also greatly benefitted from the efforts of Joanne Slike, copyeditor, and Anand Shekhar, indexer.

Last but not least, a special thanks to Claire Le Pape, textile artist, for the striking image of her artwork on this volume's cover. I sincerely hope that the ideas in this book and its spirit of collaboration will inspire readers to further explore the 'material subject' in their own work.

Urmila Mohan
Honorary Research Fellow,
Department of Anthropology, University College London

Foreword

Laurence Douny and Urmila Mohan are uniquely qualified as academic brokers to bridge the gap between several scholarly traditions in continental Europe and the anglophone world. Their background, publications and commitments give them first-hand access to anthropological studies in technology, material culture and bodily techniques that have developed in various quarters, in a dialectic way, or more or less independently from each other, as is sometimes the case in global academia.

In this edited volume, they seek to bring to an anglophone readership interested in those topics an intellectual tradition that has developed mostly – but not only – in France since the late 1980s, around a group of scholars who gathered together under the banner of *Matière à Penser* (for 'food, or matter, for thought'). Since I belonged to that group right from the start, I have the privilege to provide a Foreword in which I will sketch the issues that prompted its development.

In 1985, I was recruited as a Professor of anthropology at Université Paris-Descartes. Ten years previously, as I was doing research in Cameroon, I met with Michael Rowlands of UCL, and we joined hands to work together in the same places, with the same people, on the same topics that ranged from the evolution of social systems to the workings of regional hierarchies, trade and material culture. This encounter had its own logics since the two of us had been working on those topics from quite different angles and in different intellectual settings, though, having done my PhD at the University of Pennsylvania under the direction of Igor Kopytoff, I was already acquainted with some of the themes developed subsequently. Mike Rowlands opened up entirely new avenues ahead of me, especially regarding material culture studies in which UCL had become quite prominent.

To make a long story short, when I began teaching in Paris, I introduced material culture studies in the curriculum. I presented the students with a broad spectrum of authors, from Fernand Braudel on the 'material civilisation' of capitalism, to Roland Barthes and Jean Baudrillard on the semiotics of consumption and to the scholars at UCL. Looking back at those years, I can see how unsophisticated my teaching was. Yet, it was new, and it attracted the interest of some students and colleagues, I think mostly

xviii *Foreword*

because I gave them access to a number of anthropological and sociological issues that had been left fallow in France for quite some time and that called for investigation, particularly during the annual internship of field research training for third- and fourth-year students. The topics ranged from thrift markets to local culinary traditions, hunting, rubbish disposal, the lace industry in Calais, the recycling of second-hand consumer goods at Emmaüs, etc. As far as I am concerned, around 1988–1990, I had started working in earnest on the bodily techniques of Cameroonian kings as containers of ancestral substances, and on the material culture they used in that context.

A handful of colleagues, PhD candidates and students felt the need to meet and discuss those issues together. Two of them – Marie-Pierre Julien and Céline Rosselin – soon named the group *Matière à Penser*, quite explicitly focused on material culture and at the same time calling for more thought and for more theoretical sophistication. As we came together, it became clear that the conceptual tools we used were inadequate as regards the topics we were trying to analyse. Recycling (F. Hoarau), inhabiting one room, a frequent occurrence in Paris, especially with students (C. Rosselin), the sewage system in the town of Montpellier (A. Jeanjean), producing Chinese furniture in Paris (M.-P. Julien), a Cameroonian kingdom (J.-P. Warnier) to name but a few of those topics. Each of us brought to the floor whatever theory, notion or monograph could help with our common research. Years later, it is no longer easy to date, let alone give credit to this or that contribution or to such and such member of the group. In our limitless ambition to produce a new grand paradigm in anthropology, we even contemplated dissolving the identity of each of us into a single label, just as the group of mathematicians who collectively publish their contributions under the blanket signature of 'Bourbaki'.

Two things became clear in the early 1990s: the first one was that we were wavering between two anthropological objects: material things, and the body. We failed to establish any clear conceptual connection between the two, except through the kind of cultural technology first developed by M. Mauss and A. Leroi-Gourhan. But few of our objects could be considered as belonging with technology. The second was that previous approaches, such as semiotics, failed to take into account the dynamics of bodies and objects so prominent in the work of Leroi-Gourhan around the technical gesture. Calling on the dynamic sociology of G. Balandier and the Manchester School, Céline Rosselin was the first to open up this perspective focused on dynamics, mobility, motions and motricity – how bodies and things are on the move.

In subsequent years, we read and discussed extensively M. Merleau-Ponty, P. Schilder, P. Bourdieu, various authors in the neurocognitive sciences, Leroi-Gourhan, etc. We collaborated with Pierre Parlebas, a colleague at Paris-Descartes, who introduced us to his praxeologic approach first

Foreword xix

developed by Espinas. We invited the psychoanalyst S. Tisseron who was working on bodily conducts that combined with the sensorium, emotions and motor habits, in the symbolisation process relating to the material environment. It would be far too long to give a complete list of the authors we read and discussed. It is in that context that we read once more the famous article published by Marcel Mauss in 1936 on the techniques of the body. This text is emblematic of the main theoretical issues we were facing at the time. Mauss separates material culture from the bodily techniques and discards the former because, he says, it is a mistake to consider that there are techniques only when material tools are involved. This is not so, because, says Mauss, the body is the tool of all tools, and should be considered first and foremost on its own rights. In that text, Mauss keeps the body and material culture separate, without conceptualising any possible connection between the two.

This seemed to be the case almost all around the academic landscape. The body had its journals *(Body & Society, Quel Corps?)*, specialists, teaching programs, textbooks. The same situation is obtained with material culture and its journals *(Journal of Material Culture, Techniques & Culture)*, specialists, teaching programs and textbooks. In France, around 1970, the body raised more and more interest in philosophy and the social sciences, with a gradual and steady increase in the number of publications. In the 1990s, Dominique Memmi and Florence Bellivier devoted a seminar to the epistemology of the body and the history of its study that resulted in the publication of an edited volume, *La Tentation du Corps* in the social sciences.[1] On the side of material culture, what was readily available in France was the anthropological study of techniques by the *Techniques & Culture* research unit and journal. But it was only concerned with efficacious action to transform matter, not human beings. It had, from its inception, a Marxian agenda.

Our main theoretical challenge was to conceptualise the way bodily techniques and material culture are on the move together, with what implications and what results. I am sitting at my desk. I am writing with a pen in hand on a sheet of paper that is lying in front of me. Once in a while, I put down my pen and reach for my mug of tea. My sensorium, my bodily techniques of writing while sitting form one and the same system – on the move – with the table, chair, paper, pen, cup of tea, but also the desk lamp, the radiator without which it would be freezing cold in my study. How can we articulate together such a material culture and the body geared to it, a bodily-and-material-culture as it were, into a single theoretical perspective? In the sewage system of Montpellier, the Cameroonian sacred kingship, the recycling practice at Emmaüs, bodily and material culture on the move belong together in a systemic manner. If the 'MaP' group made any specific contribution, it is on that very point – a point that is still far from being generally accepted in 2020 in the social sciences, when scholars keep studying xx *Foreword*

the body as if it were in a material vacuum and material culture as if it were not manipulated, incorporated and disincorporated at a turn by embodied subjects.

The result of our intellectual venture is clearly explained by Laurence Douny and Urmila Mohan who have access not only to the contributions by the MaP group but – what is most important in the case of academic brokers, to the readership for which their book is designed. Let me just mention a last piece of information: we had criticised Marcel Mauss for failing to provide a conceptual status to material culture, though he mentions its presence at every twist and turn of his article (spades, slipper, musical instruments and marching, etc.) Yet, the same Mauss provides a conceptual tool to bring back together bodily techniques and material culture – that is, the very awkward and strange notion of a 'total man', a 'bio-psycho-social' synthesis including the body ('bio'), the cognitive and emotional component ('psycho') and the social one ('socio'), since all bodily techniques differ from society to society. We have had to translate this jargon into something more accessible to contemporary scholars. This is where the 'subject' and Michel Foucault come in handy as a means to conceptualise what takes place in a sewage system, an African kingdom, an organisation such as Emmaüs, and so on in which 'total men' alias 'subjects' are subjected and subjectified by the bodily techniques, their cognitive and emotional capabilities, and the social dimension of bodily-and-material-cultures. Consequently, *'Matière à Penser'*, for 'food for conceptualisation', provides a paradigm that can be transposed as matter for religion, politics, warfare, training, sports, and so on.

There has been a brisk turnover in the research group, especially since some of its members were students who scattered upon graduation. There was never any orthodoxy. It was informal and open. Each participant developed particular lines of thought according to his/her own interests. We discussed the sociology of innovation and the ANT of B. Latour, the various implementations of the phenomenological tradition from Husserl to Merleau-Ponty and to contemporary attempts at a phenomenological anthropology by Csordas, Tilley and others, the many different ways Foucault can been read, the historical and comparative political sociology as developed by Jean-François Bayart, etc.

Around 2005, the group dispersed for good. Later on, it turned into a lively international network, especially thanks to Urmila Mohan. Yet, we are still far away from what we had meant to achieve, that is, a merging of studies in material culture and bodily conducts because this is what we can see in the real life of human beings. Let us hope that this book will contribute by putting this question squarely to its audience, and bridging various national academic traditions in Europe and the anglophone world. Laurence Douny and Urmila Mohan have achieved a brilliant and consistent presentation of this intellectual venture, for which they must be heartfully thanked.

Jean-Pierre Warnier
Honorary Professor, Centre d'Etudes Africaines, Paris

Note

1. D. Memmi, D. Guillo and O. Martin (eds.) (2009), *La tentation du corps: Corporéité et sciences sociales.* Paris: Ed. de l'EHESS.

Introduction

1 Subjects, their bodies and their objects

Laurence Douny and Urmila Mohan

The material subject: a *Matière à Penser* approach

Since the mid-1990s, the study of Material Culture has witnessed an increasing interest worldwide in social sciences and beyond. In France, distinctive trends in material culture studies have emerged since the early twentieth century[1] with approaches oscillating between an attention to consumption or production (Naji and Douny 2009), including the domain of gift and exchange founded by Mauss (2007[1925]). Production[2] appears to be more prominent from the 1950s onward with the work of archaeologist André Leroi-Gourhan (1943, 1964–1965) on the role of gestures and tools as efficacious actions upon matter[3] in the development of the human mind. Influenced by Mauss' foundational essay, *Techniques of the Body* (1936), in France, Leroi-Gourhan launched the consolidation of studies of cultural technology or techniques, developed further in the 1970s. Simultaneously, sociologists such as Pierre Bourdieu (1979) and Jean Baudrillard (1968, 1996) were influenced by Marxism and paved the way for a study of consumption as a principle of distinction of social class and as a social critique of modern society, respectively. Scholars, such as Michel de Certeau (1980), saw consumption as the production of meanings through creative practice where users culturally appropriated and 'misappropriated' objects *(détournement des objets)*. This body of work inspired studies in the 1990s on everyday life and the home, with a focus on objects of daily use and through them issues of class, kinship, gender relations and intimacy, and the theme burgeoned (Chevalier 1992, Kaufmann 1992, Segalen and Le Wita eds. 1993, Semprini 1995, Faure-Rouesnel 2001: 245).

Against this backdrop, in the 1990s, the research group known as *Matière à Penser* (MaP)[4] or 'thinking through material culture' (with the double meaning 'food for thought') was formed in Paris by a group of anthropologists including Marie-Pierre Julien, Céline Rosselin-Bareille, Agnès Jeanjean and Jean-Pierre Warnier.[5] This informal research group has developed different approaches to the study of the subject around Mauss' core paradigm of 'techniques of the body' (1936), adding material culture to this paradigm as an essential component of bodily conducts. This group

4   *Laurence Douny and Urmila Mohan*

is perhaps less well-known outside French-speaking countries both for the fact that most of its original publications were in French as well as because MaP is not a formal group or a laboratory depending on an institution of higher learning or research as is the usual practice in France. There are no formal criteria of belonging, no registration processes and no institutional boundaries, and MaP is therefore a decentralised group with people engaging with its ideas in different ways. Despite the various publications released by MaP associates,[6] there is much more to be done in bringing the group's contribution to material culture studies into dialog with other strands of material culture studies in the English-speaking world (Buchli 2004, Tilley et al. 2006, Hicks 2010). This edited volume is a significant step in that direction while emphasising the group's focus on studying people as *subjects*, constituted through their bodies' incorporation and disincorporation of 'object dynamics'. As a 'subject', the human body is the object of a person's actions as well as an entity subjected to the actions of a network of other subjects. Through the present volume, we hope to contribute to a global discussion on the socio-anthropology of the body *and* of the subject, and, by framing MaP's work as a 'multimodality' and 'cloud of ideas', to open dialogues on these themes.

MaP's study program as 'multimodality'

Dynamics of casual discussions, the testing of ideas in the field and the subsequent picking up, discarding or merging of ideas in a search for coherence are integral to the development of MaP's ideas as a decentralised study program. MaP's anthropology is strongly grounded in fieldwork but is also an open network research program, employing a range of methods, systems of thoughts and approaches from the domains of social, historical and cognitive sciences. As such, this is probably best defined as multimodality, a term pointing both to the form and method by which something exists, is perceived and is experienced. Approaches from related domains take on different modes and thereby theoretical configurations over time as they are gathered around discussions of the body/subject in relation to materiality. By extension, in this volume, the term multimodality also invokes how French theories have been used and developed by MaP over time. In this book, MaP uses theoretical and analytical concepts developed in a specific milieu by considering the history of ideas that precedes them. Therefore, the ideas presented here are framed as concepts that we try to some extent to embed in the history of the people who produced them, including the relationships between people, elements of their biographies and the events of that time and space that influenced scholars (see, for instance, the work of Nathan Schlanger [2006, 2012] on Marcel Mauss).

Grounded in social sciences, MaP's material culture study program situates itself within the French tradition of material culture studies alongside the cultural technology movement. Myriem Naji and Laurence Douny have

Subjects, their bodies and objects 5

followed the particular program that allies MaP's approach to the 'technology of the subject' with cultural technology and therefore sees 'making' as a production system alongside 'doing' or the usages (and consumption) within the same material paradigm (Naji and Douny 2009). MaP shares with anglophone studies of material culture[7] a common interest in consumption themes (Warnier and Rosselin 1996), but also in concepts of materials and materiality (Rosselin-Bareille 2017). MaP's approach is probably best defined in terms of opening a dialogue between multiple schools of thoughts and domains of research to (1) cross-culturally address the question of the subject's formation in societies and (2) maintain a focus on the subject's relationships to the material world.

MaP's approach seeks interdisciplinary debates, aiming at theorising a science of material and motor cultures that are *specifically grounded in the subject*, rather than in the object as anglophone and cultural technologists suggest.[8] Within this framework, MaP defines the subject in its relation to objects via bodily conducts, including movements, gestures, senses and affects, that is, 'the subject, his/her body and their objects in action' (Warnier 2009a: 151). In other words, the subject does not only *have* a body but he/she *is* a body (ibid, 151), that is, a thinking, perceiving, feeling and moving body that constitutes itself through its relation to the dynamics of materiality, including objects, materials and substances. Finally, the subject makes himself/herself through a process of subjectification or subject-fashioning (also known as *subjectivation* in French)[9] resulting from accumulative micro-processes of 'incorporation' and 'disincorporation' of object and material dynamics (see Figure 1.1). Thus, this volume mediates

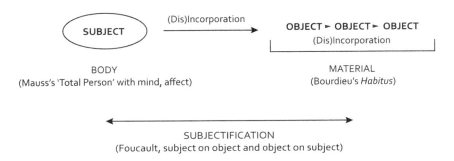

Figure 1.1 Diagram of MaP's focus on the subject and subjectification process, illustrating how it draws from the ideas of Foucault, Mauss and Bourdieu, among others, as well as the specific manner in which the bodily and material are combined.

Illustration by the authors.

6 Laurence Douny and Urmila Mohan

different scales of engagement through its focus on practices and connects the study of physical properties, both humans and objects, and gestures to larger questions of how people as subjects are connected with their environment, as well as each other through actions. Terms such as subjectification, objectification and incorporation are central to this discussion, and will be explained in greater detail later.

The history of ideas in social sciences including French theory has inspired the development of a MaP theory of what has on occasion been termed the 'bodily-and-material', bringing together influential contributions stemming from psychoanalysis [Schilder (1935), Lacan (1986) and Anzieu (1985)], philosophy and sociology [Foucault (1988) and Bourdieu (1977)], alongside sociology of sport and psychomotricity (Parlebas 1999), cultural technology or techniques [Leroi-Gourhan (1964-1965) and Sigaut (2003)] and anthropology [Mauss (1936, 1939)] to name but a few influences. MaP has also long benefited from international sources on the subject, its bodies and their relationship to objects such as Bateson (1936, 1972), Bateson and Mead (1942), Gell (1998), Miller (1998), Appadurai (1986), Löfgren (1996), Rowlands (2002), Bayart (2007) and Argenti (2007). In this respect, it is important to note that MaP brings new perspectives about subjects and their bodies into anthropological theory by bringing a level of methodological and analytical focus on subjects' culturally specific relations to objects and materials. That is, how subjects are fashioned via these interactions, and how these relationships are shaped by the domains of power and governance, gender, kinship, religion, craft and work as demonstrated by the authors in this volume. Over time, MaP has advocated for a greater consideration of the material dimensions of the social world in the study of cultures and of their subjects at large and, therefore, for a better integration of such an approach towards materiality within the social and political sciences. This stance was also taken by Faure-Rouesnel (2001: 245), who concluded her review article on French material culture with the need for a better inclusion of material culture studies within social anthropology both through theorising objects as well as through empirical field research – a program that we emphasise repeatedly in this volume.

To put it succinctly, 'the material subject', as we term it, describes cross-cultural processes of subject-making through the bodily-and-material. This book offers a collection of chapters that highlight MaP's concepts, but also challenge their scope by introducing new perspectives on the material fashioning of subjectivities that emerge from specific ethnographic contexts. Thus, this book sets up new ground for further debates across disciplinary domains on the question of the subject as constituted in its relations to other subjects or groups, and mediated through materiality. From a pedagogical perspective, this volume aims at connecting different spheres of knowledge, approaches and methods through a combination of: (1) contextualising theoretical concepts in French such as *'faire corps avec l'objet', 'mise-en-objet'* and *'incorporation',* as well as those that already exist in English such as 'subjectification' and 'objectification' (2) Gathering and analysing nuances from a diversity of case studies from various areas of the world to better theorise subjects as the intersection of the bodily-and-material within social anthropology.

Bodies and objects on the move: embodiment as (dis)incorporation

In the 1980s, the body became a central issue in the social sciences and anthropology in Europe and beyond. Material culture also became a topic of some relevance that was given increased attention a decade later in the United Kingdom at University College London in particular through the works of scholars such as Michael Rowlands, Susanne Küchler, Christopher Tilley, Christopher Pinney, Nicholas Saunders and Daniel Miller, as well as in North America (examples include Pocius ed. 1991, Schlereth 1992, Lubar and Kingery 1997).[10]

However, topics of the body and material culture were kept separate and, according to MaP, still remained as such in the social sciences. In the mid-1990s, based on the 'dynamic sociology' of Georges Balandier (1963) and influenced by the Manchester school, Céline Rosselin-Bareille of the MaP group proposed the dynamics of the bodily-and-material system as to how they are on the move (Warnier 2012: 7). As Warnier explains, 'motricity was the key issue and we needed to improve on the tool kit needed to study the way human bodies move together with objects in a material world' (ibid.). Thus, the fundamental issue raised by MaP from that time onward was *how* bodies and objects move together, one with the other, against or together and very close to each other (Julien and Rosselin eds. 2009). MaP's joint analysis of material culture and body dynamics, movements and motricity further developed when they started to work with Tisseron (1999) on his 'sensori-affective-motor conducts' (*conduites sensori-affectivo-motrices* or SAM), critically examined Mauss 'techniques of the body' (1936) and also focused on Parlebas' (1999) praxeology that seemed quite relevant as regards motricity and movement. Maussian techniques of the body became crucial with its notion of *l'homme total* that could bring together the body on the move and material culture on the move all together with the body of the 'total man' or 'whole person'. The group later replaced the expression with the concept of the 'subject', a decision that, as we shall explain later, was more in tune with contemporary thought and opened the door to new theoretical developments in the domain of politics (*Matière à Politique*, e.g., Bayart and Warnier 2004).

MaP locates its approach to material culture in the body *vis-à-vis* its relation to objects, and in particular in the dynamic of 'embodiment'. The term embodiment is widely used in anglophone scholarship (Csordas 1990; Stoller and Olkes 1989; Lock 1993; Marchand 2003, 2012; Geurts 2003; Mascia-Lees ed. 2011; Okely 2007) and can be glossed as anything with a body. However, MaP brings a heightened level of theoretical and methodological clarity to this study by focusing on the bodily-and-material simultaneously, and therefore interrogating processes of (dis)incorporation or (de)coupling (in French *couplage/découplage*) between objects and subjects. In the human species, there is hardly any technique of the body that takes place in a material vacuum (Warnier 2007: 11–12) or without some kind of 'propping'. By propping, we refer to the fact that practically all our sensori-motor conducts are geared to particular objects. Moreover, as Paul Schilder (1935) underscored in his seminal work on the image of the body, the bodily schema does not stop at the limits of the human coetaneous envelope. It extends beyond it and includes the objects at hand. A greater emphasis is placed by MaP on embodiment as the ability for subjects to incorporate objects and their dynamics in their bodily schemas. In other words, the incorporation or coupling of objects and their dynamics into the subject occurs when both interact, for instance, through use of an artefact, and disincorporation or 'decoupling' takes place when the usage or interaction stops. Through perception, motion and emotions they become an integral part of bodily synthesis and, therefore, of the subject.

Since people interact with a myriad of objects in their everyday life, it is important to look at how people practice embodiment through means (tactics and techniques) of (dis)incorporation, something Bourdieu (1977) defines as *habitus* through his study of material habituations and dispositions that are continuous and subconscious in a person's life. Through a fine description and analysis of actions, gestures, perceptions, affects and movements, researchers may study a sequence of actions in a daily routine, over a life-time and in various situations (at work, at school, while using a computer or playing football, etc.). Similarly, analysing Mauss' (1936) observation of the *kabyle* slipper-wearer, Warnier concludes that the slippers did not come off the man's feet since they were incorporated into his body schema through *habitus* (Julien and Rosselin eds. 2009: 96).

Through their 'coupling' and 'decoupling' relationship to objects, subjects come to identify themselves with these objects through a process of ongoing incorporation of object dynamics or *mise-en-objet*, what we could define as material habitus. The latter is best explained as a process close to that of objectification as put forth by Daniel Miller (1987) in his account on Hegel, dialectics and material culture. MaP proposes the idea of *mise-en-objet* as 'putting something into an object or preparing', a total process through which the subject and the object are constructed together and for each other. For instance, Schilder (1935: 203) proposes that the blind person feels the obstacles at the tip of the cane and not in his/her hand, which means that the bodily schema has extended all the way to the tip of the cane. This example was also put into good use by Merleau-Ponty (1945: 167; 1964: 178) and Bateson (1972: 318). Similarly, a soldier identifies himself with his weapon (Julien and Rosselin eds. 2009: 103) to become a new kind of entity, that is, a 'man-with-weapon' as historian Audoin-Rouzeau (2009) states by bringing together the body of the fighter, and the materiality of warfare and weaponry (see, for instance, Warnier 2011).

This emphasis on incorporated bodies can take us into the study of new areas, such as 'post-human bodies' (Haraway 1991), 'body hacking' (Duarte 2014) and the use of prostheses and enhancements (Hogle 2005), and what happens, for instance, when technologies become too invasive and intrude onto the body and the mind to control them. There is one kind of prosthetic that aims at replacing/enhancing a missing body part or function, for example, a conventional hearing aid that works as a medical device to compensate for hearing loss due to birth defects, disease or old age. There are also prosthetics, such as body sensors of various kinds, that are purposefully inserted or altered by wearers to extend their sensory capacities. Examples include RFID sensors inserted under the skin to be wirelessly accessed by a smartphone (Barfield 2015: 169). But at another level, technology and material culture are fully incorporated to control the body and, therefore, are more than just interfaces that extend people's abilities to interact with the world. Just where this line is between extending or heightening the body's capacities and controlling the body to the detriment of the 'human' is unclear. For example, in the case of an Amazon warehouse worker, productivity may be enhanced by hand prostheses, such as wristbands, that not only track the worker's movements but also correct his/her gestures for efficiency by using vibrations to nudge them in different directions (Solon 2018). Another example is how texting changes our hands and fingers morphology and how these new bodies affect subjects. At its extreme, such enhancement of productivity results in the dehumanisation of workers and invokes the issue of hegemonic power as one that is also integral to MaP's more recent concerns.[11]

The subject and its body: material culture turned inside-out

As we have briefly summarised, MaP's interest lies in the role that material culture, and thus materiality, plays not only in the constitution of the body but also of the subject. How important is a bodily experience of things to the making of a subject? That is the question that the MaP network has explored since the mid-1990s. However, it is really over the last decade that the group has refined its theoretical positioning by considering the subject and his/her body as two programs that run together (see Julien and Rosselin eds. 2009 and Galliot 2015, Gowlland, 2011, Naji and Douny 2009) by drawing on the heritage of Schilder (1935) on the *Körperschema*, Merleau-Ponty (1945) on the phenomenology of perception, the cognitive neurosciences and the Foucauldian philosophy of the subject.

Subjects are considered as those human entities which are the object of their own actions as well as being the result of (or subjected to) a network of other subjects acting on them. Thus, subjecthood is the result of a process by an individual as well as a group entangled with material culture. In a MaP approach, the definition of a subject encompasses several theoretical

10 *Laurence Douny and Urmila Mohan*

perspectives including Michel Foucault's idea of the subject which rejects the Cartesian *cogito* as the ontological substance of the subject and refuses to consider that the subject has any substance at all. He underscores the fact that the subject is an *event* (Foucault 1966: 356). It may happen or not. It is never where one thinks it is. It may disappear and come again. In other words, it is elusive and therefore quite difficult to grasp, says Foucault, because it is always engaged in actions by other subjects or by the self.

This notion is close to what Lacan called a subjective division which operates at a very different level from the notion of the 'self' as developed by US scholars (e.g., Hartmann, Kris and Loewenstein 1964). With his notion of the subject, Lacan rejected the Cartesian approach to the subject as that which is the result of consciousness and thought and replaced it with that of the genesis of the subject: What is it that constitutes a subject who can relate to others, to oneself and have an organised psychic life? It is an event that takes place in the early life of the subject when it begins to distinguish between self and image of the self, or, in Freudian terms, between conscious thought and the unconscious as repressed. The Lacanian subject is in a relation of alterity towards itself as well as being in an intimate and entangled relation with objects that fully integrates the dimension of praxis and the subject's relationships to the material world (Julien and Rosselin eds. 2009: 149, Warnier 2009b). Thus, the notion of the subject is a more inclusive one since it encompasses the dimensions of the body's biology, anatomy, mind and material (Warnier 2009a: 152). By contrast, according to MaP, the notion of the 'individual' or the 'person' (as a single human being) tends to erase fundamental characteristics of a human, marginalising the body that is perceiving and feeling, with a subconsciousness, etc. By following a MaP's definition of the subject, the authors in our volume critique the notion of the self-managing individual with disembodied thought and rationalised choice as put forth by several Western scholars (for instance, Coleman 1986, Schumpeter (1983 [1954] and Simmel (1987 [1900]).

Objects, materials and substances in MaP are considered as agentive 'interfaces' between subjects, groups and other objects. But this notion of agency differs from the notion of object agency as put forth by Alfred Gell (1998) and Bruno Latour's concept of non-humans (2005), where also objects can be considered as actors in their own right.[12] Gell's views are in consonance with MaP but the difference is that according to them the Gellian notion of 'agency' lacked flesh since it did not pay much attention to bodily techniques and sensori-motor conducts. As such, what is missing in both the Gellian and Latourian view is the subject and the body, that is, the 'total man' as envisioned by Mauss.

MaP takes very seriously the various intellectual traditions and the concepts and theories they have elaborated, without erasing their edges. Part of this is noting the incompatibilities between various notions of, for example, materiality (*pace* Ingold *vs.* Tilley), the subject (*pace* Foucault *vs.* Sartre or Descartes), the actor (*pace* Lemonnier *vs.* Latour) and objectification (*pace*

Miller *vs.* Baudrillard). Each of these concepts can be traced to different, often contrasting, intellectual traditions. MaP does not want to collapse them into the topos of the subject/object divide that everyone wants to avoid. MaP's theoretical option is deliberately Foucauldian and grounded in the key notion of a subject with its various dimensions that need careful and accurate elaboration (*dispositif*,[13] the body, governmentality, etc.). Simultaneously, the notion of the embodied subject is a holistic entity because it considers the body with its sensorium, mind, drives and pains that are engaged in relationships with others (Mauss 1936, Bourdieu 1977, Foucault 2001, Latour 1992, Warnier 1999, 2011).

As an example of different intellectual traditions, consider the candidacy of the 'subject' as an alternative to the concept of the actor. According to MaP, the actor in Bruno Latour's 'Actor Network Theory' is one where the idea of a body and notions of embodiment are not essential (Mohan and Warnier 2017: 376). To further clarify this comment, Jean-Pierre Warnier explains[14] that Latour aptly constructed the subject in his earlier research in the sociology of innovation in Research and Development units, in which he needed this key concept to introduce, not only a symmetrical analytical *beginning* in his investigations,[15] but to establish (in his view) the fact that the non-human actor has an agency of its own, distinct from that of the human one within a 'collective'. This meaning is conveyed in Latour's famous quote: 'You are different with a gun in your hand; the gun is different with you holding it. You are another subject because you hold the gun; the gun is another object because it has entered into a relationship with you' (Latour 1999: 179). Here, Latour underscores the fact that the gun is another object in your hands from what it is in the armory. By being in someone's hands, the gun has acquired an agency of its own. The MaP approach states that it is exactly the same gun in both cases and that it does not exercise any agency of its own. MaP clearly differentiates the Latourian notion of the human actor from the Foucauldian subject as MaP claims that the notion of a non-human actor is central in the thought of Latour. Instead, MaP wants to use the Foucauldian subject as a key concept to its approach by claiming that there is no such thing as a 'non-human subject'. Consequently, MaP does not have the same notion of the material object incorporated and disincorporated by the subject. Thus, MaP suggests that attention should be paid to the Foucauldian subject as distinct from the Latourian actor, the individual of most of the sociological tradition, the person of Mauss or the self of the psychological tradition.

Following this, persons, individuals or agents are subjects constituted by objects and other subjects (Julien and Rosselin eds. 2009) and material culture is turned *inside out* by a combination of object and subject dynamics (Rosselin-Bareille 2017). For instance, Warnier (2007) in his book, *The Pot-King*, shows how things are brought inside and outside the subject and body via his concept of 'containers' and 'envelopes'. This movement of substances from inside the body to outside and vice versa with a focus on the subject

12 *Laurence Douny and Urmila Mohan*

is what we phrase as material culture turned inside out. While processes of objectification and subjectification coexist, in the MaP approach, the focus is on the dynamic of subjectification whereby the object is brought into the subject's dynamic by a process of incorporation.

Subjectification processes: the fleshiness of empowerment and embodied governmentalities

Foucault's work from the history of sexuality (1975) to his later works on the hermeneutics of the subject examines the many ways by which subjects takes themselves as the objects of their own actions, shape their identity and implement techniques of the self.[16] MaP proposes subjectivation as a fleshy, visceral process by which the subject is the focus of his/her own actions and governs itself, and by which others act on the subject at the very point where the subject governs itself through its relation to the object world, that is, through continuous actions of incorporation and disincorporation. Such a process does not imply that the subject becomes 'complete' or 'new' but that he/she is constituted over time through the vector of material and bodily habituations (Julien and Rosselin eds. 2009: 104). Therefore, 'subjectification' (or subjectivation for Foucault) raises questions about power and more precisely about empowerment, that is the process by which subjects not only gain power as agency but overall how subjects embody power in their bodies and thereby in their very matter. Foucault's *'technologie du sujet'* or *'technologie du soi'* is therefore central to the group's theoretical positioning on the subject's identification, shaping of one's identity and action and in particular in their examination of 'power' or 'empowerment' as a material process engaged in bodily praxis or actions mediated by objects. As Foucault (1975) suggests, penitentiary, medical but also educational institutions are material structures of power, exemplified in some cases by panopticons.[17] The latter are architectural structures of control developed by Jeremy Bentham in the eighteenth century by which subjects are continuously observed by keepers standing from a single vantage point, located at the centre of the structure. In such institutions, subjectivities that are systematically controlled become normalised or institutionalised as subjects that are obedient. Yet, the power of materialities in shaping subjectivities also transcends what we are conscious of in everyday life (see Rosselin-Bareille and Julien, in Chapters 2 and 4).

The notion of governmentality was proposed by Foucault as 'the art of government' that concerns subjects and institutions using techniques of power and thus, of social control through the development of material means including prisons and schools as we have touched upon. In addition, Foucault keeps noticing how governmentalities achieve results that were not intended or conscious. Therefore, he provides a detailed account of what is intended in, say, the Panopticon or the pastoral power of the Church, and then tries to unfold all the non-intended effects of what it achieves and the

Subjects, their bodies and objects 13

historical transformations of the governmentalities to which such techniques belong. Similarly, in his ethnography of governmentalities in the Cameroon Grassfields, Warnier (2007) explains that objects and the sensori-motor conducts associated with these materialities played a compelling role in the king's mediation of power in his chiefdoms. For instance, they ensure the king's reproduction of power and of lineage while maintaining his control over his community. In Warnier's analysis, the king as a container of ancestral substances disseminates them to his subjects through praxis, such as spraying raffia wine mixed with his saliva onto his subjects that amounts to a micro-technology of power incorporating the subjects into the single body politic of the kingdom – a non-verbal, bodily conduct that does not express in so many words what it achieves but still does it efficiently. Thus, the workings of power in the Grassfields and their actions as a 'governmentality of containers' reveal themselves through material practices instead of speech. The Foucaldian concept of governmentality or sovereignty is elaborated in the work of Warnier as a governmentality of containers in relation to motor conducts and the habituation of performance through specific and powerful gestures, resulting in not only making a political statement, but acting upon subjects. The power of the king is even more *compelling*, as Warnier notes, since the king's speech is markedly different in its egalitarianism from the realities of a kingdom, where all resources are controlled by the ruler. The difference between the registers of knowledge involved in such compulsion will be discussed in greater detail in the next section.

Finally, MaP's 'technology of the subject' based on Foucault's 'technology of the self' also meets and engages with Maussian 'techniques of the body'. In fact, techniques or technologies of the subject are mediated by the incorporation and disincorporation of material culture dynamics in the subject's body while in movement. This can happen, for instance, through using objects (Warnier 2009a: 148, Nourrit and Rosselin-Bareille 2017), and, by extension, by making or producing them (Naji and Douny 2009) and thereby, through the subject's identification with materiality. The relation between matters/materials and the body as embedded in multiple processes of learning within/without institutionalised contexts is explored in Céline Rosselin-Bareille (2017), a collection of ethnographies that investigates how the body is used or how techniques of the body are altered in the process of *making*. This also includes insights from Ingold (2013), where making is seen as a process of incorporation of materialities into the body and through a reciprocal shaping of the subjects, their bodies and matter.

The praxic value of objects: motor conducts and techniques of the body

In their critique of social sciences, MaP underlines not only the lack of consideration about the role that objects play in the making of subjects and societies,[18] but also the absence of praxis (implying reflexivity, reciprocity and participation) in a world made of subjects and objects. Central to MaP's approach to bodily motor conducts is Marcel Mauss' (1936) techniques of the body. His famous essay focuses on the ways people use their body rather than objects and tools, the latter being forms of material culture that could be considered as 'instrumental techniques' or *techniques à instruments* (see, for instance, Bartholeyns and Joulian eds. 2014). These techniques imply the body as the source are traditionally transmitted, and vary across time, space and cultures (Warnier 1999: 22). Paradoxically, although it systematically occurs throughout his text, Mauss misses out the idea of objects as a mediation of bodily techniques, and it is upon this idea that Jean-Pierre Warnier (1999: 24) and MaP based an anthropology of material culture.

Mauss' (1979: 101–102) concept of a 'Whole Person' (*l'homme total* or total man) encompasses the three aspects of the bio-psycho-social, that is, biological or the anatomo-physiological dimension of the body, the psychological or the emotional-cognitive dimension and social or, as Mauss says, techniques of the body. (The latter differ from society to society and thus constitute a phenomenon that is socially constructed.) The three are articulated together by the notion of 'cogwheels' in a relation of causality. In a similar way, Warnier (2001: 18) proposes the articulation of actual bodily conducts and representations in relation to materiality – an articulation that the subject operates through a material culture of bodily habits that include bodily and instrumental techniques.

Objects can be used for a myriad of purposes and so they have affordances (Gibson 1979, Ingold 2010, Norman 2013). However, the latter are context-specific and primarily ascribed to specific motor cultures *(culture motrice)*. In other words, people construct the material world based on their sensori-affective and motor conducts *(les conduites motrices)*. For example, a bucket can be used as a seat but is initially made to contain and transport things or matter in its liquid or solid form. Thus, the real or initial function of a bucket, that is, as an object to be carried by hand or on top of the head is defined as the praxic value *(la valeur praxique)* of the container and this marks the ways by which the subject and object become entangled, and what they do with the object (Warnier 2009a: 158). For instance, as African women demonstrate, carrying a bucket of water on the head is an action that is accomplished within an object-subject relation. On the one hand, the object has to be perfectly positioned to a part of the body to prevent it from falling off the head and, on the other hand, the body necessitates a specific posture and walking pace to carry the bucket of water without spilling it – a skill that is learned through practice. Further, the praxic value of objects can be articulated with its sign value *(la valeur signe)* within a system of communication and representation, such as a bucket of sodas cooling down in ice connotes summer time and outdoor parties, but one should not be mistaken for the other. To clarify, in a system of agency, the 'praxic value' refers to practice or actions and thus to bodily conducts as opposed to the 'sign value' in a coded system of connotations, representations and communication. MaP attempts to answer the question: How do you analyse and theorise the real bodily and material cultures instead of their representations? In this context, the term 'Magritte effect' (Warnier 2007: 6–13, 2019) refers to the confusion between a thing and its representation wherein scholars need to be more circumspect regarding the cognitive gap (theirs as well as others), between the praxeological 'things' of a tradition and representations of those things. Thus, there are two kinds of values that must be considered here. Sign or representational value and praxeological (bodily-and-material) value. Scholars, such as David Morgan (2018) and Chris Pinney (2004), have indeed proposed useful ways of studying the embodied agency of images but more work is needed along these lines.

We had previously discussed how the power of a Cameroonian king is rendered compelling since the king's speech is markedly different in its egalitarianism from the realities of a kingdom where all resources are controlled by him. The difference between the registers of knowledge involved in such exercise of power invokes yet another aspect of MaP's tool kit – the difference between verbalised and procedural knowledge. MaP calls on the cognitive neurosciences to establish a distinction between knowing *that*, and knowing *how* (Kosslyn and Koenig 1995). The first type of knowledge (verbalised) concerns verbal expressions, discourse and ideas that can only be expressed in so many words. The second type, procedural knowledge, is always the result of an apprenticeship, whether to a person or process, often a protracted one, as in the use of a musical instrument. These observations are particularly relevant to studies of domains, such as religion, where 'to locate the study of religion exclusively in … the accordance between scripture and performance is to misunderstand the compelling potency of religious compliance' (Mohan and Warnier 2017: 372). Attention must be paid to 'tensions, deviations and potential contradictions between verbalised knowledge, on the one hand, and, on the other hand, embodied, procedural knowledge embedded in the material world' (ibid). Practices are not just orthopraxy, but 'something slippery, uncertain and inconsistent that requires constant social and cultural work on bodies-and-materials' (ibid; also see Mohan 2019).

The distinction between verbalised and procedural knowledge is by no means a theoretical innovation. Head and Holmes (1911–1912), Schilder (1935) and many others had established this point in the early twentieth century. Gregory Bateson (1972: 179–181) put these two forms of knowledge at the heart of his theory of cognitive gaps, double binds and schismogenesis, following his analysis of the Naven ritual (1936, revisited in the 'Epilogue 1958') and his study of mother-child interactions conducted in Bali together with Margaret Mead (Bateson and Mead 1942). For Bateson, the fact that two or more subjects could interact through two different media, that is, speech and bodily conducts and material culture, provided the potential for gaps and contradictions between verbalised and procedural knowledge, and pointed to the compelling nature of such relationships. More recent and spectacular developments in the cognitive neurosciences have validated this conceptual distinction (Berthoz 2000, Berthoz and Petit 2006) by

16   *Laurence Douny and Urmila Mohan*

demonstrating that verbalised and procedural knowledge do not rest on the same neuro-physiological processes although there is a fair amount of connection between the two. Yet, procedural knowledge is far more involved with the sensorium and with bodily and material culture. The two kinds of human capabilities – verbalised and procedural – do not simply duplicate the Cartesian divide between body and mind. Verbalised knowledge depends on the brain no less than the action of driving a car or singing religious songs in a church. Both are equally human. Often, they are implemented simultaneously. Yet, all too often, scholars rely solely on verbalised descriptions to have access to the bodily-and-material cultures of the subject when forms of direct participant observation and documentary media (photography, video) are needed to record actions and emotions.

The corporeal turn (Sheets-Johnstone 2009) that emerged in the late 1980s and 1990s was characterised by the embodiment paradigm (Csordas 1990, Le Breton 1990) and phenomenology in anthropology, for instance, Desjarlais and Throop (2011), a review of the approach in anthropology. The inclusion of phenomenology in anthropology had an impact on the development of Material Culture Studies in the anglophone world, for instance, Tilley's famous *A Phenomenology of Landscape* (1994), where the multisensorial dimensions of the materiality of the landscape are explored as a process of being-in-the-world and of objectification. In MaP's view, these trends have predominantly focused on individual's or researcher's verbal expression by providing descriptions of their experiences of the lived world and seem to miss out the neuro-physiological or cognitive aspects of subjects' bodily experience of the world (Berthoz 1997, Petit 1997, Gallagher 2005) that empirically acknowledge the functioning of the senses as well. For instance, by breaking away from Western dichotomy between the mind and the body, Kathryn Geurts uncovers Anlo-Ewe of Ghana's theoretical and sensory model that encompasses the dimensions of bodily feeling, balance and intuition in relation to the material world (Geurts 2003, Geurts and Adikah 2006). By drawing on Csordas' embodiment paradigm and following Johnson's (1987) idea of 'the body as the ground for cognitive culture' (Geurts 2003: 73), Geurts proposes an Anlo-Ewe approach to bodily and sensory experience of the world that also describes inner states that she explains in terms of 'kinesthesia'. At the turn of the twentieth century, Edmund Husserl, the founder of phenomenology, proposed that kinesthesia accounts for the subject's perceptual experiences as situated in the lived body. Perception is not a passive phenomenon, but the result of tension between the subject and the outside world. Thus, kinesthesia as a merging of the senses that are culturally and politically constructed across time occurs in the moving and perceiving body that makes sense of the 'lived world' (Classen and Howes 2014).

Within a MaP approach, the praxic and procedural value of materiality enables us to understand subjectivities as a configuration of subjects and collectivities, and their identification with materiality as a transformative process implying a mutual shaping of subject-object. For instance, the lacquering of French furniture by Chinese immigrants living in France since the 1970s is described by Julien and Rosselin (2003) as the articulation between Chinese tradition and French modernity. Traditional Chinese motifs painted on wood are covered by chemical varnish applied in layers and by using lacquering techniques invented in France. The process is a means by which Chinese craftsmen adapt to the French furniture market and come to identify with French culture. (Other examples could include playing a musical instrument or walking with high-heeled shoes.) Within this perspective, the subject's engagement with its material environment, the appropriation of objects and the resulting transformations are central to the subject's but also the group's constitution. These three points – interaction, appropriation and (transformation as) shaping of subject – are 'factors of identity in the same way as a religious or a social affiliation' (Julien and Warnier eds. 1999: 11).

Praxeology as a 'cloud' of intersecting ideas

While body dynamics encompassing sensori-affective and motor habits can be verbalised, they may also often remain unspoken from the moment the subject has fully incorporated an object's dynamic through practice (Warnier 2009a, 2009b). This may result in automatic daily actions which take place spontaneously and bypass conscious thinking, and are also often impossible to explain. Using the *chaîne opératoire* as a method of observation, collection and analysis of field data allows us to study the sequences of gestures and actions upon matter and apply a cultural technology perspective to archaeology and anthropology (Douny 2014).[19] Also see, for instance, the works of Ludovic Coupaye (2009, 2013) in which this approach helps him uncover implicit meanings associated with bodily practices (Lemonnier 1992, 2012).

Central to MaP's approach is praxeology as a science of actions or motricity that derives from Paul Schilder's work (1935) and his interpretation of Alfred Espinas (1897). It is also largely inspired by Parlebas' lexicon (1981) in motor praxeology that he developed in the context of sport sciences and games, and that provides over 100 concepts and definitions of motor conducts. Motor actions *(action motrice)* as motor logics or 'ethnomotricity' help us to critically investigate the relationships between, on the one hand, propositional or descriptive knowledge expressed through language and, on the other hand, procedural knowledge revealed through the body's relations to materiality. The latter derives from a hands-on approach to materiality produced by doing actions such as lacquering wood (Julien and Rosselin 2003), making pottery (Gowlland 2017), or diving (Rosellin 2015). In other words, praxeology links the practical knowledge of a community, that is, knowing *how* to do something, with the analyses of socio-cultural concepts and values attached to actions (knowing *what* to do and *why* to

18 *Laurence Douny and Urmila Mohan*

do it). According to Warnier, 'materiality in its relation to subjects' motor conducts, is a subjectification matrix' that enables one 'to think through one's fingers, in action' (Warnier 1999: 16–17 citing Mauss 1974 [1939]: 162 after Maurice Halbwachs). It is worth reiterating that Warnier distinguishes praxeology and 'praxic value' as practice, that is, actions and bodily conducts in a system of agency from 'sign value' that exists within a coded system of connotations and communication.

In this MaP volume, praxeology or bodily practice is examined as such or as combined with other approaches,[20] such as embodied cognition as a 'matter of knowledge' (see Munz and Gowlland), and applied to domains as a 'matter of religion' (see Mohan and Naji), 'matter of politics' (see Warnier and Bertrand), 'matter of heritage' (see Roustan and Douny) and 'matter of work and technology' (see Rosselin-Bareille, Jeanjean and Julien). Drawn from different domains of knowledge, the chapters in this volume use MaP as a flexible cloud of multimodality and connectivity bringing together such different analytical contributions as the Maussian approach to the techniques of the body (1936), the praxeology of Parlebas (1981), various inputs from the cognitive sciences such as distributed cognition (Hutchins 1995, Petit 1997, Gallagher 2005), the study of movement (Berthoz 2000), theory of agency (Gell 1998), developments in phenomenology (Berthoz and Petit 2006), Foucault on the subject, power and body (1975), etc. Further, even while grounded in French studies of Material Culture, this volume includes different research traditions, Mauss 1936, Bourdieu 1977, Gell 1998 (also see Pinney and Thomas 2001, Chua and Elliott 2013, Küchler and Carroll 2021) and Bateson 1972, and schools of thought. We hope that the need for more studies of the 'material subject' will engender new collaborations.

This volume shows the international dimensions of MaP's approach with ideas and contributions from different domains of expertise and knowledge, such as religion, politics, technology, work, etc., disciplines including museology and heritage studies, sociology, anthropology, archaeology and art history, and geographical regions from Europe, Africa and Asia. However, our contributors also share something important that should be emphasised again: bodily techniques should not be considered apart from material culture. This is the crucial point that MaP has been insisting on right from the start. We should also note that although the dimensions of a body/mind/object perspective may be explored analytically and theoretically, in anthropological texts, a combination of the three rarely occurs from a practical point of view. That is, anthropologists in the field rarely conduct their research using specific methods such as kinesthetic/cognitive survey/object analysis for each of the three aspects of body/mind/objects. Thus, the strength of MaP as an anthropological approach to the study of subjects, societies and cultures is its holistic dimension in lines with the Maussian project of the 'total man' or 'whole person'. In keeping with this proposition, the various inter-disciplinary chapters in this volume offer empirical studies grounded in participant observation and reflexivity, and also develop theoretical positioning as a divergence of choices and perspectives on the shaping of subjectivities through bodily-and-material conducts. The collections of chapters in this volume thus bring together contributions that either contrast through their respective approaches to MaP or bring new dimensions to it.

The material subject: opening dialogues with MaP

MaP provides plenty of 'food for thought' by offering many concepts, approaches and themes applicable to the domains of religion, politics, economics, art, kinship, etc. MaP's key idea is the inclusion of materiality in the study of human phenomena and the integral role of material culture in constituting subjects through bodily interactions and material interfaces. This also includes the technologies by which people engage with the world via their body dynamics, including their senses, movements, gestures and emotions. These dynamics occur in many contexts such as professional work, museums and collections; craft production; religious ceremonies; entertainment and leisure; food consumption and gardening; politics and waging war. Accordingly, the chapters in this volume show the implementation of MaP approaches to the material subject with theories and concepts grounded in detailed ethnographies and empirical materials collected in various cultural areas. MaP prepares the ground for an ethnography of objectification *(mise en objet)*, but focuses on an anthropology of subjectification/subjectivation and governmentalities via material culture. Therefore, MaP sees fieldwork as the driving force from which researchers develop conceptual tools to analyse given field situations in the manner of a Foucauldian archaeology of knowledge (1966).

The upcoming chapters provide an overview of how subject-object relationships in the contemporary material world may be explored in specific cultural contexts and geographical areas such as Europe, South and East Asia, and North and Sub-Saharan Africa. They situate themselves methodologically either within or beyond praxeology to explore the construction of the subject through a bodily approach to the material world. The chapters are informally grouped by themes, such as work and technology, heritage, politics, religion and knowledge, but this ordering acts more as a suggestion – both of MaP's reach as well as its ability to cross-fertilise domains through ideas and relationships. In the Afterword, Nathan Schlanger draws on the chapters of this volume to propose a general overview on the notion of material culture, its historical sources and implications.

Céline Rosselin-Bareille shows that French professional divers, employed in public works and who belong to a specific work organisation, harness particular material substances and objects that construct them as precarious workers. While using an approach that concentrates on the divers' processes of incorporation of material culture through their sensori-motor and emotional conducts, Rosselin-Bareille proposes that through their

20 Laurence Douny and Urmila Mohan

progressive integration into networks of actions on other subjects' actions, these workers subjectify themselves.

Agnès Jeanjean examines residual practices and waste objects from which health and hospital workers in France elaborate meaning, and transmit and express values and knowledge based on a tangible, socialised relationship. By paying attention to the transformations of these practices, she questions what 'management' does to technique. Jeanjean opens her ethnography to a broader reflection on contemporary organisations by following the trail of the discarded and lost, and by focusing on irregularity and singularity in the form of the subject and desire.

In her study of clothing of children aged 9–13 years old in Eastern France, Marie-Pierre Julien employs a Foucauldian approach to the study of clothing choices and habits that she describes as a process of subjectivation, which emphasises concepts of knowledge, power and governmentality. While clothes and clothing techniques are means by which the process of 'growing up' is experienced, performed and asserted by these children, Julien also shows the many power issues that underlie forms of know-how that are required and embedded in this process, and the networks of actions upon actions of which they are a part.

Mélanie Roustan's chapter offers some methodological and theoretical reflections on French museums in postcolonial contexts at the turn of the millennium. She proposes that museum objects are shaped *through* and *by* the actions on them, such as collecting and conserving, and that their cultural and heritage value and significance is a result of these actions. By a process of subjectivation, actions transform not only museum objects and environments, but also those who engage with them, ranging from curators to visitors, thereby establishing their role in the domain of heritage. Roustan analyses these actions in terms of a power chain that articulates the struggle of minorities for their political rights, but also reproduces the symbolic domination of a cultural elite on a society.

In her ethnography of Marka-Dafing women's production and wearing of wild silk wrappers in Western Burkina Faso, Laurence Douny proposes an analysis of the subjectivation process by which these women harness the power of the wild silk as means to 'shine in society', a process by which this prestige-conferring material has become over time a form of heritage and identity. She suggests that subjectivation as a process of incorporation of wild silk's material properties and qualities is also a technique by which women acquire charisma. Hence, in a Marka-Dafing conception, charisma as an aura or body envelope stems from the sheen of the silk called *daoula* that enables women to not only make themselves visible in public and private settings but also to attract the benevolence of the invisible world.

From a more theoretical perspective, Jean-Pierre Warnier develops the Foucauldian critique of functionalist political theory by drawing upon *The Pot-King. The Body and Technologies of Power*, a monograph of a Cameroon kingdom at the end of the twentieth century. In his view, political analysis

Subjects, their bodies and objects 21

often fails to take into account the dynamics of the bodily and material cultures as technologies of power, that is to say the subject who *has* a body and *is* a body, who takes himself/herself as the object of his/her own action, is subjected to the action of others and combines autonomy with a good deal of heteronomy. He elaborates such concepts in light of territorialisation of space (for instance, through the making of various kinds of 'containers') and by providing a historical overview that exemplifies how such processes are enacted over time via dynamics of change and continuity.

Romain Bertrand's chapter develops the importance of ethnography in historical research. It exposes the *privileges of subjectivation*, used in the Foucauldian sense of the term as 'practices of self on self', in colonial situations in Java in which the hierarchies of daily life gave or denied privileges to certain social groups. By focusing on the various registers and practices of subjectivation of Javanese nobility *(priyayi)* – asceticism as well as abundance – Bertrand demonstrates how colonised elite subjects in Indonesia used processes of state formation to pursue their own growth and ascendency. Bertrand adopts an ecological approach to show how *priyayi's* access to a range of goods, as well as repertoires of postures, at a particular moment and place, helped them legitimately objectify themselves.

Myriem Naji explores the materiality of weaving as subjectified by female carpet weavers of the Sirwa region in southern Morocco. Naji combines a praxeological approach with Gibson's theory of affordance to investigate how female conceptions of the body, sexuality and the occult are deeply interwoven in the making of these textiles. Naji's use of the concept of affordance takes into consideration the potentiality of objects in human action. She describes materiality as dynamic and active, that is, as acted upon by human gestures, as well as emphasising the reciprocal action of materiality on the subject. For Naji, the agency that weavers attribute to the loom and its materiality is thus inherently connected with the gestures and movements that weavers perform upon woollen materials.

Urmila Mohan offers a 'material religion' approach to Hindu devotional practice in the context of the universalising 'International Society for Krishna Consciousness' (ISKCON) at the Chandrodaya temple in Mayapur in West Bengal, India. She explores how devotees, in specific, non-Indian foreigners, are made as particular Hindu subjects, that is, as 'Krishna Conscious' entities through the sect's practice of devotional love *(bhakti)* and service *(sewa)* in the hope of salvation. By combining Mauss' techniques of the body and Gell's agency, she considers deity care as subjectifying practices with tangible, material efficacy for the practitioner as believer. Devotion is produced through the 'efficacious intimacy' of home worship, a bodily-and-material relationship between householders, gurus, the community and a sentient deity.

Hervé Munz's chapter provides a study of Swiss watchmaking framed within an anthropology of knowledge and techniques that places an emphasis on the importance of the relationships between the body and artefacts

22 *Laurence Douny and Urmila Mohan*

in human interactions in the processual dimension of knowledge. Munz examines how craft knowledge is learned and therefore passed on, in the apprenticeship and daily activities of multiple practitioners in training and industrial organisations. He exposes craft learning and practice in the light of concepts of corporeality and materiality that help him to provide a better understanding of the notion of 'transmission', that is, what is effectively a knowledge *in the making*, and by breaking away from oppositions between academic and vocational knowledge.

In the final chapter of this volume, Geoffrey Gowlland considers two paths to becoming a skilled person, *Pulima* and *Shifu*, among the Paiwan indigenous people of Taiwan. He examines how these paths are enmeshed with building practices and ways of being indigenous in a settler society. Gowlland suggests that becoming skilled for people called *pulima* (meaning 'having many hands' and whose gift emanates from the power of ancestors) and the *shifu* workers (whose name means 'to possess specialised skills' in relation to a specific trade) is closely intertwined in makers' subjectivities both in terms of experience, but also as subjects in relations of power. *Pulima* and *shifu* are enskilled through engagements with materials and procedures, whilst becoming particular subjects within the community, and in relation to the Taiwanese state and market forces.

Notes

1. For a more detailed view of trends in France (including museology, cultural patrimony, etc.) see Faure-Rousnell (2001) in English, and Diasio (2009) and Julien and Rosselin (2005) in French.
2. Over time, the study of production was coordinated by an interdisciplinary research group founded by Robert Creswell in 1982 and developed around the peer-reviewed journal *Techniques & Culture*. The group is dedicated to the study of cultural technologies and has notably included François Sigaut, Jean-Luc Jamard, Madeleine Akrich, Pierre Lemonnier, Olivier Gosselain and Frédéric Joulian as past and current members.
3. This principle is based on Mauss' famous formula of techniques as 'traditional efficacious action' upon something (2013: 371–372); also see Sigault on Mauss' formula (2003).
4. The decision to use MaP as an abbreviation, instead of MàP, speaks to the meaningful use of this term in English as a form of 'mapping'.
5. The history of this group is described in the Foreword of this book by Jean-Pierre Warnier. We reference his work in the Introduction repeatedly both because he was a core member of MaP as well as somebody whose work is more accessible to anglophones.
6. The associates include Marie-Pierre Julien, Céline Rosselin-Bareille, Agnès Jeanjean, Jean-Pierre Warnier, Myriem Naji, Joël Candau, Frédérique Menant, Jean-Luc Jamard, Francois Hoarau, Nicolas Auray, Mélanie Roustan, Frédérique Lecoeur, Pierre Parlebas, Richard Pottier, Tim Putnam, Valérie Swales, Jean Ferreux and Julie Poirée.
7. For instance, see Warnier (2009b).

Subjects, their bodies and objects   23

8. Ibid.
9. While the terms subjectification and subjectivation are used interchangeably in the following chapters, we favour the term subjectification in the Introduction.
10. In this context, we note that material culture studies in the United States have a different history from that of the United Kingdom with various shifting paradigms (Fowles 2016, Martin and Garrison 1997, Whalen 2001–2002). We hope that this book will generate dialogue that leads to these different histories being compared and related across the anglophone world.
11. These themes feature among the research interests of the group developed in the colloquium 'Matières à Savoir-Faire. Propriété, Circulation et Formation des Savoir-faire', 14–15 December 2018, Paris 1 Sorbonne, and in Arnaud Dubois and Céline Rosselin-Bareille's forthcoming publication in *Ethnologie Française* titled *'Gestes (dé)possédés'*.
12. See Gowlland's succinct summary (2011: 210–211) of the manner in which MaP critiques three approaches in material culture: as a sign to be decoded, things as agents on par with human agents, and the concept of 'material culture studies' initiated by Daniel Miller.
13. *Dispositif* is the term used by Foucault for the various institutional, physical and administrative mechanisms and knowledge structures which enhance and maintain the exercise of power within the social body.
14. Personal communication with Jean-Pierre Warnier, 24 August 2018.
15. Ibid. Warnier points out that Latour himself has not elaborated on the notion of the subject as it is not part of his theoretical tool kit except in the blanket expression that denies the subject/object divide.
16. 'Technologies of the self' and 'technologies of the subject' are both used by Foucault in French as *'techniques de soi'* and *'technologies du sujet'*. Since the publication of his seminar in California on 'Technologies of the Self' (1988), Foucault's work has often been read through the lens of the psychology of the self which may result in a deep misunderstanding since technologies of the self may be misunderstood as the 'Californian cult of the self'. In fact, 'Cult of the Self' was the title of three lectures Foucault delivered at Berkeley in 1983.
17. A study of Foucault's examination of the role that material structures or a certain material culture plays in the process that he describes as subjectivation has not yet been explored by the group.
18. Exceptions to these include works by Anglo-American sociologists/psychologists on material culture (e.g., Csikszentmihalyi and Rochberg-Halton 1981, Hindmarsh and Heath 2003, Molotch 2003, Shove 2003, Dant 2005). See also Dant (1999) for a critique of sociology that fails to notice the role of objects in the social world.
19. *Chaîne opératoire* consists of a sequence of operations that describes step-by-step an action or activity that involves the production and usage of things within a particular socio-cultural context. This field method of data collection and analysis is used by both anthropologists and archaeologists.
20. In Douny's (2014) work on container forms and containment practice, body movements, gestures and actions upon matter are analysed within a praxeological and phenomenological perspective that also include elements borrowed from a linguistic approach. Semi-structured interviews and the collection of essential indigenous terms that people use in a given activity are means for her to underline deep localised forms of knowledge about material practice as well as the semantic of bodily practice and material epistemologies.

References

Anzieu, D. (1985), *Le Moi-Peau*, Paris: Dunod.

Appadurai, A., ed. (1986), *The Social Life of Things: Commodities in Cultural Perspective*, New York: Cambridge University Press.

Argenti, N. (2007), *The Intestines of the State: Youth, Violence, and Belated Histories in the Cameroon Grassfields*, Chicago: University of Chicago Press.

Audoin-Rouzeau, S. (2009), *Les armes et la chair. Trois objets de mort en 14–18*, Paris: Armand Colin.

Balandier, G. (1963), *Sociologie actuelle de l'Afrique noire. Dynamique sociale en Afrique central, Deuxième édition mise à jour et augmentée*, Paris: Presses Universitaires de France.

Barfield, W. (2015), *Cyber-Humans: Our Future with Machines*, New York: Springer.

Bartholeyns, G. and F. Joulian, eds. (2014), 'Le Corps Instrument – Introduction', *Techniques & Culture*, 62. [DOI:10.4000/tc.7287]

Bateson, G. (1936), *Naven: A Survey of the Problems Suggested by a Composite Picture of the Culture of a New Guinea Tribe Drawn from Three Points of View*, Stanford: Stanford University Press.

Bateson, G. (1972), *Steps to an Ecology of Mind: Collected Essays in Anthropology, Psychiatry, Evolution, and Epistemology*, London: Chandler Publishing Company.

Bateson, G. and M. Mead (1942), *Balinese Character: A Photographic Analysis*, New York: New York Academy of Sciences.

Baudrillard, J. (1968), *Le système des objets*, Paris: Gallimard.

Baudrillard, J. (1996), *La société de consommation*, Paris: Gallimard.

Bayart, J. -F. (2007), *Global Subjects: A Political Critique of Globalization*, Cambridge: Polity.

Bayart, J. -F. and J. -P. Warnier (2004), *Matière à politique: Le pouvoir, les corps et les choses*, Paris: Karthala.

Berthoz, A. (1997), *Le sens du movement*, Paris: Odile Jacob.

Berthoz, A. (2000), *The Brain's Sense of Movement*, Cambridge: Harvard University Press.

Berthoz, A. and L. Petit, (2006), *Phénoménologie et physiologie de l'action*, Paris: Odile Jacob.

Bourdieu, P. (1977), *Outlines of a Theory of Practice*, Cambridge: Cambridge University Press.

Bourdieu, P. (1979), *La distinction, critique sociale du jugement*, Paris: Coll. le sens commun, Les Éditions de Minuit.

Buchli, V. (2004), *Material Culture: Critical Concepts in the Social Sciences, Vols. 1, 2 and 3*. London: Routledge.

Certeau (de), M. (1980), *L'invention du quotidien. Arts de faire*, Paris: Gallimard.

Chevalier, S. (1992), *L'ameublement et le décor intérieur dans un milieu populaire urbain – Approche ethnographique d'une vraie-fausse banalité*, Nanterre: Thèse de doctorat Université Paris X.

Chua, L. and M. Elliott, eds. (2013), *Distributed Objects: Meaning and Mattering after Alfred Gell*, New York: Berghahn.

Classen, C. and D. Howes, (2014), *Ways of Sensing: Understanding the Senses in Society*, London: Routledge.

Coleman, J. S. (1986), 'Social Theory, Social Research, and a Theory of Action', *American Journal of Sociology*, 91: 1309–1335.

Coupaye, L. (2009), 'Ways of Enchanting: Chaînes Opératoires and Yam Cultivation in Nyamikum Village, Maprik, Papua New Guinea', *Journal of Material Culture*, 14 (4): 433–458.

Coupaye, L. (2013), *Growing Artefacts, Displaying Relationships: Yam Technology in Nyamikum Abelam (ESP, PNG)*, New York: Berghahn Books.

Csikszentmihalyi, M. and E. Rochberg-Halton (1981), *The Meaning of Things*, Cambridge: Cambridge University Press.

Csordas, T. (1990), 'Embodiment as a Paradigm for Anthropology', *Ethos*, 18: 5–47.

Dant, T. (1999), *Material Culture in The Social World: Values, Activities, Lifestyles*, Buckingham and Philadelphia: Open University Press.

Dant, T. (2005), *Materiality and Society*, Maidenhead and New York: Open University Press.

Desjarlais, R. and J. C. Throop (2011), 'Phenomenological Approaches in Anthropology', *Annual Review of Anthropology*, 40 (1): 87–102.

Diasio, N. (2009), 'La liaison tumultueuse des choses et des corps: Un positionnement théorique', in M. -P. Julien and C. Rosselin (eds.), *Le sujet contre les objets … tout contre: Ethnographies de cultures matérielles*, 21–83, Paris: Éditions du CTHS.

Douny, L. (2014), *Living in a Landscape of Scarcity: Materiality and Cosmology in West Africa*, London: Routledge.

Duarte, B. N. (2014), 'Entangled Agencies: New Individual Practices of Human-Technology Hybridism Through Body Hacking', *NanoEthics*, 8 (3): 275–285.

Espinas, A. (1897), *Les origines de la technologie*, Paris: F. Alcan.

Faure-Rouesnel, L. (2001), 'French Anthropology and Material Culture', *Journal of Material Culture*, 6 (2): 237–247.

Foucault, M. (1966), *Les mots et les choses. Une archéologie des sciences humaines*, Paris: Gallimard.

Foucault, M. (1975), *Surveiller et punir. Naissance de la prison*, Paris: Gallimard.

Foucault, M. (1988), 'Technologies of the Self', in L. H. Martin (ed.), *Technologies of the Self: A Seminar with Michel Foucault*, 16–49, Amherst: University of Massachusetts Press.

Foucault, M. (2001), *Madness and Civilization: A History of Insanity in the Age of Reason*, translated from the French by Richard Howard; with an introduction by David Cooper. London: Routledge.

Fowles, S. (2016), 'The Perfect Subject (Postcolonial Object Studies)', *Journal of Material Culture*, 21 (1): 9–27.

Gallagher, S. (2005), *How the Body Shapes the Mind*, Oxford: Clarendon Press.

Galliot, S. (2015), 'Ritual Efficacy in the Making', *Journal of Material Culture*, 20 (2): 101–125.

Gell, A. (1998), *Art and Agency: An Anthropological Theory*, Oxford: Clarendon Press.

Geurts, K. L. (2003), *Culture and the Senses: Embodiment, Identity, and Well-being in an African Community*, Berkeley: University of California Press.

Geurts, K. L. and E. G. Adikah (2006), 'Enduring and Endearing Feelings and the Transformation of Material Culture in West Africa', in E. Edwards, K. Gosden and R. Philips (eds.), *Sensible Objects. Colonialism, Museums and Material Culture*, 35–60, London: Bloomsbury.

Gibson, J. J. (1979), *An Ecological Approach to Visual Perception*, Boston: Houghton Mifflin.

Gowlland, G. (2011), 'The 'Matière à Penser' Approach to Material Culture: Objects, Subjects and the Materiality of the Self', *Journal of Material Culture*, 16 (3): 337–343.

26   *Laurence Douny and Urmila Mohan*

Gowlland, G. (2017), *Reinventing Craft in China: The Contemporary Politics of Yixing Zisha Ceramics*, Canon Pyon: Sean Kingston Publishing.

Haraway, D. J. (1991), *Simians, Cyborgs, and Women: The Reinvention of Nature*, New York: Routledge.

Hartmann, H., Kris, E. and R. M. Loewenstein (1964), *Papers on Psychoanalytic Psychology*, New York: International Universities Press.

Head, H. and G. Holmes (1911–1912), 'Sensory Disturbances from Cerebral Lesions', *Brain: A Journal of Neurology*, 34: 102–254

Hicks, D. (2010), 'The Material-Cultural Turn: Event and Effect', in D. Hicks and M. C. Beaudry (eds.), *The Oxford Handbook to Material Culture Studies,* 25–99, Oxford: Oxford University Press.

Hindmarsh, J. and C. Heath (2003), 'Transcending the Object in Embodied Interaction', in J. Coupland and R. Gwyn (eds.), *Discourse, the Body, and Identity*, 43–69, Palgrave, Basingstoke.

Hogle, L. F. (2005), 'Enhancement Technologies and the Body', *Annual Review of Anthropology*, 34 (1): 695–716.

Hutchins, E. (1995), 'How a Cockpit Remembers its Speeds', *Cognitive Science*, 19: 265–288.

Ingold, T. (2010), 'Bringing Things to Life: Creative Entanglements in a World of Materials', Working Paper No. 15, *Realities*, ESRC National Centre for Research Methods, University of Manchester.

Ingold, T. (2013), *Making: Anthropology, Archaeology, Art and Architecture*, London: Routledge.

Julien, M. -P. and C. Rosselin (2003), 'C'est en laquant qu'on devient laqueur. De l'efficacité du geste à l'action sur soi', *Techniques & Culture*, 40 (1): 6–6.

Julien, M. -P. and C. Rosselin (2005), *La culture matérielle*, Paris: La Découverte.

Julien, M. -P. and C. Rosselin, eds. (2009), *Le sujet contre les objets... tout contre: Ethnographies de cultures matérielles*, Paris: Éditions du CTHS.

Julien, M. -P. and J. -P. Warnier, eds. (1999), *Approches de la culture matérielle: Corps à corps avec l'objet*, Paris: L'Harmattan.

Johnson, M. (1987), *The Body in the Mind: The Bodily Basis of Meaning, Imagination and Reason*, Chicago: University of Chicago Press.

Kaufmann, J. C. (1992), *La trame conjugale – analyse du couple par son linge*, Paris: Coll. Essais et Recherches, Nathan.

Kosslyn, S. M. and O. M. Koenig (1995), *Wet Mind: The New Cognitive Neuroscience*, New York: The Free Press/Macmillan.

Küchler, S. and T. Carroll (2021), *A Return to the Object: Alfred Gell and the Anthropology of Art,* London: Routledge.

Lacan, J. (1986), *Le séminaire, Livre VII. L'éthique de la psychanalyse*, Paris: Seuil.

Latour, B. (1992), *Aramis ou l'amour des techniques*, Paris: La Découverte.

Latour, B. (1999), *Pandora's Hope: An Essay on the Reality of Science Studies*, Cambridge: Harvard University Press.

Latour, B. (2005), *Reassembling the Social: An Introduction to Actor-Network-Theory*, Oxford: Oxford University Press.

Le Breton, D. (1990), *Anthropologie du corps et modernité*, Paris: Presses Universitaires de France.

Lemonnier, P. (1992), *Elements for an Anthropology of Technology*, Ann Arbor: University of Michigan.

Subjects, their bodies and objects 27

Lemonnier, P. (2012), 'Technology', in N. Thieberger (ed.), *The Oxford Handbook of Linguistic Fieldwork*, 298–316, Oxford: Oxford University Press.

Leroi-Gourhan, A. (1943), *L'homme et la matière*, Paris: Albin Michel.

Leroi-Gourhan, A. (1964–1965), *Le geste et la parole, 1. Technique et langage* [archive], 2. *Mémoire et les rythmes* [archive], Paris: Albin Michel, coll. 'Sciences_d'aujourd'hui'.

Lock, M. (1993), 'Cultivating the Body: Anthropology and Epistemologies of Bodily Practice and Knowledge', *Annual Review of Anthropology*, 22: 133–155.

Löfgren, O. (1996), 'Le retour des objets? L'etude', *Ethnologie Francaise*, 35 (1): 140–150.

Lubar, S. and D. W. Kingery (1997), *History from Things: Essays on Material Culture*, Washington: Smithsonian Institution Press.

Marchand, T. (2003), 'A Possible Explanation for the Lack of Explanation; Or "Why the Master Builder Can't Explain What he Knows": Introducing Informational Atomism Against a "Definitional" Definition of Concepts', in A. Bicker, J. Pottier, and P. Sillitoe (eds.), *Negotiating Local Knowledge: Power and Identity in Development*, 30–50, London: Pluto Press.

Marchand, T. (2012), 'Knowledge in Hand: Explorations of Brain, Hand and Tool', in R. Fardon et al. (eds.), *SAGE Handbook of Social Anthropology*, 260–269, London: Sage.

Martin, A. S. and J. R. Garrison (1997), 'Shaping the Field: The Multidisciplinary Perspectives of Material Culture in American Material Culture', in A. S. Martin and J. R. Garrison (eds.), *The Shape of the Field*, 1–20, Knoxville: University of Tennessee Press.

Mascia-Lees, F. E., ed. (2011), *A Companion to the Anthropology of the Body and Embodiment*, Malden: Wiley-Blackwell.

Mauss, M. (1936 [2006]), 'Les techniques du corps', *Journal de psychologie*, 32: 271–93. Translated by B. Brewster and reproduced in M. Mauss, *Techniques, Technology and Civilisation* (edited and introduced by N. Schlanger), 77–95, Oxford: Berghahn books.

Mauss, M. (1974 [1939]), 'Conceptions qui ont précédé la notion de matière', in M. Mauss, *Œuvres 2*, 161–168, Paris: Les Éditions de Minuit.

Mauss, M. (1979), *Sociology and Psychology*, translated by B. Brewster, London: Routledge and Kegan Paul.

Mauss, M. (2006), *Techniques, Technology and Civilisation*, edited and introduced by Nathan Schlanger. New York: Durkheim Press/Berghahn Books.

Mauss, M. (2007 [1925]), *Essai sur le don. Forme et raison de l'échange dans les sociétés archaïques*, Paris: Presses Universitaires de France (Collection 'Quadrige Grands textes').

Mauss, M. (2013), *Sociologie et anthropologie*, Paris: Presses Universitaires de France. [DOI: 10.3917/puf.maus.2013.01]

Merleau-Ponty, M. (1945), *La phénoménologie de la perception*, Paris: Gallimard.

Merleau-Ponty, M. (1964), *Le visible et l'invisible* (suivi de Notes de travail, Avertissement et postface de Claude Lefort), Paris: Gallimard.

Miller, D. (1987), *Material Culture and Mass Consumption*, Oxford: Blackwell.

Miller, D., ed. (1998), *Material Cultures: Why Some Things Matter?* Chicago: Chicago University Press.

Mohan, U. (2019), *Clothing as Devotion in Contemporary Hinduism*, Brill Research Perspectives E-Books Online. Leiden: Brill. [DOI:10.1163/9789004419131]

Mohan, U. and J. -P. Warnier (2017), Editorial: 'Marching the Devotional Subject: The Bodily-and-Material Cultures of Religion', *Journal of Material Culture*, 22 (4): 369–384.

Molotch, H. (2003), *Where Stuff Comes From*, New York: Routledge.

Morgan, D. (2018), *Images at Work: The Material Culture of Enchantment*, New York: Oxford University Press.

Naji, M. and L. Douny (2009), 'Editorial', *Journal of Material Culture*, 14 (4): 411–432.

Norman, D. A. (2013), *The Design of Everyday Things*, New York: Basic Books.

Nourrit, D. and C. Rosselin-Bareille (2017), 'Incorporer des objets: Apprendre, se transformer, devenir expert', in C. Rosselin-Bareille, (dir.) *Matières à former. Socio-anthropologie*, 35: 93–110.

Okely, J. (2007), 'Fieldwork Embodied', *Sociological Review*, 55 (1): 65–79.

Parlebas, P. (1981), *Contribution à un lexique commenté en science de l'action motrice*, Paris: INSEP.

Parlebas, P. (1999), *Jeux, sports et sociétés. Lexique de praxéologie motrice*, Paris: INSEP.

Petit, J. -L. (1997), *Les neurosciences et la philosophie de l'action*, Paris: Vrin.

Pinney, C. (2004), *"Photos of the Gods": The Printed Image and Political Struggle in India.* London: Reaktion Books.

Pinney, C. and N. Thomas, eds. (2001), *Beyond Aesthetics: Art and the Technologies of Enchantment*, New York: Berg.

Pocius, G. L., ed. (1991), *Living in a Material World: Canadian and American Approaches to Material Culture*, St. John's: Memorial University, Institute of Social and Economic Research.

Rosselin-Bareille, C. (2017), 'Matières à former', *Socio-anthropologie*, 35, Paris: Publications de la Sorbonne.

Rowlands, M. J. (2002), 'The Power of Origins: Questions of Cultural Rights?' in V. Buchli (ed.), *The Material Culture Reader*, 115–134, Oxford: Berg.

Schilder, P. (1935), *The Image and Appearance of the Human Body: Studies in the Constructive Energy of the Psyche*, London: Kegan Paul (trad. fr.: L'Image du corps. Paris, Gallimard, 1968).

Schlanger, N., ed. (2006), *Marcel Mauss: Techniques, Technology and Civilisation*, Oxford: Berghahn.

Schlanger, N. (2012), 'Une technologie engagée: Marcel Mauss et l'étude des techniques dans les sciences sociales', in M. Mauss, *Techniques, technologie et civilisation*, 17–134, Paris: Presses Universitaires de France.

Schlereth, T. J. (1992), *Cultural History and Material Culture: Everyday Life, Landscapes, Museums*, Charlottesville: University Press of Virginia.

Schumpeter, J. A. (1983 [1954]), *Histoire de l'analyse économique*, Paris: Gallimard.

Segalen, M. and B. Le Wita, eds. (1993), *Chez soi – objets et décors: Des créations familiales*, Paris: Coll. Autrement, Série mutations, 137.

Semprini, A. (1995), *L'objet comme procès et comme action: De la nature et de l'usage des objets dans la vie quotidienne*, Paris: L'Harmattan, Coll. Logiques sociales.

Sheets-Johnstone, M. (2009), *The Corporeal Turn: An Interdisciplinary Reader*, Exeter: Imprint Academic.

Shove, E. (2003), *Comfort, Cleanliness, and Convenience*, Oxford: Berg.

Sigaut, F. (2003), 'La formule de Mauss', *Techniques & Culture*, 40. https://journals. openedition.org/tc/1538; [DOI: 10.4000/tc.1538]

Simmel, G. (1987 [1900]), *Philosophie de l'argent*, Paris: Presses Universitaires de France.

Solon, O. (2018), 'Amazon Patents Wristband that Tracks Warehouse Workers' Movements', *The Guardian*, 31 January. Available online: www.theguardian.com/technology/2018/jan/31/amazon-warehouse-wristband-tracking (accessed 21 August 2019).

Stoller, P. and C. Olkes (1989), 'The Taste of Ethnographic Things', in P. Stoller, *The Taste of Ethnographic Things: The Senses in Anthropology*, 15–36, Philadelphia: University of Pennsylvania Press.

Tilley, C. (1994), *A Phenomenology of Landscape: Places, Paths, and Monuments*, Oxford: Berg.

Tilley, C., W. Keane, S. Küchler, M. J. Rowlands and P. Spyer, eds. (2006), *Handbook of Material Culture*. London: Sage.

Tisseron, S. (1999), *Comment l'esprit vient aux objets*, Paris: Aubier.

Warnier, J. -P. (1999), *Construire la culture matérielle: L'homme qui pensait avec ses doigts*, Paris: Les Presses Universitaires de France.

Warnier, J. -P. (2007), *The Pot-King: The Body and Technologies of Power*, Leiden: Brill.

Warnier, J. -P. (2009a), 'Technology as efficacious action of objects ... and subjects', *Journal of Material Culture*, 14 (4): 459–470.

Warnier, J. -P. (2009b), 'Les technologies du sujet', *Techniques & Culture*, 52–53. http://journals.openedition.org/tc/4853; [DOI: 10.4000/tc.4853]

Warnier, J. -P. (2011), 'Bodily/material Culture and the Fighter's Subjectivity', *Journal of Material Culture*, 16 (4): 359–375.

Warnier, J. -P. (2012), *Cameroon Grassfields Civilization*, Mankon: Langaa Research & Publishing CIG.

Warnier, J. -P. (2019), 'The "Magritte effect" in the Study of Religion, Part I and II', *The Jugaad Project*. 27 July. Available online: www.thejugaadproject.pub/home/the-magritte-effect-in-the-study-of-religion-part-i-and-ii (accessed 21 August 2019).

Warnier, J. -P. and C. Rosselin (1996), *Authentifier la marchandise: Anthropologie critique de la quête d'authenticité*, Paris: Éditions L'Harmattan.

Whalen, C. (2001–2002), 'American Decorative Arts Studies at Yale and Winterthur: The Politics of Gender, Gentility, and Academia', *Studies in the Decorative Arts*, 9 (1): 108–144.

Matter of work
and technology

2 Making do and wanting: The professional diver's predicament[1]

Céline Rosselin-Bareille

The third section of a wrecked Roman barge that was laying ten meters deep in the Rhône River has been lifted without any mishap in spite of a strong wind and the doubts voiced by the crane operator concerning the intervention. Standing a few centimetres above a trailer on which it must be laid down – the wood made brittle by 2000 years spent under water – the barge is surrounded by the diver-workers who are looking for a device to prevent the precious wreck from being damaged when put into contact with the metal. Gazes furtively search here and there, get lost on the wharf where the operation is taking place; hands grope around the place, feel their way tentatively; a foot pushes a stone to assess its form. In the end, pieces of plywood and polystyrene found at the back of a shed will make do as protections. What a contrast between the wreck, as an archaeological treasure, and such materials! Isn't it the same contrast that obtains between divers and archaeologists compelled to cohabit on the work site and whose motor habits and ways of relating to the materials are so different? (From field notes, August 10, 2011).[2]

In France, professional divers employed in public works are familiar with the experience of wanting: lack of time, of space, of tools and raw materials – to the point of scarcity. This compels them to consider any object or material as potentially usable. A working site may thus be analysed as a space for 'bricolage', for poaching (de Certeau 1990), for recycling (Corteel and Rétif 2013), do-it-yourself (Jeanjean 2006) and 'catachresis' (Rabardel 1995, Clot and Gori 2003, Poussin 2011). However, what has been perceived by sociologists and ethnographers alike as a daily art of doing, and, at the same time, as a rehabilitation of its artisans/artists, is not devoid of ambiguity in a work context. Workers lament that, by putting up with this situation, they serve the interests of their boss. What is at stake in their relationship with recycled, discarded and reused objects, is the construction of power relationships. However, what I would name the work on leftovers belongs by the same token with the construction of those who have to do with such material things.

In the perspective of a *'Matière à Travail'* – Matter for Work – approach, I will propose an interpretation of some *connections* between the observations

34 Céline Rosselin-Bareille

and discourses I have met in the field: on the one hand, unavoidable work of recycling, a necessary 'doing with'. And, on the other hand, the remark by a woman-boss reported by a professional diver: 'The divers, they are a consumable of sorts! You kick a garbage can, and a hundred of them will spill out!'

On this question, one can find several interpretative logics that may even coexist in a more or less accepted way:

1 A confusion between the men and the matters they work with would be connected with the representations of purity and defilement (Douglas 1966/2003). Such an assimilation, according to Lhuilier (2005) would be due to the gaze cast by the others, that the researcher would adopt. However, how does the collapse of the object-waste on the human-waste operates? By similitude or resemblance? By contamination, contagion or contiguity? By physical or symbolic contact? So to speak by magic (see Frazer evolutionist work in *The Golden Bough*, first edited in 1890), would it be enough to have such a proximity with undetermined, always potentially dispensable, matter to allow the divers to become a 'Kleenex of work' of sorts?

2 Or else, is it by some sort of comparison that this collapse is achieved, as regards the parallel trajectories of the biographies of objects and subjects according to the analytical model put forward by Kopytoff (1986)?

Such kinds of approaches are useful, in particular to belabour the borders, the sometimes porous limits, between the statuses of subject and object, but they seem to obfuscate the co-construction of subjects and objects in action.

In order to validate an approach claiming that humans, by incorporating material culture thanks to their sensory-motor and emotional conducts and through their integration in networks of actions on other subjects' actions subjectify themselves,[3] I will show that professional divers are included in a specific work organisation, geared on particular material substances and objects, that construct them as precarious workers, and consequently as 'disposable men'.

Working on an indeterminate matter

In France, the Public Work Divers are recognised as a registered profession since a by-law dated 13 February 2014. Until then, they were considered as public work labour if not quite like others. Indeed, as specialists of sub-aquatic works, subjects to the Labour Code, they are allowed to dive down to 50 metres subsequently to a certification and a professional licence. They intervene on immersed structures, to inspect them, cast concrete, weld, cut up all kinds of materials, in environments defined as hostile, in which dangers may pop up any time. In addition to their three statutory hours per day spent under water, fed with fresh air by a narghile while keeping in touch with a communication room, they also operate as emergency divers, diving supervisors and public works labour while at work, conducting all those activities at a turn during the intervention. A majority of them (most of them are men) work temporarily, but for the time being, they experience far less competition among themselves than the *ad interim* workers studied by Rosini (2014). Consequently, I will leave aside the labour shortage mentioned in public statements and its effects on the maintenance of precarious labour conditions obtaining in building and public works (Jounin 2008). Therefore, the divers' work is not primarily defined in terms of recuperating or dealing with waste. By contrast, divers' frequent contacts with such matters and material objects open up several avenues for an understanding of the identification processes they experience.

The liquid element in which the divers immerse themselves is neither the kind of clear, springtime water mentioned by Bachelard (1942), nor a pure and cleansing one, but rather a deep, heavy, sometimes violent, toxic and dark one: it belongs with canals, rivers, seas, in which the bridge pillars, the dams, the locks on which the divers operate are found to rest; as well as the nuclear power plants and the filtering stations: a kind of pasty water when (at best) it is mixed with soil (ibid., 122). Immersing oneself in filthy water may be tolerated by beginners, but it becomes suspect as time goes on: 'do you still go into shit, do you? (B., 40 years old, certified in 1998, pulling a face of disgust, with an embarrassed grim, addressing R., 35 years old, certified in 2004, a colleague thus more recent in the trade). I myself now refuse to do it!', thus drawing a line between those who can chose their mission and those who can't.

The open-air work sites and those under water are shared spaces, on which some perform their tasks, but that may be used as passageways by others. Their possible openings, accessibility and occupation sometimes imply that they may have to be tidied up prior to any intervention. Thus, the Paris divers find shopping carts, bicycles, washing machines and even cars in the canal: 'the other day, we had to lift 8 cubic metres of caddies and bikes before we could control the optic fibre' (D., 57 years old, certified in 1991). Quite a few actions conducted as part of the divers' job could thus mislead us on their very manly dimension– claimed as such[4]– of their activity: vacuum cleaning, tidying up, cleaning up, sorting out, recycling, patching up, throwing down, a true catalogue of actions worthy of the theory of housekeeping as developed by Kaufmann (1997). But the objects, the materials and the bodily culture that go along with them have nothing to do with the latter: the mud is sucked with a sucker (an underwater vacuum cleaner), the diameter of which requires it to be grasped with both hands; the diving suit, quickly worn down by friction, torn off by objects on which it gets caught, is patched up with neoprene; the materials are recuperated in their raw state.

The rubbish that is extracted, fished out, brought to the surface, saved from oblivion, may be turned into relics; an old Singer sewing machine, a piece of wood hardened up under water, but also mobile phones or weapons

Figure 2.1 A suit to be patched up. Arles, France, July 2011.

Photo by author.

(toys or not). The actions performed on those objects are quite diverse: thrown down into a garbage dumpster tip-lorry; reintegrated into the public space (as is the case with self-service urban bicycles); put aside and somewhat piled up on the window still of the workshop; photographed and exhibited to the visitors on Heritage Day in Paris; put in one's pocket carefully wrapped into cloth to find its place into the private sphere of whoever has found this desirable object.

No object is *a priori* considered as rubbish or as an object. As underscored by Hoarau (1999), the very action on such matters will contribute to defining its status. The rubbish category is not limited to its symbolic dimension that would define it as something out of place,[5] it is also produced 'by the action of throwing down' the objects (ibid., 98). And throwing down is not performed the same way with all and every object (carefully, violently, in an irreversible way or not, etc.), according to different situations. Similarly, the opposite action of recuperating and recycling tilts the categories around. Recycling amounts to pulling out the object from its rubbish status. It often goes along with putting it aside to be dealt with at a later date. (I will come back on this point). It also means spending some time to restore it as new, just as a stained outfit is recovered. Thus, T. (50 years old, certified in 1991) recovers a metallic ashtray found by the underwater work place and devotes 24 hours to restore it during his supervision time.

The definition of rubbish, of what can be disposed of or recovered, depends in the end on finding its place in a particular repertoire of bodily conducts and in a network of actions on other people's actions. In the case of the recovery of the barge wreck mentioned above, the old stuff (clay amphoras, jewellery, coins, little glass flasks some 2,000 years old) is no more for the divers than rubbish to be dealt with as such (even if quickly enough not to be heard by archaeologist colleagues): they have working goals from which they do not deviate (that is, remove the mud around the wreck in order to allow for its extraction, and organise the latter). They do not have enough time to waste on an archaeological object. The boss is always there to remind them that they must bring the work to completion in the shortest time possible.

The experience of wanting

The material culture that is recovered at the end of a previous worksite – found, collected, put aside, acquired in a different context – is mostly constituted by all-purpose raw materials that may be put to good use on demand: threads, ropes, straps, pipes, tape rolls of various colours, tire tubes, pieces of wood, plywood, polystyrene, metal. J. (38 years old, certified in 1992) reminds us that 'Everything may be recycled!' To such an extent that any object that is recuperated amounts first and foremost as a raw material of sorts. It is only at a later stage that actions on such a material transform it into an affordable object for the diver. This transformation will provide the object with a new name (for instance, an old rope, once re-worked and integrated into the bodily conducts of the divers becomes a *bout* in nautical parlance).

There exists hardly any material that would be specific to the trade of the diver: the tools used while working under water or above are the same; the rubber gloves used as isolators when welding are those used in dish-washing or surgery; there are gloves specifically designed for diving but the nature of the work is such that they will be quickly torn town, as will the diving suit known notoriously for needing patches of neoprene at the knees, elbows and back after having been used just a few times.

One has to consider that by and large on the work site, materials are lacking: 'in our job, you dive with your prick and your knife', says this diver who works in harbours. Thus Jounin (2008: 55) has underscored that, on standard building sites, to procure equipment amounts to 'stealing it or appropriating it unobtrusively, picking up, tapping, borrowing' thus generating competition among the workers. Even if I have not met with such explicit competitive logics in the work places of the divers, the shortage or want of all sorts of things is a commonly shared working condition.

Scarcity is a bodily experience, the senses being constantly activated on the work sites. Sure enough, first and foremost, one must avoid stumbling on a newly made step or a pipe, or bumping on a beam that is too low to allow for an easy passage. But, above all, the senses are permanently alert and on the lookout: investigating with one's sight, bending double,

Figure 2.2 A diver with his dish-washing gloves. Arles, France, August 2011.

Photo by author.

picking up, touching, grasping, getting hold, assessing, weighing usable materials, putting them down again, listening to the noises in the working place (Thibaud 1991); sorting out the smells related to the work in progress. All this provides so many bits of information on the ongoing work, and consequently, on the probable availability of tools and spaces. Motor conducts are somewhat hesitant for whoever is searching, groping about, improvising.

All the workers allude to the fact that they have learned to make do with nothing: lacking material resources is often associated with putting oneself at risk.[6] Accordingly, questions of security are often mentioned in discussions on the necessity of having to obviate shortages. In one case, fire caught unexpectedly when a worker had to fashion metallic blades on an improvised bench. Some inflammable glue used to mend the diving suits had been used on the bench and stood next to the welding equipment used to attach stoppers at both ends of the blades. People improvise, engage in bricolage with matter, with time, with regulations, with their own know-how. Jeanjean and Rosini (2013) aptly mention a position of technical insecurity when time (or the lack of it) and the multi-tasking imposed on *ad interim* workers prevent them to find acceptable compromise. However, as underscored by Jounin (2008: 183), 'part of the workers' know-how consists in assessing where, when and how to abide by the rules of security so as to respect the schedule' that generates the lack of time.

Making do: adaptability, interchangeability, disposability

'One must make do and one makes do' (qualified workers' labour on a building work Six 1997: 11). 'Make do', that is, make do while abiding to 'woolly prescriptions in work organisation' (in French, OTPF).[7] Duc characterises this as follows: 'a low prescription level concerning "the work to be done"; the work site manager must "make space for alternative solutions"' (ibid., 119); and 'promote innovative behaviour in taking care of the variations in the activity'; 'establish a frame and structure, in particular the interactions and coordination required by such a management in such a hazardous environment.'

Thus, making do, for the *ad interim* workers studied by Rosini (2014: 290),[8] means 'to adjust to the spaces they get acquainted with, to compromise with the materials they manipulate, to get used to the tools they use, etc.', 'together with constantly changing material elements and colleagues' and that 'constitute as many obstacles to be overcome at every new assignment'. By resorting to *ad interim* labour, OTPF induces 'a quick integration on the work site and within the work collective' (Mashkova 2008: 394).

Accordingly, this type of work organisation may be analysed as a particularly flexible network of actions on other people's actions furthermore including a multitude of subjects whose motor habits are shaped in a number of different ways, incorporating equally different material cultures (those two components going along together): engineers in their studies, when designing a metallic bar that will fill up with water and become too heavy under water and that divers must rework; the boat pilots who do not always slow down when sailing past a work place and are likely to generate dangerous waves impacting those at work in the water; the boss who will not pay extra hours but requires that the work be completed swiftly; the divers who stop the daily production of a factory when changing a damaged water pump, etc., turn the work site into a space in which power is exercised and the material culture into the matter for politics (Bayart and Warnier 2004).

Recuperating objects/materials takes place in this network, and making do allows for a constant adaptation to the work situations: realising with metallic pipes that only need to be welded together a structure that will prevent stepping over the narghile given the particular layout of the worksite; inventing a thread designed to cut off the dense mud in which the stern of the wreck is stuck; conceiving and producing a basket to lift amphoras to the surface or a bell to ring the colleagues who stand on the deck and cannot be seen from the wharf down below; all this is accomplished with materials found on the spot.

In each material, in each object, a potential is produced and maintained as such. In the Paris municipal workshop whom divers work for, a large shed is dubbed 'the hall of whatever may be put to some use'. In it are kept in store old pumps, clutches and scale models and materials of all kinds. Catachresis is so frequent that it recovers its original linguistic meaning: a

40 *Céline Rosselin-Bareille*

Paris diver has coined the name 'schibouzette' for any object whose name does not exist or has been forgotten. A name that someday may be put to good use...

The unpredictability of OTPF; the hostile environments in which divers operate and the associated shortages are considered as toilsome, and appreciated by the workers at the same time: 'I always learn something new' (P., 50 years old, certified in 1980); 'what I like in this job is that you constantly have to invent solutions. You never get bored. It is fascinating. I have quit the factory very early in my life. Well! I do not regret it!' (D., 57 years old, certified in 1991). 'It is never twice the same thing; there are so many parameters: visibility, water. It is such a force of nature; one constantly has to imagine, find tricks and schemes. All the while one has to avoid straining oneself. One has to find the easiest solution' (J.-P., 45 years old, certified in 1997). 'One has to adjust constantly' (T., 50 years old, certified in 1991). To be a good bricoleur is thus a compliment among divers.

This versatility is enforced by the different situations encountered and reinforced by the many activities that keep the diver busy during a day's work, under water or at the surface. It is appreciated for the sake of resourcefulness *(débrouillardise)*. Recognised by M. de Certeau (1990) as an 'art of doing', by Clot (2003) as a 'power to work at a task', by Rosini (2014) as a 'know-how with...', is such an undeniable competence recognised and considered as legitimate?

Working on the leftovers in the kitchen, for instance, requires a real competence. Yet a competence that is acquired in a large or a needy family as regards children (a pedagogy to stay clear of squandering food perhaps) is not the same competence for a chef. Working on waste in a work site means bricolage, and bricolage is a virtue in lower class households (Bonnette-Lucat 1991: 62). More than that, doesn't such a competence fall back upon the workers when making do also amounts not only to avoiding squandering resources but also to serving the interests of the boss who will thus draw some benefit from scarcity?

Therefore, it may be the divers' remarkable capacity for adaptation that we may consider as a true competence and because of their versatility that the divers are interchangeable, consumable and, in the end, can be discarded.

Wanting: the ambiguity of being a jack of all trades

Several scholars have concerned themselves with bricolage. They underscore its ambiguity in a professional context. Thus Erikson (2002) shows that:

> The possibility of recycling one's professional qualifications for private uses is highly valued. It constitutes an important criterion to assess the technical competence of each and every one. Paradoxically, such an attitude does not preclude, on a working site, despising the obligation

to resort to such trivial activities as, precisely, pure and simple bricolage. Mid-way between work and leisure, bricolage thus provides real satisfactions, but that are nevertheless perceived as unworthy of a genuine electrician, the nobleness of which comes from the more technical gestures he is lead to accomplish.

Bonnette-Lucat (1991: 62) goes even further when the author states that the bricoleur 'is not a professional. Consequently, he is not the man of a single trade. If his productions are to be measured against his competence, in principle, he will win a poor mark. Jack of all trades, master of none, he cannot expect to be respected by others'. In the desire expressed by many youth who are being trained to do welding under water, one may probably see a more or less conscious means to acquire a specialisation being set against the awareness they acquire progressively, transmitted by their teachers, that being a diver means knowing how to do everything. And knowing how to do anything is not a real know-how.

Knowing how to do anything, accepting the hazards due to shortages and showing a good level of resistance to them by making do everything also entails confronting and passing beyond the arduousness of the diver's trade, whatever the means employed to achieve this. Besides, one has got to perform anyway and do so well, say the divers.

Figure 2.3 Materials on hand (neoprene) for improvised solutions. The 'thing' with the correct dimensions to protect the barge from the metal. Arles, France, August 2011.

Photo by author.

42 *Céline Rosselin-Bareille*

As underscored by Gallioz (2006): 'the hardship of work as a criterion built around the use of physical strength is still a structural component of the gendered identity of the labour force in the building industry. Its gender is the male one, the reason being that the working conditions are debasing and constructed as physically arduous'. The construction of the divers in a setting made of materials to be specified, redefined, provides a lot of opportunities for bricolage, for improvisation, for the search for technical solutions that goes along with the construction of a male subject, a construction that has unnerving perverse effects: would each and every man be naturally a bricoleur, just as women would be naturally skilful with precision tasks (Gallioz 2006, Maruani 2011)?

Such a possible naturalisation of the making do raises the question of a difficult reconciliation between recognising a given subject as a male or as a professional with specific qualifications. The discussions around their wages draw on quite a different justification than in the more classical wage claims: indeed, they tend to emerge as counterpoint to the potential absence of recognition of their specific qualifications. Thus, at the end of his training, one of the occasional teachers at 'Institut National de Plongée Professionnelle' (INPP) with a rich record on various work sites including off-shore ones, explains to the new graduates: 'if you accept to work for nothing, it means that you are no good'. Making do, all right, but not for nothing. During a labour union meeting,[9] looking at their meagre pay slips as compared with the work they had done, the divers explain: 'we are bloody stupid! We are whores!' And indeed, how can you make do and not be satisfied with it?

At a time when qualifications are recorded in some businesses by means of censuses and information cards, in order to safeguard and transmit whatever particular know-how is likely to vanish, the divers' work is pushed off balance. Indeed, the want of time, materials, men, as well as the potential bestowed on recuperating objects and matters often leave the technical gestures in abeyance, uncertainty and, as it were, by the side. It compels one to prove oneself against new situations, all the more since the status of temporary worker defines the workers as subject to dismissal at any time (Jounin 2008).

In such a context, it is hard to sort out the gestures considered as being specific to the trade and to formalise them, to such an extent that one may question what Roux and Brill (2006) names a trade-identity since it rests on the identification of technical gestures. The divers criticise their employers for saving on equipment. But is it not indirectly an economy made on wages? Material shortages compel the divers to act as bricoleurs and consequently to be deprived of claiming any qualification that would increase their wages. Thus, what is at stake is the issue of maintaining the divers within the confines of such a status.[10]

Therefore, in the eyes of the main actors in this network of actions on other people's actions, the capacity to make do goes along as a corollary with the fact of being without any clear qualification, and knowing how to work under water and above, under the conditions exposed here, does not seem to suffice.

Conclusion

Shortages, together with recycling, bricolage, 'woolly prescription' in work organisations, and resorting to *ad interim* labour go along with constructing precarious subjects. In the case of divers working in public works, it seems that the analysis put forward by Poussin (2011) or Jeanjean (2011) as regards the sewage workers is being turned upside down. As a matter of fact, with the sewage workers, recuperating is perceived as promoting 'various forms of rehabilitation of work and of the worker through retrieving' and recycling (Jeanjean 2011: 298). In the case of the divers in public works who are not expected to intervene on waste but come to it given the nature of their tasks on the work site, the analysis of what is really performed shows that the experience of shortage, the necessity of being a Jack of all trades making use of everything and nothing, imposes ways of working that win insufficient recognition and maintain the precariousness of those workers. Materials, objects, and the divers define each other in a network of actions on other people's actions specific to the work site as potentially exploitable and disposable. Working on disposable materials does not lead to become disposable by contagion, imitation or assimilation. It leads to developing a group of qualifications inscribed in the body that are not acknowledged because they are deemed too versatile and 'naturally' bestowed on men. Accordingly, divers are defined as interchangeable workers and as disposable.

Notes

1. The translation of this text has been done by Jean-Pierre Warnier, who is very much thanked here. I also thank Laurence Douny and Urmila Mohan for their outstanding editing work.
2. This chapter is a work grounded on a field research with divers conducted between 2011 and 2018, without any participant observation, without any immersion in the strict sense of the term for a number of reasons: medical problems, age, security connected with the work activity. Nevertheless, accessing the fieldwork setting is not made all the more difficult since the divers share with public work labour studied by Ghasarian (2001) a common nomadic sociability (39), 'a particular sociability grounded on parting and coming back together again' (46): public work sites are often located far away from the living quarters of the workers. They impose an ephemeral togetherness where evenings in hotels and B&Bs, and the three daily meals provide opportunities to discuss techniques, to debrief the work accomplished during the day and to organise the next one, but also to discuss regional origins and life histories conjured up if delicately. Such moments offer privileged opportunities to the ethnologist to collect relevant narratives. In addition to this, the presence of numerous *ad interim* workers creates the habit of meeting newcomers and to quickly integrate them into the work teams. If the observer abides by the security rules on the work site, such as wearing the individual

44   *Céline Rosselin-Bareille*

protection devices, then the doors get wide open to the extent that s/he may become a resource person above water (to locate a tool, a person, to guide a crane, to transmit an information). Thus, the presence of a stranger is quickly accepted, even if being a woman leaves little doubt about her non-diver status, since there are so few of them in the trade.

3. See for example, Warnier (1999), Julien and Rosselin (2005, 2009).
4. Whereas J. (certified in 1992) cannot dive for health reasons, he has been occupying the communication room for several days, which serves as a meeting place for the divers under many circumstances during the day. When he finds out the state of disorder obtaining in the room in which he has to settle down in order to monitor his diving colleagues, he gets annoyed: 'plastic coffee cups, cigarette butts, no pen. I am fed up with playing the maid!'
5. This model, inspired by the famous *Purity and Danger* (Douglas 1966/2003) that analyses pollution through the lens of the cultural codes of purity and impurity, constitutes the basic reference of many works concerning waste. The *a priori* representations are then taken into account at the expense of the gestures applied on materials as contributing to direct the objects towards either one of the two categories, although, in addition to this, purity and impurity are constantly in the process of being re-defined, in a given situation, while integrating many a subtlety that escape the grasp of generalising categories, just as with those students having to produce a scale model for a school kitchen and who invent the 'semi-dirty' and 'not quite so clean' categories.
6. However, the question of risk in building works is not limited to shortages or wanting.
7. In the original French: *Organisation du travail à prescription floue* (OTPF), an expression coined by Duc (2002).
8. A whole chapter of his dissertation is devoted to making do.
9. There is no obligation to join a union. In France, the precarious employment category includes temporary work, fixed-term contracts, apprenticeship and State-aided Contracts, as opposed to open-ended contracts (the form considered normal and general of the employment relationship).
10. This domain has been undergoing a process of professional qualification since 2015. And if it is not yet possible to see its effects with the newly trained divers, it is not inconceivable that the ways of making do and, consequently, the divers themselves, may experience a change.

References

Bachelard, G. (1942), *L'eau et les rêves*, Paris: Librairie José Corti.
Bayart, J. -F. and J. -P. Warnier, eds. (2004), *Matière à Politique. Le pouvoir, les corps et les choses*, Paris: CERI-Karthala.
Bonnette-Lucat, C. (1991), 'Les bricoleurs: Entre polyvalence et spécialisation', *Sociétés contemporaines*, 8: 61–85.
Certeau (de), M. (1990), *L'Invention du quotidien. Arts de faire, Tome 1*, Paris: Gallimard.
Clot, Y. (2003), 'La catachrèse entre réel et réalisé. Contribution d'un psychologue du travail', in Y. Clot and R. Gori (eds.), *Catachrèse: Eloge du détournement*, 11–26, Nancy: Presses Universitaires de Nancy.
Clot, Y. and R. Gori, eds. (2003), *Catachrèse: Eloge du détournement*, Nancy: Presses Universitaires de Nancy.

Corteel, D. and S. Rétif (2013), 'Réduction des déchets et requalification des objets. La construction de la valeur dans le secteur du 'réemploi' ', 5ᵉ congrès de l'Association Française de Sociologie, Réseau Thématique Sociologie Economique, Université de Nantes.

Cru, D. (2014), *Le risque et la règle. Le cas du bâtiment et des travaux publics*, Toulouse: Erès.

Douglas, M. (1966/2003). *Purity and Danger*, London: Routledge.

Duc, M. (2002), *Le travail en chantier*, Toulouse: Octarès.

Erikson, P. (2002), '"Tout ce qui ferait fuir un âne..." L'amour du métier chez les électriciens du bâtiment', *Terrain*, 39: 69–78.

Gallioz, S. (2006), 'Force physique et féminisation des métiers du bâtiment', *Travail, genre et sociétés*, 16 (2): 97–114.

Ghasarian, C. (2001), *Tensions et résistances. Une ethnographie des chantiers en France*, Toulouse: Octarès.

Hoarau, F. (1999), 'Trier, transporter à Emmaüs. Ethnographie, sens et sciences de l'action', in M. -P. Julien and J. -P. Warnier (eds.), *Approche de la culture matérielle. Corps à corps avec l'objet*, 97–106, Paris: L'Harmattan.

Jeanjean, A. (2006), *Basses oeuvre: Une ethnologie du travail dans les égouts*, Paris: CTHS.

Jeanjean, A. (2011), 'Entre contagion, secret et transmission, ce que l'on se passe aux abords des déchets', in D. Corteeland and S. Le Lay (eds.), *Les travailleurs des déchets*, 279–303, Toulouse: Erès.

Jeanjean, A. and P. Rosini (2013), 'Ce que la multi-activité fait aux sujets: Une perspective ethnologique. Assainissement et intérim', https://halshs.archives-ouvertes.fr/halshs-01275137 (last accessed 2016).

Jounin, N. (2008), *Chantier interdit au public. Enquête parmi les travailleurs du bâtiment*, Paris: La Découverte.

Julien, M. -P. and C. Rosselin (2005), *La culture matérielle*, Paris: La Découverte.

Julien, M. -P. and C. Rosselin, eds. (2009), *Le sujet contre les objets... tout contre. Ethnographies de cultures matérielles,* Paris: Éditions du CTHS.

Kaufmann, J. -C. (1997), *Le Cœur à l'ouvrage. Théorie de l'action ménagère,* Paris: Nathan.

Kopytoff, I. (1986), 'The Cultural Biography of Things', in A. Appadurai (ed.), *The Social Life of Things*, 64–91, Cambridge: Cambridge University Press.

Lhuilier, D. (2005), 'Le "sale boulot"', *Travailler*, 14 (2):73–98.

Mashkova, E. (2008), 'Travail stable, travail précaire: confrontation productrice de risques. L'hypothèse mise à l'épreuve dans le secteur du bâtiment', *Revue Française des affaires sociales*, 2 (2–3): 391–8.

Maruani, M. (2011), *Travail et emploi des femmes*, Paris: La Découverte.

Poussin, N. (2011), 'La réorganisation de leur travail par les éboueurs: De la nécessité d'une prescription pour pouvoir y répliquer', in D. Corteel and S. Le Lay (eds.), *Les travailleurs des déchets*, 191–205, Toulouse: Erès.

Rabardel, P. (1995), *Les hommes et les technologies*, Paris: Armand Colin.

Rosini, P. (2014), *Temporaires en permanence: Une ethnologie du travail intérimaire 'non-qualifié'*, Thèse de Doctorat (sous la direction d'A. Jeanjean), Université d'Aix-Marseille.

Roux, V. and B. Bril, eds. (2006), *Stone Knapping: The Necessary Conditions for a Uniquely Hominin Behavior*, Cambridge: McDonald Press.

46   *Céline Rosselin-Bareille*

Six, F. (1997), *La préparation du travail. Un enjeu pour la sécurité et la calorisation des compétences*, Rapport 'Etudes et Expérimentations, Chantier 2000', Lille: GERN.

Thibaud, J. -P. (1991), 'Temporalités sonores et interactions sociales', *Architectures et comportements*, 7 (1): 63–74.

Warnier, J. -P. (1999), *Construire la culture matérielle, L'homme qui pensait avec ses doigts*, Paris: Presses Universitaires de France.

3 'Management' and its refuse

Agnès Jeanjean

Looking at waste from a political angle ... with the body

What does MaP contribute?

Anyone studying waste in the West will inevitably come across famous quotes, in which rubbish is considered as a path leading to truth. Victor Hugo expressed this idea in *Les Misérables,* as he reflected on the sewers or piles of refuse: 'The sewer is the conscience of the city' or 'The heap of crap has this going for it, it is not a liar' (Hugo 1862). Lacan declared: 'Where there is an accumulation of waste in disorder, there is something human. (...) The pile of rubbish is one side of the human dimension that should not be ignored' (Lacan 1986: 273–274). Another quote worth mentioning is from Jean Gouhier, founder of *rudologie*,[1] which he defines as the science of waste from goods and decommissioned areas: 'An examination of the margins provides information on the meaning, the rhythms and the foundations of decommissioning and recommissioning' (Gouhier 1999: 80). The scientific interest archaeologists have shown for waste (also referred to as refuse, garbage, rubbish, etc. in this chapter) is also repeatedly emphasised. One of them, Colette Pétonnet (1991: 108), trained by André Leroi-Gourhan, notes:

> We would know nothing about the way hunters of the Upper Paleolithic lived, if all we had found was a flint tool with a lost handle. But blade debris scattered around the anvil, compacted ashes from the hearth found an arm's length in front of it, and bones from wild game, sliced to extract the marrow and thrown behind it, allowed prehistorians to reconstruct the number, arrangement, size and shape (circular) of the tents. While tools indicated only a certain degree of material civilization, the Magdalenian waste bins, as an irony of history, were the only items that provided a first clue about their organization.

The waste archaeology program set up in 1973 in the United States by William Rathje and Cullen Murphy is another example. The program, named *Garbage*, was organised in collaboration with the City of Tucson's

48   *Agnès Jeanjean*

Urban Sanitation Service. Researchers examined the contents of rubbish bins and extracted information from them on consumption patterns as well as dietary and sexual practices. The premise was that waste bins do not lie. Researchers considered that what they found in them could be used to rectify data obtained from interviews with the inhabitants. They insisted on the exotic nature of what they called 'the world of garbage': 'The garbage itself was an unknown world – everything learned about it was new – and thus held the fascination that a trip up the Congo in the nineteenth century would have' (Rathje and Murphy 1992: 59). Mary Douglas (1970) and many writers after her highlighted the political and symbolic dimensions of waste and more particularly of dirt. Douglas considers dirt as 'matter out of place'. She highlights the subversive and creative power of this *disorder*. It threatens existing arrangements, current categories and established limits and is therefore unlimited and endowed with infinite creative power. The gestures of cleanliness are then considered as rites that restore order, both politically and symbolically. Waste contributes to the construction of social identities and territories. Some authors also insist on the temporal dimension of refuse: 'Nothing is absolute and final in the rejection and removal from the system (...). The margin is located between the centre of power and the void, and is the expression of an intermediate space and time between different and even contradictory assessment systems' (Gouhier 1999: 81). This is also what Michael Thompson demonstrates in his book: *Rubbish Theory. The creation and destruction of value* (Thompson 1979). He considers that refuse has a relative value, that depending on the time and social context, it can acquire a new status, and become a precious object with a value of exchange or use.

Despite these major contributions, waste has long been marginalised by ethnologists and sociologists. However, interest in these objects (or this status) has been growing in recent years in France (Corteel and Le Lay 2011, Monsaingeon 2014, Debary 2019) and in the English-speaking world (Scanlan 2005, O'Brien 2008, etc.), as demonstrated by the development of 'Discard Studies'. This movement is tied to growing economic and political concern over the proliferation of waste produced by our consumerist societies. Extensive research has been conducted on issues relating to the environment, recycling and the *second life of objects* (Ortar and Anstett eds. 2017). This study offers a different perspective on these objects, by focusing the attention on their technical processing, and by examining them from the standpoint of the bodily actions and engagements they entail in the work context.

Following the path laid down by *Matière à Penser* (MaP), we will discover the political dimension of refuse and see that it is inseparable from the actions carried out by gestures and bodies. Mary Douglas (1970) adopts a radically sociological position: the *subject* is absent from her analyses. The MaP approach, on the other hand, gives us the opportunity to introduce the *subject* and body by emphasising the body-matter pair in the action, and

'*Management*' *and its refuse*   49

locating it, using Foucault's expression, in 'networks of actions on the actions of others' (Foucault 1994, Julien and Warnier eds. 1999, Julien and Rosselin 2009). The *subject-and-its-objects*, as described by Jean-Pierre Warnier (2009a, 2009b), is also a foundational concept. On the strength of these theoretical contributions and without disavowing the theses of Douglas, which are essential for studying waste from a political and symbolic point of view, we will consider refuse matter, waste and the technical activities that apply to them, from the perspective of their effects on *subjects*. I will also suggest some ideas to be explored about the political dimension of work, which, in my opinion, have a critical action on bodies and subjectivities.

In the first section, based on field studies conducted among waste workers who have been the focus of my interest for almost 30 years, I will highlight a few of the mechanisms specific to their activity. Then we will look at other workers (technicians working for healthcare facilities) also engaged in actions on refuse objects and materials. Finally, we will examine the political impact within contemporary work organisations of marginal technical activities and *bricolage*[2] (Lévi-Strauss 1962) using salvaged equipment. The data and analyses provided here are the outcome of field studies carried out over several years, during which I spent extensive time following the workers throughout their daily activities. The data collected at the hospital is the result of collective research conducted with Teresa Cruz, Cyril Laudanski and Philippe Rosini (Jeanjean et al. 2007).

What do waste workers teach us?

In the course of my field studies, I have met waste workers (sewer cleaners, street cleaners, garbage collectors, sweepers, ragmen) from various backgrounds, mainly from France and Morocco, both women and men. They had one thing in common: they were regularly and physically in contact with socially rejected substances, objects and tools which caused disgust. I will not analyse the effect of disgust any further in this contribution, but will point out that Norbert Elias (1939) following Sigmund Freud (1971) showed how much, in the Western world, civilisational mechanisms are based on the repression of instincts and the repression of the pleasure attached to natural functions. In addition, members of society are conditioned in such a way that, when faced with these functions, they feel negative emotions, anxiety, shame and disgust. The latter can then be considered as the manifestation of psychic life (Butler 1997) and physiological power (Jeanjean 2011a).

Waste workers have to touch what their societies want them to stay away from. They perform transgressive acts daily. The knowledge and techniques they use are unpopular and are developed and transmitted within work communities which are usually pushed back into spaces and temporalities cut off from public life. Contact with refuse matter and fear of contagion (in its physical and symbolic dimensions) determines their position in space and creates a physical distance in relation to bodies, places and objects

50 *Agnès Jeanjean*

protected from this contact. At the heart of this opacity and from this *place* where they 'touch and think what no one else touches' (sewer cleaner), the workers develop values and know-how kept under a seal of secrecy and adopt specific view points on society: 'We gain a psychological and socio-logical knowledge about people's lives, and what we see of them is not always pretty. (...) We discover the other side of things and people'. The knowledge they acquire and to which they assign a subversive power is accompanied by questioning. They wonder about the meaning of their lives and their psychological balance. For example, they wonder why they accept these bodily engagements that shape their affects, their bodies and their social relations. The workers talk about times when they feel anxiety and when meaning is elusive: 'When I start to think that I might smell like the sewers, and that people might notice it, I feel completely paralysed' (sewage treatment plant worker, 38 years old, Lunel, south of France). 'It raises a lot of questions in my mind [...]. I never would have imagined doing this kind of work. I can't find any logic to it' (sewer cleaner, 45 years old, Antibes, south of France).

Words, and more particularly their socially accepted uses, seem to have very little hold on the issue. Their effectiveness is regularly questioned. Sewer cleaners explain, for example, that metaphorical uses of terms for waste make it difficult for them to use the words literally. They have to deal with euphemisms and other rhetorical expressions that lead to a denial of what is real *[le réel]* in their activity. They explain that they cannot find the words to talk to those who do not practice their trade about 'shit that stinks, sticks and sinks' (sewer cleaners in Jeanjean 2006): 'Even if the word "clean" is written on our lorries, they are still shit pumps and we're in them' (sewer cleaner to Jeanjean).[3]

Waste workers consider that their field of activity can only be understood and the technical efficiency and subversive knowledge that goes with it can only be acquired if there is a physical engagement with refuse matter: 'To understand shit, you need to touch it' (sewer cleaners). This point of view is absolutely, and in a disturbing way, consistent with that of Rathje and Murphy (1992). These authors describe the physical engagement of research-ers in the same terms, word for word, as the sewer cleaners: 'Garbage is not mathematics. To understand garbage you have to touch it, to feel it, to sort it, to smell it (...)' (Op. Cit: 9).

Observation shows that such physical engagement does not necessarily contribute to developing 'haptic knowledge' and to collecting information on the substances worked, unlike what happened to the deep-sea divers studied by Céline Rosselin (Rosselin, Lalo and Nourrit 2015). But it leads to a bodily engagement beyond disgust and to a shared recognition that the activity is real (Jeanjean 2006). This recognition then makes it possible to think about the matter and the technical equipment handled, and there-fore, to develop effective actions. In his research, François Sigaut, consid-ers technical action as a 'reciprocal relationship between what is real *[le réel]*, me and others'. He insists on the central role of what is real in this triangular relationship: '(...) the analysis of alienation forms has forced us, in an unforeseen way, to place what is real *[le réel]* (the technical skills and the equipment) at the very centre of the social structure' (Sigaut 1990: 174). He also considers that what is real *[le réel]* only gains in solidity and consistency to the extent that it is socialised. Only on this condition can the actions of individuals become effective and provide meaning as well as identity. By touching refuse matter while collectively assigning meaning and value to this contact, waste workers socialise this transgressive experience. They protect themselves from the misleads[4] potentially contained in each of their actions.

Discussions among the MaP community and observations of this bodily engagement have led me to consider the technical activity, particularly when it is carried out in a work context, as an action on matter in which the workers act on themselves and on others at the same time as social positions are created and incorporated. I noticed that by acting on refuse matter, the (re)signifying dimension of gestures is emphasised. This also contributes to building space-times at the margin, marked by transgression, secrecy and subversion. Bodies and specific relationships with order, morality and institutions then unfold from these 'places'. We will explore this idea, by focusing on other workers and other gestures, also carried out on the back stage filled with castoff objects.

Action on refuse matter as critical pluralism

Workshop kitchens: meaning, desire and waste

We will now move on to the workshops used by the technical staff of two healthcare facilities: a hospital and a spa. Both are located in the south of France. The technicians are in charge of maintaining and repairing buildings and technical devices. Their work activities require tools, machines (welding machine, workbench, drill, electric saw, etc.) and specific work areas: workshops. These are removed from the spaces assigned to care (used by patients and caregivers). Most technicians consider themselves as the invisible part of the facilities in which they work and thus qualify themselves, as a spa technician stated, 'staff from below'. By assigning themselves to different zones and separate temporalities, they collectively develop peculiar ways of defining their institutional space. Similarities with the mechanisms described above are obvious in this case.

Along with Erving Goffman, we could describe the workshops, and the storage rooms attached to them, as 'free zones'. In fact, they can be defined as 'prohibited areas in which surveillance and prohibition are clearly loosened' (Goffman 1961: 286). These places, associated with the presence of tools and the spatial expression of social positions, allow workers to carry out their own activities and rearrange their space. They give them a certain

52 *Agnès Jeanjean*

leeway, a degree of control on their work and provide meaning to their technical activities. Refuse also plays an important role in this context.

The spa technicians have set up a kitchen in a corner of their workshop. They designed the layout, mounted the partitions and installed sinks. 'The windows were closed up. We have the tools, so we used them. We used our screwdrivers to unblock them and make it breathable in here'. At the hospital, the electrical technicians built a mezzanine in the workshop; the carpenters installed partitions and added a door in theirs to create a kitchen and the telecom technicians turned a cubbyhole into a 'coffee room'. These rooms are equipped with household appliances salvaged by the workers. Some of the items were donated – by friends, neighbours, employees of another department – because they were no longer working. Others were found in rubbish bins, or on sidewalks after being thrown away by their owners. This characteristic clearly expresses the limit placed by technicians on the financial investment they are ready to make. However, the capacity to repair broken-down appliances is a recurring theme that obviously reflects the workers' specific trades.

> Someone from the hospital gave me the fridge. I was in his home, making some repairs. He said to me: 'I'm throwing it away,' I said 'Don't throw it, I'll take it.' 'We found the TV in a rubbish bin, the remote control and everything was with it. I took it and repaired it. We know how to do it, it's our trade! Nothing was wrong with it. There was just a push button that needed to be fixed. It was on the sidewalk next to a litter bin' (hospital electrical technician).

'I found these desk chairs. Office people wanted to throw them away. We fixed the feet' (spa technician).

Using these objects gives the technicians the opportunity to show their skills and to affirm different values from those they assign to society around them. What distinguishes them is the capacity to repair and to control technical objects and programmed obsolescence, while others are ultimately powerless before them. They also express their attachment to the practical value of the objects, their usefulness.

In these cases, the salvaged objects do not come from the work environment, but the activities associated with them are tied to the workers and their work and how they fit into the wider environment, to their autonomy, and the effectiveness of their tools. Sometimes, when the agents feel that they are sidelined and not provided the means to fully exercise their professional activity, the break rooms become the place where they enjoy putting into practice what they claim to be their trade, because of the actions on matter developed there and the creativity behind them.[5] Something happens in these rooms that corresponds to 'oeuvre' in the sense given to it by Arendt (1958); as artefacts building a human world with opportunities to develop thought and action in a long temporality beyond the short time of consumption. This was the case

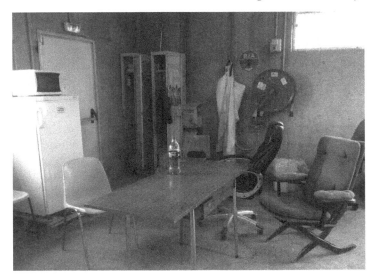

Figure 3.1 Workshop kitchen for spa technicians. South of France, 2015.

Photo by author.

for the hospital carpenters, who built a table from salvaged walnut boards. One of them explains that unlike the melamine or kit furniture that they have to assemble for the hospital, the table they built for themselves requires professional skills and corresponds to the idea they have of their trade. They were able to achieve what they collectively call 'beautiful handiwork' (literally: *[beau geste technique]* a beautiful technical gesture). The table is proof of it. The aesthetic dimension of the gestures used refers to values that are inseparable from the notion of trade and of skill. In these kitchens, the workers give their tools a different use than the prescribed ones. They apply other techniques, other gestures or the same ones but in a different context. This obviously has effects on meanings. Although we are dealing here with activities developed on the workplace, we find a similar mechanism to what Florence Weber (1989) described as 'work on the side'. On the fringes of their assigned work, the agents develop technical activities, transform matter and rework work. These bodily engagements, and the feelings associated with them, renew the concepts of work, pleasure, effort and their collective values. As these objects are shared and used, these values are circulated, incorporated and maintained. The workshop kitchens contribute to the construction of the workers' bodies.

This is achieved, as mentioned previously, by technical gestures and a technical bodily engagement, but also by the way these workers use the objects they have repaired or built. These objects are tailored to the needs of the community and meet their expectations in terms of comfort, taste

54 *Agnès Jeanjean*

and pleasure. Meals are regularly shared in each of the locations studied. Technicians enjoy eating the same things together rather than individual meals. Workshop kitchens are an alternative to professional canteens. The workers we have considered so far do not feel at home in these canteens for a variety of reasons relating to their place in the institution, to the fact that their bodies are in contact with 'dirty' objects and places, to the disgust that they provoke and the shame they feel as a result. They believe that meals shared, prepared and eaten in the workshop prove that their group functions well: 'Everyone feels good in our group, so we all eat here' (hospital electrical technician).

The food and its origin confirm the values of the group, the shared tastes, origins and territorial attachment (Jeanjean 2011b). The fact that the workers are eating well, comfortably installed in a space suited to their bodies, violates the abstraction imposed on their bodies by the work organisation. In these break rooms, their bodies are at the centre of an arrangement that takes into account their specific pains, injuries, professional deformities and singularity as well as their pleasure, desire and enjoyment.

In the renovated functional objects, their uses and what is said about them, we find the expression of pleasure, which relates to what Olivier Schwartz assigns to worker 'tactics' and qualifies as 'the art of making something with almost nothing' (Schwartz 1990: 115 and 416). This 'worker art' is not devoid of humour and poetry. Jokes are made about these contraptions. The cleverness, repurposing, transformation (even of food) and the incongruous but technically effective associations provoke emotions and allow workers to distance themselves from the prescribed use. Workers in these kitchens develop, maintain and express a *taste* for work, self-esteem and recognise 'working skills' (Schwartz 1990: 416) associated with aesthetic judgements. These practices also confirm the technician's feeling of autonomy.

This last observation leads me to mention other practices which are also associated with the workshops and contribute to rearrange work places and temporalities. One of these practices is to store objects and used materials whose status as waste or potentially useful object is undecided or suspended.

Workshop storehouses: suspended time and controlled future

These objects with no market value, kept because 'they can always be useful', are the manifestation of a link between desire, time and refuse. Washer rings, handles, rods, planks, etc., salvaged when the opportunity arises, are used to make the alterations inevitably required in the workers' technical activities.

But they also give workers some leeway with respect to the rhythms and temporalities imposed by the institution and the administration. At the hospital, for example, workers complain about complex administrative procedures that force them to fill out forms before and after each of their operations. The purpose of these documents is to give management the means to check each individual's activities and to keep a rein on expenses. Changing a door or repairing a switch generates a whole chain of documents. These are required not only for traceability purposes but also to obtain authorisations to purchase equipment. These procedures give workers the impression that they are wasting their time, that they are not as free, not as autonomous as they wish to be. They feel that their actions are hindered. Having a storehouse allows them to do their work 'without asking anyone'. They defend a temporality of their own, defined by priorities that correspond to the idea they have of their trade and of their assignments. According to the procedure, the forms and authorisation requests have precedence over the workers' actions. This chronological order demeans their work by giving them a secondary place. However, by keeping a few tools and salvaged objects under hand, which 'can always come in handy', they can circumvent the administrative web. Storehouses allow technicians to defend their own point of view and rhythms. The storage of discarded objects, useless in the immediate future but which may be useful someday, suspends time. Between the past (they are used, sometimes broken), the present and the future, discarded objects materialise both an interrupted time and an open future on which the workers can keep a certain control. They help them accept uncertainties and keep a grip on the future. They offer a way to resist a precarious situation.

Figure 3.2 Workshop with tools and store of supplies. South of France, 2015.

Photo by author.

Figure 3.3 Spoon and rope fashioned into an alarm for the machine that sorts bath robes. South of France, 2015.

Photo by author.

All these observations highlight the freedom and fresh perspective offered by actions on refuse matter under certain conditions. Through storage, repair, cooking and leisure activities, the workers rearrange their workshops and fit their activity into time and space. They use skilled gestures recognised by their community and develop rhythms of their own. The presence of refuse, because of its open nature, contributes to the existence of spaces and temporalities where workers are allowed to develop 'other' perspectives on their work; places and times in which action on matter and bodily engagement contribute to subjectivation processes which oppose those imposed by the work organisation. Pluralism finds a place in the debris, the refuse, the waste … which carry in themselves contradictions, but also *the* contradiction.

These practices confirm what Michel de Certeau (1987: 86) writes:

> Any autonomous order is founded upon what it eliminates; it produces a 'residue' condemned to be forgotten. But what was excluded re-infiltrates the place of its origin – now the present's 'clean' *[propre]* place. It resurfaces, it troubles, it turns the present's feeling of being 'at home' into an illusion, it lurks – this 'wild', this 'ob-scene,' this 'filth,' this 'resistance' of 'superstition' – within the walls of the residence, and, behind the back of the owner (the ego), or over its objections, it inscribes there the law of the other.

Conclusion: management's quest to reconquer recesses, refuse and consequently subjectivities

Both in the hospital and in the spa, I observed architectural transformations that weaken the practices we have just examined. We are witnessing a 'standardisation' of break rooms reserved for employees. Designed by architects, these new rooms are furnished and equipped before employees are admitted. They comply with strict rules of hygiene and their content does not include opacity. Glass partitions are preferred, as are openings that allow outside observation to check the activities that take place inside and the time spent, rather than opaque partitions. New equipment does not tolerate bricolage and other informal architectural transformations, nor does it tolerate the disorderly presence of worn, broken objects with an ambiguous status. Cooking activities are limited to the use of microwaves to heat meals prepared elsewhere, outside of working hours. There is no room for *andouillettes*, *planchas*, baked mushrooms and other specialties, nor for the smells they generate. No room either for mismatched and patched chairs, adjusted by the workers to their bodies, their singularity and their idea of comfort. These new places leave no space for criticism of the work, nor for the development of *reserved territories*.

Interstitial areas with unclear uses are eliminated and even fought. This considerably reduces the possibility for workers to develop ways of acting on themselves that escape imposed activities and therefore to collectively introduce their own goals and values at the heart of production sites. These architectures and arrangements not only prevent the expression of these values but also condemn them as illegitimate. Compared with the ideas of order and beauty that dominate in these places, readjusted, repurposed and re-used objects, 'workers' art', become a source of disorder, dirt, disharmony and ugliness. They acquire a negative value, including aesthetically.

This diminishes the possibility of reintroducing, into the heart of the technical action, collective modes of recognising what is real *[le réel]*, and consequently subjectivation modes other than those dominated by the work organisation. This also applies to the resources that make it possible to live at work and thus to make work liveable (Flamant and Jeudy-Ballini 2002).[6] These are the conclusions that can be drawn from an ethnology of work that is mindful of the tensions that arise from refuse and is convinced, like Jean-Pierre Warnier and Jean-François Bayart, that '(...) the analysis of the political scientist and anthropologist must take into account the subject, its sensorimotor behaviours, its inventories of embodied material culture, its likes, dislikes and passions' (Bayart and Warnier 2004).

Notes

1. Jean Gouhier inaugurated this field of study in the 1980s in France.
2. The term bricolage according to Levi Strauss has no precise equivalent in English.

58 *Agnès Jeanjean*

3. Georges Knaebel (1991) posits that excrement can only be expressed when it is depreciated, derided and denied.
4. They consider themselves very courageous and strong in the face of fear or disease caused by waste matter and excrement. Sometimes, they enjoy frightening people who express disgust or scorn.
5. Many work places have breakrooms. They contribute to the existence of communities, and determine how they fit in time and space. Recognition by the group is particularly important in trades we qualified as 'from below', which do not receive public recognition and where the reality of the activity is an object of denial, including by the work organisation.
6. 'Ways of living work are first and foremost ways of living at work. Transcending the simple relation to the productive activity itself, they can be considered as the different individual or collective approaches used to put this activity at a distance, to organise off-work activities, to organise the space, to highlight the divisions, to accommodate knowledge, to define references in terms of identity, to build social connections, to reactivate a history, to tinker strategies or to express self-esteem, for example – the ways of living work are finally just ways of making work liveable' (Flamant and Jeudy-Ballini 2002: 16).

References

Arendt, H. (1958), *The Human Condition*, Chicago: University of Chicago Press.
Freud, S. (1971), *Malaise dans la civilisation*, Paris: Presses Universitaires de France (1st ed. All. 1930).
Bayart, J. -F. and J. -P. Warnier (2004), *Matière à politique. Le pouvoir, les corps et les choses*, Paris: CERI-Karthala.
Butler, J. (1997), *The Psychic Life of Power: Theories in Subjection*, Stanford: Stanford University Press.
Corteel, D. and S. Le Lay (2011), *Les travailleurs des déchets*, Toulouse: ERES.
Certeau (de), M. (1987), *Histoire et psychanalyse*, Paris: Gallimard.
Debary, O. (2019), *De la poubelle au musée, une anthropologie des restes*, Paris: Créaphis éditions.
Douglas, M. (1970), *Purity and Danger: An Analysis of the Concepts of Pollution and Taboo*, London: Routledge and Kegan Paul.
Elias, N. (1939), *La civilisation des mœurs*, Paris: Calmann-Lévy.
Flamant, N. and M. Jeudy-Ballini (2002), 'Le charme discret des entreprises', *Terrain*, 39: 5–16.
Foucault, M. (1994), *Dits et Écrits, IV. 1980–1988*, Paris: Gallimard.
Goffman, E. (1961), *Asylum: Essays on the Condition of the Social Situation of Mental Patients and Other Inmates*, New York: Doubleday.
Gouhier, J. (1999), 'La marge entre rejet et intégration', in J. -C. Beaune (ed.), *Le déchet, le rebut, le rien*, 80–89, Paris: Champ Vallon.
Hugo, V. (1862), 'L'intestin du Léviathan', in *Les misérables*, 313–320, Paris: Livre de Poche.
Jeudy-Ballini, M. (2002), '"Et il paraît qu'ils ne sont pas tous sourds ?" Le travail comme exploit et résistance au quotidien', *Terrain*, 39: 17–32.
Jeanjean, A., T. Cruz, M. Ducerisier, C. Laudanski, M. Occelli and P. Rosini (2007), *Etude ethnologique des hôpitaux Pasteur et Saint-Roch. Mars 2005-Janvier 2007*, rapport remis au service culturel du CHU de Nice.

Jeanjean, A. (2006), *Basses oeuvre: Une ethnologie du travail dans les égouts*, Paris: CTHS.

Jeanjean, A. (2011a), 'Travailler à la morgue ou dans les égouts: que faire du dégoût', *Ethnologie Française*, 2: 59–66.

Jeanjean, A. (2011b), 'Entre contagion, secret et transmission, ce que l'on se passe aux abords des déchets', in D. Coortel and S. Le Lay (eds.), *Les Travailleurs des Déchets*, 279–303, Paris: Eres.

Julien, M. -P. and J. -P. Warnier, eds. (1999), *Approches de la culture matérielle: Corps à corps avec l'objet*, Paris: L'Harmattan.

Julien M. -P. and C. Rosselin, eds. (2009), *Le sujet contre les objets … tout contre: Ethnographies de cultures matérielles*, Paris: CTHS.

Knaebel, G. (1991), 'Le rangement du résidu', *Les Annales de la Recherche Urbaine*, 53: 23–31.

Lacan, J. (1986), *Le séminaire livre VII*, Paris: Seuil.

Lévi-Strauss, C. (1962), *La pensée sauvage*, Paris: Plon.

Monsaingeon, B. (2014), *Le déchet durable. Eléments pour une socio-anthropologie du déchet ménager*, Thèse de doctorat, Paris 1 Panthéon-Sorbonne.

O'Brien, M. (2008), *A Crisis of Waste? Understanding the Rubbish Society*, New York: Routledge.

Ortar, N. and E. Anstett, eds. (2017), *Jeux de pouvoir dans nos poubelles. Economies morales et politiques du recyclage au tournant du XXIe Siècle*, Paris: Editions Petra.

Pétonnet, C. (1991), 'Le cercle de l'immondice', *Les annales de la recherche urbaine*, 53: 108–111.

Rathje, W. and C. Murphy (1992), *Rubbish. The Archaeology of Garbage*, New York: Harper Collins publishers.

Rosselin, C., Lalo, E. and D. Nourrit (2015), 'Prendre, apprendre et comprendre. Mains et matières à travailler chez les scaphandriers', *Ethnographiques.org*, 31. http://www.ethnographiques.org/2015/Rosselin-Lalo-Nourrit (last accessed 04.06.2019).

Scanlan, J. (2005), *On Garbage*, London: Reaktion Books.

Schwartz, O. (1990), *Le monde privé des ouvriers. Hommes et femmes du Nord*, Paris: Presses Universitaires de France.

Sigaut, F. (1990), 'Folie, réel et technologie', *Techniques & Culture*, 15: 167–179.

Thompson, M. (1979), *Rubbish Theory: The Creation and Destruction of Value*, Oxford: Oxford University Press.

Warnier, J. -P. (2009a), 'Technology as Efficacious Action on Objects… and Subjects', *Journal of Material Culture*, 14 (4): 459–470.

Warnier, J. -P. (2009b), 'Les technologies du sujet: Une approche ethno-philosophique', *Techniques & Culture*, 52–53: 148–167.

Weber, F. (1989), *Le travail à-côté. Étude d'ethnographie ouvrière*, Paris: EHESS-INRA.

4 Clothing choices and questioning the incorporation of *habitus*[1]

Marie-Pierre Julien

Introduction

In the 1970s, Quentin Bell ([1976] 1992) developed a general sociology of clothing demonstrating the importance of clothing in the socialisation of humans in any society, and putting into question the functionalist paradigm which claims that the aim of clothing is to replace the hair with which other mammals are covered. In order to support his demonstration, Bell relied on the work of Thorstein Veblen ([1899] 1909) who from the beginning of the nineteenth century onwards had looked at clothes through the perspective of the movements they authorise, limit or prevent, seeing them as a way to affirm one's distinction from others, by taking the example of the ostentatious clothing style of the American *bourgeoisie* (leisure class) of his time. Later on, Pierre Bourdieu (1980b) looked at fashion, relying both on Veblen's work concerning distinction, and on the more semiological studies of Roland Barthes (1957, 1967) on clothing and fashion. This in spite of the fact that from the beginning of the twentieth century onwards, the German researcher Georg Simmel ([1908] 1998), who had worked on fashion and clothing, reacted to Veblen's approach by insisting that individuals are constantly oscillating between imitation and distinction from other members of the group. For Simmel this to-and-fro shows the possibility for norms to be incorporated through socialisation, and to be transformed by the individuals who experience them. However, none of these authors tackles the question of youth or children's clothing, except for Dan Cook (2004), whose work concerns the consumption of products aimed at children and youths. Cook shows how first adolescence and then pre-adolescence have become marketing categories built to increase target consumer markets, and how teenagers and tweens have now appropriated these categories and reclaim them as naturally appropriate.

When clothing does not serve the main purpose of regulating body temperature, is it still a sign of distinction or imitation, or is it merely the result of economic and symbolic power relations between producers, distributors and consumers? What happens to the materiality of clothes and of the bodies they dress, bodies which grow and age continuously, and which have a

62   *Marie-Pierre Julien*

central place in the status changes of subjects[2] in society, throughout their lives? Moreover, how do clothes accompany these social changes?

As shown in the Balinese field work of Gregory Bateson and Margaret Mead (1942), social age is completely disconnected from biological age. Like Norbert Elias ([1939, 1969] 1973) who uses the notion of 'civilisation process', the authors argue that body functions are part of the process of cultural denaturalisation of the body. This process mobilises body techniques that are socially and culturally normed, as Marcel Mauss ([1934, 1950] 1993) also underlines. As part of the CorAge ANR[3] project which aimed to study the modes in which children aged 9–13 imagine, perceive and govern their bodily transformations through everyday practices, I focused on how these children manage clothing. How do clothes help to experience, perform and affirm 'growing'? Which forms of know-how are necessary for clothing, what are the power issues that underlie clothing and what are the networks of actions upon actions of which it is a part?

Mauss' concept of socialisation through body techniques has its weak points (Julien 1999, Warnier 1999), as Alain Prout (2000) also underlines. Prout criticises Mauss for having looked at children's and adolescents' socialisation with a single-minded focus, considering it merely as a result of incorporated normative dispositions that are passively and gradually accumulated in order to obtain access to the plenitude of the adult world. However, for the past thirty years a number of French (Sirota 1988, 2006, Delalande 2001, Diasio 2004, 2010) and Anglo-Saxon (James 1993) studies in child sociology and anthropology have refuted several assumptions on which Maussian theory relies.

The approach taken by the *Matière à Penser* (MaP) research group centres on the materiality of clothing and bodies, and is grounded in the writings of Michel Foucault, who joins knowledge[4] and power and subjectivation and government. This article looks at the know-how that is acquired in connection with clothing, and which is part of the networks of actions[5] that constitute a subject's social construction. In this approach, clothes are seen as tools to build knowledge about oneself and about others, providing information about a body which changes in size and shape, and about the social consequences of these changes.

I will look here at the body as an entity that encompasses its objects – in this case clothes and accessories like bags, caps or shoes – through action (Warnier 1999, Julien and Rosselin eds. 2009), in a paradigm that is the outcome of a longstanding anthropological tradition (Diasio 2009). The hypothesis is that both the choice of clothing and the body techniques that are necessary for individuals to be clothed in a certain way allow them to integrate various groups of play, age and gender. These techniques require learning and practice in front of the bedroom or bathroom mirror, performed before the other cohabitants of the home, during the neighbourhood walk, the party or among the school community. Depending on the situation, the opinion of peers and adults has an important role to play in

Clothing choices and questioning   63

the establishment of this know-how, linking it to the network of actions that relate governmentalities through complex connections and allow the social construction of subjects. In this chapter, the first part will focus on the performative know-how of clothes as tools for social and material measure, and as 'techniques of the self' on the self and on others, in a Foucauldian sense, while the second part shows how the networks of actions upon actions, which include objects and the know-how they generate, are established, looking at clothes from the angle of the 'technology of the self', in the sense of the government of the self and of others.

Clothes and techniques of self: tools to measure and know oneself and others

Knowledge of the self and about the self through socially determined procedures is a daily activity that is indispensable to young people for two reasons: firstly, their bodies are changing constantly and secondly, young people are constantly relearning social rules that connect age and gender, because these two criteria change the norms. These techniques of the self not only allow young people to measure themselves physically and confront the social norms, they also allow them to learn about themselves and about others, and to test existing social categorisations. Michel Foucault (2001a: 1032) has described techniques of the self as 'procedures which exist in every civilisation and which are proposed or prescribed to individuals in order to establish their identity, maintain it or transform it to match a number of aims, and this is done through control of the self on the self or knowledge of the self by the self'. Translated into more anthropological terms, every piece of clothing constitutes a means for our young interlocutors to acquire knowledge of the self and of others, because of the techniques of objects (Leroi-Gourhan 1964) and of the body (Mauss [1934, 1950] 1993) which it requires in order to act.

Clothes improve self-knowledge at various levels: they allow the wearers to measure changes and create the need to reconsider the connections between biopsychological and social age, in order to define themselves in an age group that results from a combination of calendar age, morphology and gender. Indeed, one's 'age group' is not always of much help when young people of the same age vary physically and it is difficult for young people to dress according to the social criteria applied to their age. Human bodies are biologically incomplete, very different from one another and highly unstable. These particular characteristics open the doors for the social to work on the human body through *habitus* composed both of techniques of objects and techniques of the body, in order to make the subjects resemble the others in the group to which they belong (social, age and gender) more closely.

Every young person has had the experience of the favorite piece of clothing that has become 'too small', and clothes thus constitute an experience through which young people can measure themselves. Luc,[6] fourteen, lives with his mother in an apartment in the city centre of Strasbourg and showed ethnographer Chloé Buchmann[7] how he put on the jeans he wore in sixth grade with some difficulty (Figure 4.1). Arthur lives with his parents and his sister (thirteen) in an apartment in the suburbs close to Strasbourg. His mother explains[8] that her thirteen-year-old son likes to show that he's growing by wearing a piece of clothing that is slightly too small, so that the people he meets will observe his growth and congratulate him on it. A change in position in the group, and often in the family, is negotiated through clothing changes. As a tool of self-knowledge and as a means to perform this change in front of others, clothes also represent the experience of the categorisation of the self and others, and its social consequences.

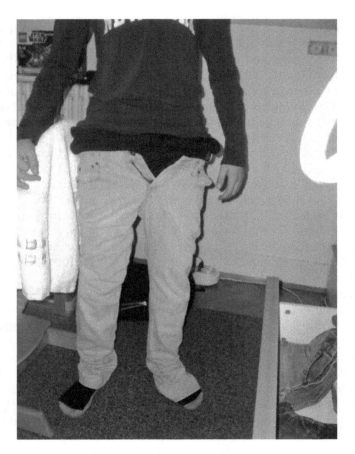

Figure 4.1 Luc shows how he puts on his jeans with difficulty. Strasbourg, France, 2012.

Image credit Chloé Buchmann.

Knowledge about oneself and others that aims to categorise

In Western society age is considered to be an objective matter, since we can measure it in the same way for everyone thanks to our capacity to identify our date of birth. However, this is very recent and dates back to the second half of the nineteenth century, when nation states needed to be able to identify every one of their citizens. At the same time there was a concern to improve medical care, with doctors working to establish thresholds of development and maturity – whether that be in bone-structure, in stature or in pubertal, mental or intellectual development. These thresholds and stages in development began to be measured, averaged and transcribed into graphs in people's medical health booklets from the eighteenth century onwards with Pierre-Jean-Georges Cabanis, MD, (Staum 1980) and later on, around the turn of the nineteenth century, with Paul Godin (1902), and form the link between degrees of development and chronological age. In the twentieth century, studies by developmental psychologists (Hall 1904, Erikson ([1959] 1994) proposed the idea that biological maturity is also linked to psychological maturity with age being biopsychological or psychophysiological. However, there is a third dimension to age, which is social, determined according to the social place the individual occupies, or is made to occupy, and the social qualities that are attributed to or demonstrated by that individual. These 'social' qualities are associated with chronological and psychophysiological age to create an age category called childhood, to which social norms are then attributed.

Lisa, ten, lives with her mother in an apartment in the city centre of a small city in the Lorraine region. She has four brothers and sisters who are all older than her. In order to describe their clothes, our interlocutors mainly apply the criteria of age and of gender, as Lisa underlines when the sociologist[9] asks whether the girls in her school dress like her. 'There's Caroline and Julia, they have exactly the same style of clothing as me. They don't like it to be too babyish. They'd rather walk around in stuff that could be worn by boys'. By tackling the complex question of age, our interlocutors bring up the way their bodies, physiologically unstable, are linked to categories of age which are not at all obvious and which, moreover, depend on gender relations. In the Christian Western world, the techniques of gathering knowledge on and by oneself are required to truthfully and coherently bring together calendar, social and biological age. Secondly, the age characteristics associated with boys are not the same as those for girls, and age will therefore depend on gender relations that are historically determined in every social environment.

Growing requires knowledge about oneself and about 'good' age norms, in order to correspond truthfully to one's age and gender, and to avoid transgressing social categories. Diva, ten, lives in an apartment with her mother in the village of the Haut-Rhin region in Trois-Frontières, Alsace.[10] She has brothers and sisters who are much older than her. Going out, she wears trousers, a cap and a shoulder strap bag, in which she puts her phone and her keys (Figure 4.2). Lucie, eleven, lives with her parents, her brother, eight and her sister, thirteen, in a house in residential area of a small city in the Lorraine region. Lucie replies to the researcher, Niloofar Shariat, when asked why she does not like dresses: 'I don't know, you can't run in them'. As has been demonstrated in a number of gender studies, these young people show by their choice in clothing that they master certain social codes, which imply, for instance, that girls should not show their underwear. In this way, if they want to play and run with the boys of the village, the girls we observed have to dress like boys, with long trousers and sometimes caps. Still, this does not at all imply that they want to be assimilated with boys. Lorraine, ten, lives with her parents and her sister (four and a half) in an

Figure 4.2 Diva in New York Yankees cap (face blurred for privacy). Haut-Rhin, France, 2011.

Image credit Siar Munckien.

apartment in downtown Meurthe et Moselle.[11] She states: 'That T-Shirt there, it's not my favorite thing. It's too boyish for me and I'm not a tomboy, hey!' Girls have to learn what the right clothes are, and have to square that with their feelings and perceptions, out of the same concern for truthfulness: to be dressed like boys in order to be able to run with the boys, but not to be 'tomboys'. In a different situation, inside the home, Diva allows her sister to apply make-up and to dress her hair, and learns how to walk with high heels that go 'clac-clac-clac' (Julien 2012b). She also reveals that these very feminine gestures require arduous learning, which is a work of the self on the self that happens under the gaze of her mother and her elder sister, a long-term apprenticeship protected by the home environment.

Subjects have the specific characteristic of being both subjected to social determiners and at the same time being the actors of their actions, which puts them in a double bind with society (being both the objects of actions and actors). The social dimension does not only act in restrictive ways on individuals who supposedly undergo these effects unconsciously, as Bourdieu (1980a) would have it, for instance. Indeed, Bourdieu defines the *habitus* as a way for individuals to be and do and which happens through an unconscious/unspoken incorporation of the objective structures of the social world. This means that Bourdieu defines the bodies of individuals, caught in the experience of the social world, as repositories of social structures, generating thoughts, behaviors, representations, tastes, etc. in the shape of dispositions. In Foucault's definition of the subject, however, the reflexivity of individuals, both on themselves and on others, is also considered, as is their implication in several networks or actions upon the actions of others.

Clothes at the heart of technologies of self

In this second part, we will look at clothing from the angle of technologies of the self. When Foucault uses the term 'technology', his arguments look at techniques from the perspective of power relations. Power is not so much a relationship between the dominated and the dominating, but rather something that 'circulates, [which] is never localised here or there, it is never in the hands of some, it is never appropriated as wealth or possessions. Power functions and power exerts itself in networks, and in those networks, not only do individuals circulate, they are always in a position of undergoing, and also exercising power; they are never the inert and consenting target of power, they are always the relay factor. In other words, power goes through individuals, it does not apply to them' (Foucault 2001a: 180). Further on, Foucault specifies his argument: 'individuals are not faced with power, they are, I believe, one of its primary effects' (ibid.). This section will therefore look at how power circulates in various networks of actions, by taking a closer look at knowing how to/being able to do something such as giving gifts, lending clothes and offering clothing advice.

68   *Marie-Pierre Julien*

Know-how as parts of networks of actions upon the actions of others

To know how to dress according to a particular social situation (activities, material context, people present) is not easy and has to be acquired through learning. Tom, thirteen, Ibanez, eleven and Maxence, eight, live in a house in a village in the Moselle region, and Tom explains to researcher, Benoit Dejaiffe, how well he manages this know-how: 'When I prepare my sports bag, if I'm being a bit careful I'll take a nice top and a nice T-Shirt... The tennis club's top: the jacket is red, to I'll pick a red T-Shirt, and when the top is black, I'll pack a black T-Shirt, it's a tennis label. And when I go mountain biking with my grandad, I take old trainers, and I'll take old T-Shirts because with grandpa we usually go in the mud!' Paul, ten, lives with his mother and his five-year-old brother in the suburbs of Strasbourg.[12] He insists on the fact that knowing how to/being able to choose cannot be dissociated from the daily chore of dealing with dirty washing, a theme that was already discussed by Jean-Claude Kaufmann (1992) in his study on couple forming: 'A while ago it was Mother, now it's me, and she says yes or no, you can wear this or no you can't wear that. It changed a few weeks ago ... Now I can manage a bit better. That one for example, I know I wore it not long ago, but I wore it only once, so I could wear it tomorrow, for instance ... Except that tomorrow I know I have sports, so I might take Bermuda pants like that one, or shorts'. It is obvious that some time is necessary to acquire the knowing how to/being able to that allows young people to choose their outfits on a daily basis. These two extracts show two of the social skills involved in clothing which young people need to be able to show their parents (in this case, their mothers): clean or dirty, and the terrain of activity as well as associated weather.

The awareness and the management of this know-how are techniques of the self which, through the socialisation processes that are proper to each society, allow young people to constitute themselves as subjects. However, this know-how is not just a *techné*, it also touches on the *bios*, as Foucault (2001b: 466) explains: through these practices, subjects learn about the world around them and through that experience, they learn to know themselves. The morality of clothing as a 'technology of power', which as bio-power relies on the body and its techniques, can be distinguished in three of the arguments used by adults (parents or educators) to justify the choice of clothing which they impose on young people: the activities of the day, the weather and the social gaze. I will limit myself here to discussing only the third. Among girls, the idea is to fight against 'vulgarity' and among boys, it is about going against 'negligence'. Teenager Romane's mother is even more explicit: 'She won't be wearing both a deep-cut neckline and short skirts. I'm always making sure it's not vulgar, I hate vulgarity, especially on a fourteen-year-old girl'. Sometimes tastes are transmitted the way Romane explains it: '[I dress] normal, simple. I think skirts and dresses are really pretty, but I don't like them, it's pretty but it doesn't suit me. I don't like it, it's not me, in fact, in a skirt it's a different girl! I have always only hung out with boys so I will wear jeans or sweatpants. When I see myself in jeans, I'm not the same girl, in fact'. When we meet her, Romane seems to have adopted her mother's criteria. The transmission of morals requires unconscious incorporation as Bourdieu describes it for the *habitus* seems to work, since the girl declares that her personal taste is the fact that she does not like dresses and skirts.

For the mothers it seems clear that the moral dimensions of clothing have been fully integrated by their children. Parents, however, are not the only normative prescribers, and neither are clothing retailers. In the last part of this article, I will elaborate these exchanges between pairs within the family (siblings, cousins) or outside of it (friends, classmates or other people).

Clothes at the heart of gifts, loans and advice

Networks of exchanges of clothes and clothing advice can be divided into three categories that are distinguished according to the mode in which the exchange happens: gifts, loans and clothing advice. These three modes of exchange involve very different power relations within the various networks of actions.

Gifts of clothes usually happen from the older to the younger, as Tom explains when he discusses the piece of clothing that is too small but not worn out: 'Like I enjoy having nice T-Shirts, I take care of them, so that's why it's my brothers who then get my T-Shirts'. But the elder children can also receive the younger ones' hand-me-downs. Benjamin, fourteen and Loïc, sixteen, live in a house in a village located ten km north of Saint Dié, in the Vosges region.[13] As Benjamin's mother explains: 'Benjamin is less annoying than Loïc. You can make him wear clothes that were handed down by his cousin, girl or boy'. As Lisa's mother puts it, these gifts are links: 'It's only been a few months since Jeanne … she thinks about her little sister, because she knows her little sister is beginning to grow. And then she's so proud to wear her big sister's clothes'. Lisa also discusses this with the researcher: '[Jeanne] gave me a little cardigan that I haven't worn yet'. While they are part of the construction of a family resemblance, these hand-me-downs have advantages since, one, they did not cost anything and, two, these gifts allow the children to have clothes or accessories that the parents would not have bought retail. However, these gifts do not escape the power relations described by Marcel Mauss since 1924.

Another type of exchange is advice about clothing. This includes the classic modes of socialisation through family and peers (Darmon 2007). When it comes to family, this can include advice from parents or siblings, or from members of the wider family circle where godfathers and godmothers play an important part (Fine 1997, Attias-Donfut and Segalen 2007). Dadi, ten, lives in a house in the suburbs of Mulhouse with his parents.[14] His older sister explains: 'He will propose a few outfits and we'll tell him "yes" or "no".

70 *Marie-Pierre Julien*

Otherwise, at first it was me and my mother ... We would go and buy them with him, always checking if he liked them or not... But now he buys what he wants, it's easier for him to buy with his brother than with us, because we criticise...' These discussions emphasise the work of education and transmission of certain moral norms and values in the course of action. The networks are not impermeably separate from one another, but cross over into each other, and subjects find themselves at the intersection since they act in several networks at the same time. Florian, eleven, Jeff, nine and Pikatchu, five, live with their mother and Pikatchu's father in a social housing apartment in a village in the Moselle region.[15] As their mother underlines: 'I'd rather they are with me. To buy what they like, right. So, I can be sure they won't be afraid to wear it or ...That they should not feel silly compared to the others'.

The action of getting dressed, borrowing and choosing whether to wear clothes that were a gift, asking for advice and showing oneself dressed depending on certain situations, are acts of power and resistance within networks of actions by family, peers or school friends, which allow young people to negotiate their place in those environments. The attention that is given to the materiality of actions highlights the fact that clothes are not only signs of belonging to a group. Between performance and assignation, experimenting with this or that piece of clothing reveals what is socially accepted or not, depending on the social situation. Managing this knowledge results in integration and identification to a group of family, peers, gender, etc.

Conclusion: material object as a double link between individuals and society

In this article, the approach centred on clothing, showing how this is not only a sign of belonging to an age group or a gender, but also how clothes are at the heart of actions by which we build knowledge about ourselves and others. This is all the more important for our young interlocutors who have a body that is changing rapidly, a biological fact that is combined with a social status that changes with age. Knowledge obtained through a variety of networks confronts young people with different clothing norms, which they learn to manage little by little.

The link between age and gender is particularly obvious from our observations and pervades the discourse on clothes of these young people or their parents, as soon as the first signs of puberty appear. Adolescence implies transformations that differ greatly depending on the individual, and which not only young people and their parents and peers, but also educators and the media attempt to manage through injunctions, remarks, mockery and gazes of approval or disapproval, which are all forms of affirmation, appropriation and transformation of the norms that are in force. Still, age is often a forgotten factor in the intersectional analytical approach (Crenshaw and

Bonnis 2005), as Barry Thorne has ruefully pointed out since 2004, because age is too often considered to be a natural element, and not a cultural construct. In order to avoid the trappings of naturalisation, Marc Bessin and Marianne Blidon (2011) propose to follow up on intersectional theories and think about age in terms of domination, which is a paradigm inherited from Bourdieu's thought. They propose, on the one hand, to examine how these categories are produced, and on the other hand, to question the performativity of categories that are associated with age in contemporary society on a daily basis.

In a Foucauldian perspective, this reflexivity, which we had already observed among our youngest interlocutors (aged nine or ten) is connected to the cultural requirement for truth – which we have found here in the requirement to dress according to one's culturally normed age and gender – which is established through the acquisition of techniques of the self that lie at the heart of governmentality. Our young interlocutors' reflexivity and self-work are important elements in the acquisition and mobilisation of *habitus* as defined by Bourdieu. We fully realise that taking this reflexivity into account goes against Bourdieu's thinking, as has been underlined by Philippe Corcuff (2001) who also notices the empirical weakness of *habitus* theory, while at the same time praising the author's theoretical ambitions. More recently, Michel Burawoy (2012: 7) remarked how Bourdieu 'developed his entire theory about habitus and fields without taking into serious consideration the understanding that actors have of themselves, or the resources they have at their disposal'.

By highlighting how managing know-how allows our young interlocutors to acquire power within these networks of actions, we have underscored the double link between individuals and society, as characterised by Michel Foucault (2011b: 466). The first link is characterised by the fact that clothes, as material objects, as well as the socialised actions that clothing requires, inform young people about their age and gender, since as we have seen, neither are natural givens. The second link reveals that these young people experience the world through actions on clothing, which allows them to test the efficiency of their know-how, to test themselves and to construct themselves as subjects while at the same time fulfilling the social requirement of self-knowledge. The moral dimension of clothing thus insinuates itself in this double link that constructs young people as subjects of power, that is to say, subjects who are permeated by power which they alternately undergo, manage or exercise.

Notes

1. A first version of this chapter appeared in French (Julien 2014) for the journal *Revue des Sciences Sociales*. It was rewritten, translated and edited for the English version presented here.
2. I here use the term 'subject' in the same way as M. Foucault (1994) and anthropologists such as S. Fainzang (2001), to designate individuals who are both the actors of their actions and at the same time are subjected to powers that

72   *Marie-Pierre Julien*

are beyond them, such as socio-cultural determiners, a political context, laws and rules that are imposed upon them. For more details on the notion of the subject in the social sciences see Julien (2012a).

3. The CorAge project was funded by the ANR program 'Children and Childhoods'. This project was coordinated by Nicoletta Diasio, who set up three research teams respectively belonging to the University of Strasbourg, the University of Lorraine, coordinated by Virginie Vinel (2017) and the Ca' Foscari University of Venice (coordinated by Donatella Cozzi). Eleven senior researchers and nine junior researchers studied the ways in which children between nine and thirteen imagine, perceive and govern their bodily changes in daily ordinary practices, as well as the way in which parents, siblings and peer accompany them, the resources they apply to face these changes and their consequences when it comes to social relations and defining each other.

4. Foucault draws an important distinction between *savoir* (generally translated as knowledge) and *connaissance* (awareness, understanding). *Savoir*/knowledge designates the movement which results in greater or lesser modifications of the knowing subject. *Connaissance*/awareness refers to something entirely different: it does not consider the subject as a process but only looks at the 'objective' or 'objectual' widening of the circle of things to know (Vihalem 2011). The present translation also uses the English term 'forms or types of know-how' to translate occurrences of the French term *savoir-faire.*

5. In the Foucauldian sense, a network of actions is the sum of the actions of different individuals that are interdependent. Such a network is the place where power is exercised and at the same time resisted, in the sense that power is never exercised only as prohibition and punishment.

6. All names have been changed to protect the privacy of individuals.

7. Apart from the interviews and observations which I carried out, this article is also written on the basis of field studies by Chloé Buchmann, Benoit Dejaiffe, Nicoletta Diasio, Louis Mathiot, Estelle Reinert, Niloofar Shariat and Virginie Vinel, and I would like to thank my colleagues for the quality of their work.

8. Interviews and observations by Marie-Pierre Julien.

9. Interviews and ethnographies by Estelle Reinert.

10. Interviews and observations by Siar Munckien.

11. Interviews and observations by Estelle Reinert.

12. Interviews and observations by Marie-Pierre Julien.

13. Interviews and observations by Louis Mathiot.

14. Interviews and ethnographies by Marie-Pierre Julien.

15. Interviews and observations by Estelle Reinert.

References

Attias-Donfut, C. and M. Segalen (2007), *Grands-parents. La famille à travers les générations*, Paris: Editions Odile Jacob.

Barthes, R. (1957), 'Histoire et sociologie du vêtement, quelques observations méthodologiques', *Annales ESC*, 12 (3): 430–441.

Barthes, R. (1967), *Système de la mode*, Paris: Éditions du Seuil.

Bateson, G. and M. Mead (1942), *Balinese Character: A Photographic Analysis*, New York: NY Academy of Sciences.

Bell, Q. ([1976] 1992), *Mode et société: Essai sur la sociologie du vêtement*, Paris: Presses Universitaires de France.

Bessin, M. and M. Blidon, eds. (2011), 'Vieillir', Special Issue, *Genre, sexualité et société*, 6.

Bourdieu, P. (1980a), *Le sens pratique*, Paris: Les Éditions de Minuit.

Bourdieu, P. (1980b), 'Haute couture et haute culture', in P. Bourdieu, *Questions de sociologie*, 196–206, Paris: Les Éditions de Minuit.

Burawoy, M. (2012), *Conversations with Bourdieu: The Johannesburg Moment*, Johannesburg: University of Witwatersrand Press. http://www.contretemps.eu/lectures/théorie-pratique-quand-marx-rencontre-bourdieu (Last accessed 10.06.2019).

Cook, D. (2004), *The Commodification of Childhood. The Children's Clothing Industry and the Rise of the Child Consumer*, Durham: Duke University Press.

Corcuff, P. (2001), *Le travail sociologique de Pierre Bourdieu*, Paris: La Découverte.

Crenshaw, K. and O. Bonis (2005), 'Cartographies des marges: Intersectionnalité, politique de l'identité et violences contre les femmes de couleur', *Cahiers du genre*, 2 (39): 51–82.

Darmon, M. (2007), *La socialisation*, Paris: Armand Colin.

Delalande, J. (2001), *La cour de récréation, contribution à une anthropologie de l'enfance*, Rennes: PUR.

Diasio, N., ed. (2004), *Au palais de Dame Tartine: Regards Européens sur la consommation enfantines*, Paris: L'Harmattan.

Diasio, N. (2009), 'La liaison tumultueuse des choses et des corps. Pour un positionnement théorique de matière à penser', in M. -P. Julien and C. Rosselin (eds.), *Le sujet contre les objets… tout contre. Ethnographies de cultures matérielles*, Paris: éditions du CTHS, Coll. Orientations et méthodes.

Diasio, N. (2010), 'Le gouvernement de l'incertitude. Corps, culture matérielle et maillage des temps à l'enfance', *Mémoire pour l'obtention de l'habilitation à diriger des recherches*, Paris: Université Paris Descartes.

Elias, N. ([1939, 1969] 1973), *La civilisation des mœurs*, Paris: Calman-Levy.

Erikson, E. H. ([1959] 1994), *Enfance et société*, Neuchâtel: Delachaux et Niestlé.

Fainzang, S. (2001), *Médicaments et société. Le patient, le médecin et l'ordonnance*, Paris: Presses Universitaires de France.

Fine, A. (1997), 'Parrainage, marrainage et relations familiales dans la société Française contemporaine', *Lien Social et Politiques RIAC*, 37: 157–170.

Foucault, M. (2001a), *Dits et Ecrits II*, Paris: Gallimard.

Foucault, M. (2001b), *L'herméneutique du sujet, cours au collège de France 1981–1982*, Paris: Gallimard.

Godin, P. (1902), 'Recherches anthropométriques sur la croissance des différentes parties du corps. détermination de l'adolescent type aux différents âges pubertaires d'après 36000 mensurations', *Bulletins de la Société d'Anthropologie de Paris V Series*, 3: 717–719.

Hall, G. S. (1904), *Adolescence: Its Psychology and Its Relations to Physiology, Anthropology, Sociology, Sex, Crime, Religion, and Education, 2 Vols.* New York: Appleton.

James, A. (1993), *Childhood Identities: Self and Social Relationships in the Experience of the Child*, Edinburgh: EUP.

Julien, M.-P. (1999), 'Des techniques du corps à la "synthèse corporelle", mises en objets', in M.-P. Julien and J. -P. Warnier (eds.), *Approches de la culture matérielle. Corps à corps avec l'objet*, 15–28, Paris: L'Harmattan, Coll. 'Connaissances des hommes'.

74 *Marie-Pierre Julien*

Julien, M. -P. (2012a), 'Sujet, subjectivation, subjectivité et sciences sociales', in J. Deniot and J. Réault (eds.), *L'odyssée du sujet*, 87–106, Nantes: Lestamp-Edition.

Julien, M. -P. (2012b), 'Quel statut accorder aux savoir-faire dans nos recherches. Réflexions à partir de deux terrains récents', Congrès AFEA, http://afea2011.sciencesconf.org (last accessed 10.06.2019).

Julien, M. -P. (2014), 'Choisir ses vêtements et ouvrir la boite noire des Habitus', *Revue des sciences sociales, 'La Préadolescence Existe-t-elle?'*, 51: 134–145. http://revue-des-sciences-sociales.com (last accessed 10.06.2019).

Julien, M. -P. and C. Rosselin, eds. (2009), *Le sujet contre les objets... tout contre. Ethnographies de cultures matérielles*, Paris: éditions du CTHS, 'Coll. Orientations et méthodes'.

Kaufmann, J. -C. (1992), *La trame conjugale, analyse du couple par son linge*, Paris: Nathan.

Leroi-Gourhan, A. (1964), *Le geste et la parole. Technique et langage*, Paris: Albin Michel.

Mauss, M. (1924), *Essai sur le don*, http://www.uqac.uquebec.ca/zone30/Classiques_des_sciences_sociales/index.html (last accessed 10.06.2019).

Mauss, M. ([1934, 1950] 1993), 'Les techniques du corps', *Sociologie et anthropologie*, 363–386, Paris: Presses Universitaires de France.

Prout, A., ed. (2000), *The Body, Childhood and Society*, London and New York: MacMillan St. Martin's Press.

Simmel, G. ([1908] 1998), *La parure et autres essais*, Paris: éditions de la MSH.

Sirota, R. (2006). *Éléments pour une sociologie de l'enfance*, Rennes: Presses universitaires de Rennes.

Sirota, R. (1988), *L'école primaire au quotidien*, Paris: Presses Universitaires de France.

Staum, M.S. (1980), *Cabanis, Enlightenment and Medical Philosophy in the French Revolution*, Princeton: PUP.

Thorne, B. (2004), 'Editorial: Theorizing Age and Other Differences', *Childhood*, 11 (4): 403–408.

Veblen, T. ([1899] 1909), *The Theory of the Leisure Class – An Economic Study of Institutions*, London: The Macmillian Company.

Vinel, V. (2017), 'Se coiffer et se maquiller à la préadolescence. Enquête en Alsace-Lorraine', in M. Jacquemin, D. Bonnet, C. Deprez, M. Pilon, and G. Pison, *Enfance et genre*, 133–146, Paris: INED.

Warnier, J. -P. (1999), *Construire la culture matérielle. L'homme qui pensait avec ses doigts*, Paris: Presses Universitaires de France.

Matter of heritage

5 Museum objects in motion: Colonial leftovers and French cultural politics

Mélanie Roustan

'When men die, they become history. Once statues die, they become art. This botany of death is what we call culture': here is the opening of the astonishing and somehow prefatory film made by Marker and Resnais in 1953 *(Les statues meurent aussi)*, at the preludes of the French decolonising process.

Ideas, materials and practices of 'heritage' as contained in museum objects move and change despite the human desire for imperishability. While a yearning for immutability and remembrance may surround material traces of the past, their resistance to the wear of time and their ability to be faithful evidence or reliable witnesses may turn out to be mere illusions.

It is because matter is silent that material objects can be worded, acted and incorporated by subjects. The space created by the lack of words is filled by something else, based on a *corps-à-corps* with things, or a close contact between entities of 'bodily-and-material-culture' (Warnier 2014). Through actions with and on them, the bodily-and-material are simultaneously weighed down with, and give structure to, relational phenomena such as property, memory, power and desire. My research on museum phenomena is centred on material things: not only objects whether they are conserved in storage or exhibited in public, but also architectural spaces and scenography, as well as mediation devices and conservation technologies ranging from display boxes to computer databases. I describe objects-in-action and actions-on-objects, combining an interest in diverse social groups – visitors, curators, guides and guardians – that create museum collections and heritage value and, in turn, are shaped by them.

Here, I would like to examine the metamorphosis of some colonial museum leftovers in the French context: buildings, artefacts and human remains. Paying attention to the changes implied in terms of cultural and political subjectivities, I will explore how actions on things transform material culture, and who contributes to the process and under which conditions. Concerning museums and collections domains, researchers tend to focus either on the technical aspects of production or on the practices and uses linked to consumption. Most of these studies pertain to times predating the accession of these pieces of material culture as heritage with accompanying

78   *Mélanie Roustan*

special status and protection. However, my intent is to follow the path of their 'second life' as museum objects, that is, after they have become 'heritage', and to understand how they contribute to producing new horizons and matter for subjectivations. From this point of view, museum objects are quite interesting for two reasons that appear at first sight as research obstacles. First, the transmutation of objects into heritage elements means that they are destined to remain literally untouched (except for a few people with access such as curators) and second, even as the very physical nature of objects is lauded and even sacralised, these objects have to be thought of as parts of dynamics including living bodies, continuous actions and open-ended subjects.

This chapter aims to bring to the field of French museums in (post)colonial contexts (Dias 2017, L'Estoile (de) 2007) the methodological and theoretical reflections developed in the informal group *'Matière à Penser'* at the turn of the millennium (Julien and Warnier eds. 1999, Warnier 1999, Julien et al. 2003, Bayart and Warnier 2004, Julien and Rosselin 2005, Roustan 2007), in order to illustrate three points:

- Museum objects have no 'essence'; they are material things shaped through and *by* the actions on them – cultural value and heritage meaning do not exist prior to the process of collecting, conserving and exhibiting objects but as a result of it;
- This series of actions transforms not only material things, but also those who engage with them, by a process of 'subjectivation' (Warnier 2001) – in museum contexts, diverse groups of people establish themselves as curators, researchers, guides and guardians and also visitors, owners of, sharers and even participators in this heritage;
- This series of actions on objects, oneself and other people, may also be analysed in terms of power chains – plundering memory, reproducing the symbolic domination of a cultural elite on a society, imperceptibly renewing colonial designs, but also articulating the struggle of minorities for their political rights.

The text will unfold like an informal walk through my fieldworks in anthropological museums over the last fifteen years, focusing on three case studies: the shifting purposes, right up to today, of the former French colonial museum (built in 1931); the reshaping of ethnographic collections into primitive arts with the opening of the *Musée du Quai Branly* in 2006; and the handing over of 'French' Māori tattooed heads to New Zealand in 2012. Our journey will circle around the same topic three times. First, we will take in the wide vista, tracing the trajectories of museum objects in the three case studies, investigating their metamorphosis and displacement on the one hand, and their permanence and stillness on the other. The second tour will pay attention to the embodied actions that undergird the processes of transformation of both museum objects and subjects, and to the blurring or

Museum objects in motion   79

reinforcement of the boundary between them, depending on the context and its value system. The third and final tour will address the silence of matter and unveil the power dynamics that permeate it.

Museum trajectories and the (im)permanence of things

The seminal work *The Social Life of Things* (Appadurai 1986) and in particular, the chapter on 'The cultural biography of things' (Kopytoff 1986), is considered by many contemporary anthropologists to be a common legacy for those working on material culture (Miller 1987, 1998, Fabian 2004, Coupaye and Douny 2009).

The dynamics of heritage making

In the heritage field, the biographical approaches distance themselves from any attempt to naturalise the artistic, historical or ethnographic value of past remains, by showing how socially constructed and culturally dependant are their uses and meanings (Bonnot 2002, Julien and Rosselin 2005, Heinich 2009, Vincent ed. 2011, Debary 2019). The notion of time is central to the process. Whether a museum object seems immutable or endangered by erosion, rot or even disappearance, its (im)permanence is narrated following a timeline – and its 'life' is inserted in a conservation discourse which paradoxically desires antiquity while being wary of its changing effects. But physical (dis)placements institutionally materialise its positioning in implicit definitions and hierarchies of things. The three following examples illustrate the complex relationships between an object's tangible and intangible dimensions and reveal diverse linkages between time depth and spatial (re)location of material entities.

From colonial palace to immigration museum: a static journey?

On 5 November 1928, French President Gaston Doumergues laid the cornerstone of the *Palais de la Porte Dorée*, originally built as the headquarters for the 1931 Colonial Exhibition and named *Musée permanent des colonies* (Permanent Museum of the Colonies). It included an historical gallery, a socio-economic section, orientalist arts and literature, indigenous arts and crafts and primitive arts, ethnographic collections and an exotic aquarium. A few years later, it became the *Musée de la France d'Outre-mer* (Museum of French Overseas Territories). At the beginning of the 1960s, it was re-founded as the *Musée des Arts d'Afrique et d'Océanie* (Museum of African and Oceanic Arts) and referred to as 'MAAO'. This closed in 2002 and its collections were merged with the ethnological ones of the *Musée de l'Homme* (Museum of Man) to create the new *Musée du Quai Branly*. The building then reopened its doors in 2007 as the *Musée national de l'histoire et des cultures de l'immigration* (National Museum of the History and Cultures of Immigration). Although

80 *Mélanie Roustan*

the institutional purposes of the *Palais de la Porte Dorée* have meandered, it has always remained a museum; and a museum concerned with cultural diversity and political treatment of Otherness (Monjaret and Roustan 2013, 2017). In spite of or maybe thanks to its immutability, the place has been tirelessly called back to its ideological genesis in colonialism, by academics and even more by popular social movements (Monjaret and Roustan 2012). Social conflicts and how they have been treated institutionally reveal something of a spiral trajectory, which as it moves upwards also seems to return to the same point again and again, giving the impression that the palace – and with it, France's political approach to the Others within its borders (Stoler 2011) – undertake somewhat of a static journey.

From ethnographic artefacts to primitive art: towards both recognition and denial

The trajectory of the collections now conserved by the *Musée du Quai Branly*, is marked by physical displacements in addition to symbolic ones and identification with 'external' Others. The cultural project of this new museum, conceptualised at the turn of the twenty-first century, is based on the recognition of non-Western cultures and equality of treatment with respect to their artistic production (Taylor 2008). The whole collection of the *Musée des Arts d'Afrique et d'Océanie* and the ethnological collection of the *Musée de l'Homme* have been merged as the foundation of the *Musée du Quai Branly*, installed in a brand-new building designed, furnished and scenographed by the internationally renowned architect Jean Nouvel (Figure 5.1). The institutional arguments for such a major reshaping included the need to revalorise what had hitherto been presented as semi-forgotten artefacts. The advent of a national museum dedicated to primitive art – *'arts premiers'* in the French phrase created at the time to describe the new genre – also seriously revalued the type of objects involved from a financial point of view.

A few hundred thousand material objects were therefore moved less than ten kilometres within central Paris, some of them simply crossing the Seine from one bank to the other. However, in spite of the short distance, they underwent a major biographical rupture. Neither should this recent short trip blind us to the long journey they made to France to become museum objects in the first place. Like many ethnographic collections, those housed in the *Musée du Quai Branly* are the results of transactions linked to colonial contexts and continue to bear this violent memory – and for some of them to be contested as national heritage owned by former colonisers.

From 'French' Māori collections to New Zealander indigenous heritage: deaths and lives of memories and ancestors

Similar dynamics are at play in the third case study, which concerns the *Toi Moko* (Māori tattooed and mummified heads) conserved in French national

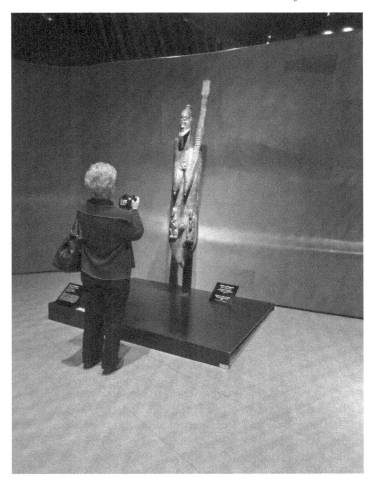

Figure 5.1 African artefact and Parisian visitor at the *Musée du Quai Branly*. Paris, 2009.

Photo by author.

collections from the eighteenth and nineteenth centuries until 2012. More than 20 in number, dispersed in several quite diverse museums (including the *Musée du Quai Branly*), the government of New Zealand claimed them, acting on an official bi-cultural national policy that has supported the Māori fight for indigenous rights since the 1970s. The heads were handed over under a French law especially voted to address this specific case (Roustan 2014). On their arrival in French museums, the mummified heads became items belonging to scientific collections, either ethnographic or naturalist, and were studied and exhibited as such until the end of the twentieth century. At the

82   *Mélanie Roustan*

turn of the millennium in Europe, a change in sensitivity occurred concerning the exhibition of human remains. Some began questioning the legitimacy of exhibiting dead bodies publicly, even in heritage contexts. Those preoccupations about the status of corpses and their consideration either as purely material things or as extensions of unique individuals opened a door to New Zealand's demand concerning the *Toi Moko*. Their hybrid status appears in the legal struggle that ended when France handed them back to New Zealand, following the vote of a special 'restitution' law – a move that was considered as a 'repatriation' of human vestiges by Māori representatives and New Zealand officials. Even more than the journey of thousands of kilometres back to where they originated, the symbolic trajectory of these 'French' *Toi Moko* is huge, from objects (museum collections) to subjects (Māori ancestors). At first glance, the trajectory of these 'French' *Toi Moko* could be viewed as a round-trip, at both the material and symbolic levels. But a global movement of heritagisation marks their social biography, as they are transformed into elements that are considered worthy of current political attention, implying the defence of a certain vision of the past and its legacy, in order to reinforce cultural identifications. Furthermore, the *Toi Moko* have had not only successive different statuses during their trajectory; they have also had simultaneous and competitive ones. The diplomatic and legal struggle that was necessary to extract them from French collections revealed profound ontological conflicts about them, concerning their very nature and also their final ownership. All this, despite an apparent consensus concerning their heritage value.

In the three examples – the static journey of a Colonial Palace in Paris, the physical and symbolic moving of exotic collections to a new museum just few kilometres away, and the much longer journey of indigenous vestiges back to the antipodes – the starting point of the described trajectories is always the forced displacement of material culture in a colonial context. This coerced 'translocation' of objects (Savoy 2015) echoes the duress and violence that were often used on colonial subjects.

Embodied actions, objects and subjects

Throughout these trajectories, objects changed status, sometimes freeing themselves from dark memories and sometimes re-enacting old scenes in new guises. Biographies of things and people seem to be entangled. Actions on objects transform these objects (in terms of their location, status, value and meaning) and simultaneously transform those who have anything to do with them: whether they made them, used them, liked them or claimed to be their owners, as in a sense, they were owned by them.

Objects-in-action as material culture

Objects have to be considered as *objects-in-action* (Julien and Rosselin eds. 2009) on the long-term and wide-space basis of their trajectories. This is the case whether it concerns the day-to-day scale of repeated gestures and interactions taking place in confined routines, familiar rituals and well-known environments or the exceptional contexts of disruptive events. Reciprocally, subjects are to be approached as *bodies-in-action*, shaping themselves and being shaped by others in a dynamic system organised by the definition and circulation of material things. A material culture approach 'in praxis' implies that objects have no essence; rather they are embodied by actions. It suggests embracing the material world from the viewpoint of its social and cultural production, and simultaneously seeing it as the core of interactions, webs of meaning and networks of desire and power that make and link people through their own materiality as bodies. It requires positioning one's research in a conceptual space where the main references are Mauss (2013 [1950]) for his views on artefacts, on 'body techniques' and on 'total social facts'; Foucault (2001) for his works on 'techniques of the self' and his theory of power as a network of actions done on the actions of others; and a glance in the direction of Becker (1963) for the way he places the social production of moral values and systems of norms at the crossroads of practices and interactions. Heritage items reflect the cultural conception and social production of the past. They are always in process and have to be looked at as materialisations of social dynamics that imply embodied actions on tangible things – actions made to change these things into legacy; actions that intimately modify the people involved in the process. Different levels of analyses may be involved in this *corps-à-corps* of objects and subjects: circulation of aura and capillarity of social status; efficiency of practices and techniques; links between senses, sensitivity and attachment.

Colonial pride and shame or the U-turn of a palace

The social biography of the *Palais de la Porte Dorée* as a place, that is to say the institutional purposes of the building and its popular uses, as well as the concrete and symbolic treatment of its architecture, decoration and furniture, reveals the changing moral economies concerning colonial legacies in recent French history (Monjaret and Roustan 2017). During the first period of its existence (1930s–1970s), curators concentrated on redefining artefacts formerly used to exemplify the richness of the French colonial empire as 'overseas' heritage, then as examples of African and Oceanic arts. These metamorphoses were linked, on the one hand, to the processes of decolonisation which the French called *'les indépendances'*, and on the other hand, to the creation of the first French Ministry of Cultural Affairs, under the leadership of writer and poet André Malraux, at the beginning of the 1960s. Curators worked on maintaining the physical integrity of collections but subsequently changed their very interpretation. In doing so, they acted also on themselves, as keepers and translators of those artefacts and benefitted from their aura. When colonial rhetoric reached its end, the stigmas had been to a certain extent 'whitewashed' with artistic value. A

84 *Mélanie Roustan*

similar process has then been applied to the building itself. The second period of the site's life (1980s–1990s) corresponds to a rising awareness of it as Art Deco heritage. Renovation was begun and the building was officially included on the French Historical Monument list for its architecture, ironwork and some pieces of original furniture – not as colonial legacy. A third period, more or less the 1990s, bears the hallmarks of a revival of the past: on the one hand, employees touched by the closure of the MAAO confided their collective memory to researchers (Eidelman et al. 2002); on the other hand, curators began a work of historicisation of the tangible remains of the colonial museum. The leftovers from the 1931 Colonial exhibition included artefacts, but also showcases, windows, dioramas and pictures. Were they to be considered as rubbish and thrown away? Or, alternatively, as relics and put in the future museum? Some items remained *in situ* as decorative elements linked to the building; others joined a newly created historical collection that came under the responsibility of the *Musée du Quai Branly*.

Reshaping the materiality of artefacts and the subjectivity of curators

Along with this newly created historical collection, all those conserved in the *Palais de la Porte Dorée* went to the *Musée du Quai Branly*. In order to become (master)pieces of *'arts premiers'*, these artefacts had to be manipulated by many people. As objects-in-action, they moved from one location to another, from two old museums whose histories are embedded in colonial science and propaganda, to a brand new one whose scope covers international arts and architecture. In between, conservation experts cleaned them, measured them, photographed them, priced them (for insurance purposes) and sometimes repaired or restored them. In the *Musée du Quai Branly*, new storage strategies, based on material preservation (instead of cultural categories), have ruled over the tangible classification of objects. Simultaneously, people have created and entered images, figures and words referring to them into databases, thus reinforcing their material existence with a digitised one, managed by computers. The curators of the collection have had to transform their professional practices, abandoning their day-to-day physical intimacy with 'their' objects in favour of a more distant relationship, mediated by screens, images and keywords, engaging the body, especially eyes and hands, quite differently (Beltrame 2012, Roustan 2016a, 2016b). This change modified not only the way people produce knowledge from objects or develop attachment to them, but also their professional role and place in the museum institution, and finally their subjectivation as curators. They lost the monopoly of access to collections and consequently a part of their prestige. They got used to producing, organising and reading pictures and data instead of material objects. They had to change the whole mode of apprehension with which they worked on and with things. The actions on objects, the forbidden, authorised or prescribed sense-based relations to them, completely redefined the articulation between the tangible dimensions of the artefacts and their intangible or elusive parts.

Becoming ancestors again

The *Toi Moko* formerly conserved in French national collections provide another example of a reconfiguration of this link between material and immaterial dimensions of 'things' (Roustan 2014). These 'trophies', by creation (keeping the head of the defeated enemy or of the venerable warrior, for ancient Māori peoples) and purpose (bringing curiosities back to Europe, for scientists and travellers), traversed across half the planet several centuries ago. They gained the status of commercial goods during the flourishing trade of the eighteenth and nineteenth centuries. This period saw the rise of middle-men and eventually a traffic of 'fake' *Toi Moko*, which were tattooed post-mortem or even made from murdered slaves. When they arrived in French museums, a series of actions on them – they were measured, drawn, written about, boxed, classified, stored, etc. – transformed them into museum objects.

Decades later, Māori claims on them as living ancestors who needed to be returned home profoundly called into question the existing perception of them, and finally modified the web of actions they are at the core of. At one stage of the process, during the ceremony held in Paris in February 2012 prior to their departure to Wellington (Figure 5.2), they were simultaneously considered as dead bodies (by the French audience members who had mostly accepted the change of status of these former museum objects) and as living ancestors (by the Māori representatives who were performing funeral rituals). Not only were *Toi Moko* moved to New Zealand, but they were taken there in a double set of actions: curated as museum objects and cared for as living ancestors. These returned *Toi Moko* are centre pieces in a cultural renaissance for the Māori, and an affirmation of the bi-cultural character of their nation for all New Zealanders.

Silent matter and power webs

The fundamental silence of matter that I discussed in this chapter gives space to plural or even conflicting interpretations. The temptation here seems to be to want to make things talk and in doing so, reveal to whom they are pledging allegiance. In addition, the undeniable central position of material objects in webs of significance and power reinforces the attribution of means of action, if not intention to act.

The effects of the unspoken and power as actions on the actions of others

Gell's (1998) concept of 'agency' has contributed to the understanding of the way in which artefacts, and especially works of art, can store and distribute the signs and traces not only of emotions but also of actions. One is touched

86 Mélanie Roustan

Figure 5.2 France and New Zealand's officials and Māori representatives during the restitution ceremony of *Toi Moko*. Paris, 2012.

Photo by author.

by a painting, and remains voiceless and immobile in front of it, arrested by one's own incapacity to reproduce the gestures of the artist that one is simultaneously feeling in one's own body. In this way, some objects are endowed with a 'power' to transform people and to organise human relations. A similar way of thinking can be found in Didi-Huberman's (1992) reflections on art, when he explores the idea that works of art are looking at us more than we are looking at them. The power chains described here do not only have to do with the potency of art; they also proceed from symbolic domination of certain social groups over others alongside very real constraints. The latter are enacted and re-enacted through actions on specific objects, which are also invariably actions on other people's actions – a phenomenon that echoes Foucault's (2001) definition of power. These webs of power result partly from inertia mechanisms linked to social reproduction of cultural hierarchising (between historical narratives, between things and between peoples) and partly from contemporary social forces engaged in fighting for moral negotiations and renegotiations of shared values such as the universality of art and indigenous rights. The heritage sphere exemplifies the struggles for the possession, definition and social uses of objects from the *past* in order to produce subjects in the *present*. In his *Anthropology of Remains*, Debary (2019) looks at museums as places where a society gathers, encloses and confines objects in order, paradoxically, to forget them. They materialise inside an outer emptiness, in a kind of sacralisation of disappearing or disappeared things – a thought that evokes Bataille's (1974) notion of 'sacrifice' as well. In 'our' cases, what kind of entanglements between the process of heritage legitimisation and the management of a painful memory can be found, when cultural recognition of Otherness (immigration heritage, primitive arts, indigenous rights), in trying to fill a gap, better underlines its stubborn existence?

The memory of stones and the 'absorption' of the other

The most recent period (2000s–2010s) of the *Palais de la Porte Dorée* starts with a liminal phase that called into question the building's destiny. Once the former African and Oceanic Arts Museum closed and its collections had gone to the *Musée du Quai Branly*, the plans for and the opening (in 2007) of a museum of immigration in this colonial monument provoked controversies and misunderstandings concerning the suitability of the chosen location, the cultural value of immigration as national heritage, and the legacy of French imperialism. Conceived to glorify the French colonial empire, the palace is a monument in itself (Lebovics 2004, Aldrich 2004, Murphy 2009). The link between its heritage function (including its tropical aquarium) and France's colonies is inscribed in its very walls: bas-reliefs and frescoes, list of conquerors. Despite the attempt of 'architectural reversal', some scholars contested the 'symbolic reversibility' of the location (Bancel and Blanchard 2007) and others challenged what they perceived as being a too direct link between colonisation and immigration (Cohen 2007).

But in 2002, when the building was the target of a demonstration against French integration policy, the public was reminded of its past with banner slogans such as 'Yesterday colonised in the south, today slaves in the north' (Monjaret and Roustan 2017). During the winter of 2010–2011, African 'undocumented strikers' claiming their rights as workers occupied the museum (Figure 5.3). By letting them stay unhindered for several months, the cultural institution contributed to their social recognition, even

Figure 5.3 The former colonial museum during its occupation by immigrant strikers. Paris, 2011.

Photo by author.

though, in the end they were forcibly evacuated. Then, by collecting, inventorying and eventually exhibiting in glass boxes some material traces of the event, curators have transformed it into a part of France's national heritage. Thus, a social movement contesting French immigration policy has been 'absorbed' by the museum, following a process of endless 'patrimonial digestion' (Monjaret and Roustan 2012) that echoes the notion of the 'cannibal museum' (Gonseth, Hainart and Kaehr 2002).

The presence of the absence as memory of the colonial encounter

When the *Musée du Quai Branly* was created, some voices arose to address the supposed universal value of the concept of art at the core of the project's philosophy, the questionable assumptions of primitivism that its aesthetics conveyed, and the ethnographic knowledge that it abandoned (Ruiz-Gomez 2006, Lebovics 2007, Price 2007, Dias 2008, Shelton 2009). Scholars have interpreted 'the Quai Branly moment' (*Le Débat* 2007) centred on redefining ethnographic collections as works of primitive art, as much as a process of cultural recognition of very distant Others, as one of how a shared scientific and political history is being denied. A study of visitors' experience of the main exhibition revealed the same ambivalence: aesthetic pleasure combined with disconcerting lack of information about the objects – which in turn led them to imagine why and how they ended up in a French national museum in first place (Debary, Roustan and Clifford 2012, Debary and Roustan 2017). The dark and mysterious scenography is evocative of an exploration of primitiveness, re-enacting racist projections and former systems of domination. But the absence of explanation about the presence of these objects here in Paris transformed their confrontation into a metaphor of colonial encounter, when things and people disappear as they go along with their forced appropriation. This suggestive presentation of colonial collections reveals its paradoxical heuristic potency: it is not by means of knowledge or information that visitors may adjust their subjective approach to the episode of violent domination in recent French history, embodied by the very presence of these 'elsewhere' objects; it is the retroactive effects of the physical 'nude' confrontation with them, here in Paris, which leads to a reflexive movement.

The politics of the indigenous

The *Toi Moko* also come with a violent memory. In addition to their genesis that is concomitant with brutal local relationships between peoples, their presence in French national collections for several centuries was evidence of former domination of imperialist Europe on this part of the world. Handing them back to New Zealand illustrates a new balance of power between the former colonisers and the colonised (even if, in this case, the link is indirect since France is not involved in New Zealand's history). The handover also exemplifies the global rise in the recognition of indigenous rights, on both a symbolic (legal) level and a very tangible one (handing them over). Finally, it reflects the French ambivalence towards both conceptions of cultural diversity in the English-speaking world and its own national political philosophy based on refusal of any particular collective rights or religious expression in the public sphere (Roustan 2017, Gagné and Roustan 2019).

Relating to the material world in (post)colonial contexts

This retrospective journey linking various attempts by museums to 'heritagise' the Other highlights the strategic role of relating to the material world in (post)colonial contexts. This heritage making relies on mechanisms of cultural legitimisation and is at the same time a way of socially managing violent or painful collective memories. It acts simultaneously as recognition and appropriation. The fact that these objects are 'here' and not 'there' is in itself an expression of domination. Their presence in French museums implies an absence elsewhere, calling into question who or what lacks or misses them. Disappearing societies, remarkable treasures, lost

90 *Mélanie Roustan*

ancestors, forced displacements: in all these cases, museums gather and shelter remains and memories left by the past that the present wants to keep. The changing purposes of national institutions in charge of ethnographic/colonial collections follow and accompany the political approaches to the cultural relationships between France and 'subaltern' countries, whether or not they were official colonies. These relationships are concomitantly also relationships with some 'inner' cultural diversity. Finding a place and places for things and peoples acts as a metaphor of the whole society and contributes to shaping it. The way they make material things speak and communicate is also a way of embodying the people who made them, traded in them, used them or cherished them – and those who do it now. Actions on material remains from the past contribute to writing history and to distributing diverse roles to social actors. By organising the circulation, access and gestures of certain categories of artefacts considered to be French national heritage despite their 'faraway' origins, museums lay out a system of objects and actions that gives matter to subjectivation processes being also a web of meanings, desires and power.

References

Aldrich, R. (2004), *Vestiges of the Colonial Empire in France: Monuments, Museums and Colonial Memories*, Basingstoke: Palgrave MacMillan.

Appadurai, A., (1986). *The Social Life of Things: Commodities in Cultural Perspective*, Cambridge: Cambridge University Press.

Bancel, N. and P. Blanchard (2007), 'Incompatibilité: La CNHI dans le sanctuaire du colonialisme Français', *Hommes & Migrations*, 112–127.

Bataille, G. (1974), *Théorie de la religion*, Paris: Gallimard.

Bayart, J. -F. and J. -P. Warnier (2004), *Matière à politique. Le pouvoir, le corps et les choses*, Paris: Karthala.

Becker, H. S. (1963), *Outsiders: Studies in the Sociology of Deviance*, New York: The Free Press of Glencoe.

Beltrame, T. (2012), 'Un travail de Pénélope au musée: Décomposer et recomposer une base de données', *Revue d'anthropologie des connaissances*, 6: 217–237.

Bonnot, T. (2002), *La vie des objets. D'ustensiles banals à objets de collection*, Paris: MSH.

Cohen, A. (2007), 'Quelles histoires pour un musée de l'immigration à Paris!', *Ethnologie Française*, 37: 401–408.

Coupaye, L. and L. Douny (2009), 'Dans la trajectoire des choses. Comparaison des approches francophones et anglophones contemporaines en anthropologie des techniques', *Techniques & Culture*, 52–53: 12–39.

Debary, O. (2019), *De la poubelle au musée. Une anthropologie des restes*, Ivry-sur-Seine: Creaphis.

Debary, O. and M. Roustan (2017), 'A Journey to the Musée du quai Branly: The Anthropology of a Visit', *Museum Anthropology*, 40: 4–17.

Debary, O., M. Roustan and J. Clifford (2012), 'Preface', in *Voyage au musée du quai Branly. Une anthropologie de la visite du Plateau des collections*, Paris: La Documentation française.

Dias, N. (2008), 'Double Erasures: Rewriting the Past at the Musée du quai Branly', *Social Anthropology*, 16: 300–311.

Dias, N. (2017), 'Ethnology, Governance, and Greater France', in T. Bennett, F. Cameron, N. Dias, B. Dibley, R. Harrison, I. Jacknis and C. McCarthy eds. *Collecting, Ordering, Governing: Anthropology, Museums, and Liberal Government*, Durham: Duke University Press, 217–254.

Didi-Huberman, G. (1992), *Ce que nous voyons, ce qui nous regarde*, Paris: Minuit.

Eidelman, J., A. Monjaret, M. Roustan and B. Plossu (2002), *Musée national des arts d'Afrique et d'Océanie (MAAO) mémoires*, Paris: Marval.

Fabian, J. (2004), 'On Recognizing Things: The "Ethnic Artefact" and the "Ethnographic Object', *L'Homme*, 25–46.

Foucault, M. (2001), *Dits et écrits. Tome II: 1976-1988*, Paris: Gallimard.

Gagné, N. and M. Roustan (2019), 'French Ambivalence Towards the Concept of "Indigenous People": Museums and the Māori', *Anthropological Forum*, 95–115.

Gell, A. (1998), *Art and Agency: An Anthropological Theory*, Oxford: Clarendon Press.

Gonseth, M.-O., J. Hainart and R. Kaehr (2002), *Le musée cannibale*, Neuchâtel: MEN.

Heinich, N. (2009), *La fabrique du patrimoine. De la cathédrale à la petite cuillère*, Paris: MSH.

Julien, M.-P., J. Poirée, C. Rosselin, M. Roustan and J.-P. Warnier (2003), 'Chantier ouvert au public,' *Techniques & Culture*, 40: 185–192.

Julien, M.-P. and C. Rosselin (2005), *La culture matérielle*, Paris: La Découverte.

Julien, M.-P. and C. Rosselin, eds. (2009), *Le sujet contre les objets… tout contre. Ethnographies de cultures matérielles,* Paris: CTHS.

Julien, M.-P. and J.-P. Warnier, eds. (1999), *Approches de la culture matérielle. Corps-à-corps avec l'objet,* Paris: L'Harmattan.

Kopytoff, I. (1986), 'The Cultural Biography of Things: Commoditization as Process', in A. Appadurai (ed.), *The Social Life of Things: Commodities in Cultural Perspective*, 64–91, Cambridge: Cambridge University Press.

de L'Estoile, B. (2007), *Le goût des autres. De l'Exposition coloniale aux arts premiers*, Paris: Flammarion.

Le Débat. Le moment du quai Branly, (2007), Paris: Gallimard.

Lebovics, H. (2004), *Bringing the Empire Back Home: France in the Global Age*, Durham: Duke University Press.

Lebovics, H. (2007), 'Echoes of the "Primitive" in France's Move to Postcoloniality: The Musée du Quai Branly', *Globality Studies Journal*, 4: 1–18.

Les statues meurent aussi (1953), [Film] Dir. Chris Marker and Alain Resnais, France: Présence Africaine Editions and Tadié Cinéma Production.

Mauss, M. ([1950]2013), *Sociologie et anthropologie*, Paris: Presses Universitaires de France.

Miller, D. (1987), *Material Culture and Mass Consumption*, Oxford: Blackwell.

Miller, D. (1998), *Material Cultures: Why Some Things Matter*, Chicago: University of Chicago Press.

Monjaret, A. and M. Roustan (2012), 'Digestion patrimoniale. Contestations autour d'un ancien musée des colonies à Paris', *Civilisations*, 61: 23–24.

Monjaret, A. and M. Roustan (2013), 'La repatrimonialisation du Palais de la Porte Dorée: Du musée des Colonies à la Cité nationale de l'histoire de l'immigration', in C. Mazé, F. Poulard and C. Ventura (eds.), *Les musées d'ethnologie. Culture, politique et changement institutionnel*, 101–126, Paris: CTHS.

92 *Mélanie Roustan*

Monjaret, A. and M. Roustan (2017), 'A Palace as Legacy: The Former French Colonial Museum - Perspectives from the Inside', *Journal of Material Culture*, 22: 212–236.

Murphy, M. (2009), *De l'imaginaire au musée. Les arts d'Afrique à Paris et à New York (1931-2006)*, Paris: Les Presses du Réel.

Price, S. (2007), *Paris Primitive: Jacques Chirac's Museum on the Quai Branly*, Chicago: Chicago University Press.

Roustan, M. (2007), *Sous l'emprise des objets? Culture matérielle et autonomie*, Paris: L'Harmattan.

Roustan, M. (2014), 'De l'adieu aux choses au retour des ancêtres. La remise par la France des têtes māori à la Nouvelle-Zélande', *Socio-anthropologie*, 183–198.

Roustan, M. (2016a), 'Des clefs des réserves aux mots-clefs des bases de données. Mutations du rapport aux objets pour les conservateurs du MAAO au musée du quai Branly', in C. Hottin and C. Voisenat (eds.), *Le tournant patrimonial. Mutations contemporaines des métiers du patrimoine*, 116–134. Paris: MSH.

Roustan, M. (2016b), 'La vague numérique et le ressac du réel. Du rapport aux sources des chercheurs en sciences humaines et sociales, enquête dans les collections patrimoniales de la BnF', in M. Roustan, A. Monjaret, P. Chevallier and J. Brault (eds.), *La recherche dans les institutions patrimoniales. Sources matérielles et ressources numériques*, 170–192, Villeurbanne: Presses de l'ENSSIB.

Roustan, M. (2017), 'Des usages de l'autochtonie dans les musées français', *Culture & musées*, 28: 151–175.

Ruiz-Gomez, N. (2006), 'The (Jean) Nouvel Other: Primitivism and the Musée du Quai Branly', *Modern and Contemporary France*, 14: 417–32.

Savoy, B. (2015), 'La mémoire restituée des oeuvres volées. Entretien avec Bénédicte Savoy', C. Terroni ed., Paris: laviedesidees.fr.

Shelton, A. A. (2009), 'The Public Sphere as Wilderness: Le musée du Quai Branly', *Museum Anthropology*, 32.

Stoler, A. (2011), 'Colonial Aphasia: Race and Disabled History in France', *Public Culture*, 23: 121–156.

Taylor, A. -C. (2008), 'Au musée du Quai Branly: La place de l'ethnologie', *Ethnologie française*, 38: 679–84.

Vincent, O., ed. (2011), *Collectionner? Territoires, objets, destins*, Ivry-sur-Seine: Créaphis.

Warnier, J. -P. (1999), *Construire la culture matérielle. L'homme qui pensait avec ses doigts*, Paris: Presses Universitaires de France.

Warnier, J. -P. (2001), 'A Praxeological Approach to Subjectivation in a Material World', *Journal of Material Culture*, 6: 5–24.

Warnier, J. -P. (2014), 'Food for Thought: The Contributions of 'Matière à Penser' to the Study of Material Culture ', Web post. First published in *Material Religions Blog*, 24 September 2014. Revised and republished in *The Jugaad Project*, 11 July 2019. thejugaadproject.pub/home/food-for-thought (last accessed 24.02.20).

6 The material shaping of women's subjectivities: Wild-silk textiles of the Marka-Dafing as a cultural heritage

Laurence Douny

While remaining largely unknown both inside and outside of Burkina Faso, wild silk is an indigenous prestige-conferring material that, according to the oral tradition of the Marka-Dafing wild-silk producers of Safané in the province of Mouhoun, has been produced by Marka-Dafing women for over four generations. Collected from the Sudanian ecological zones and the forest areas of Ivory Coast and Nigeria, the wild silk cocoons produced by the genera *Anaphe* and *Epanaphe* are processed by Marka-Dafing women who turned them into yarns (Figure 6.1). The name 'Marka-Dafing' designates a Mande-speaking people originating from the Ghana Empire [ca. 3rd century or 7th century - ca.13th century] and also found in central Mali, and is currently made up of the Marka who observe traditional beliefs system of their community and those who follow Catholicism and the Dafing who converted to Islam in the nineteenth century. In the southern region of the Mouhoun province, the wild-silk wrappers of the Marka-Dafing is a women's affair from the production to the wearing of these garments, although traders as well as dyers and weavers work on the same wrapper by following the directions of the client who is often the woman who degums the silk. Hence, these textiles are produced collaboratively amongst a network of silk specialists of whom working relationships consolidate over time. For these women, silk production is a profitable home-based economy that acts as a marker of individual and social identity. In fact, for these women who are over 50 years old and have passed childbearing age, the production of silk requires specific skills, knowledge and techniques. Accordingly, this unique craft confers not only self-worth, but also social prestige and distinction to these women who have a deep understanding of the raw material. In Marka-Dafing society, the techniques of producing and wearing this rare material become a way-of-being in which wild silk legitimates the status, power and role of women in their community as knowledge specialists and entrepreneurs, as well as guarantors of a long-standing textile tradition. In this sense, wild silk provides these women and the Marka-Dafing community as a whole with a material identity (Sofaer 2008), for which it forms an enduring cultural heritage or *laada*. The Marka-Dafing concept of *laada* encompasses knowledge systems and practices relating to the production of wild silk, such as the techniques of degumming cocoons and of beating,

94 *Laurence Douny*

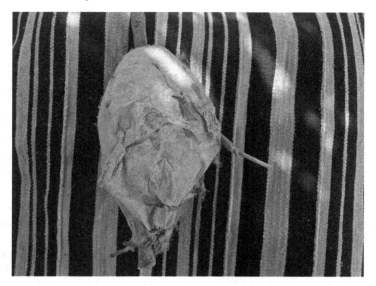

Figure 6.1 West African wild silk cocoon used in weaving Marka-Dafing women's wrappers called *tuntun*. The stripes of wild silk show as light brown.

Photograph by Laurence Douny.

brushing and spinning the silk into threads that draw on a local science of materials and a *savoir-faire*, as well as usages and customs relating to the wearing of wild silk in the form of ceremonial wrappers known as *tuntun* (see Hill-Thomas 2012) or *Marka-Dafing pon*. The heritage encompassing these techniques of the production and consumption of wild silk weaves together both symbolic and epistemological conceptions that the Marka-Dafing derive from the wild silk's materiality, such as its sheen, as a living and active property. Finally, heritage of the Marka-Dafing, as a protocol of social rules, dictates social and moral conduct, in which material and immaterial practice are highly codified. By drawing on this local definition of heritage, this chapter investigates the role of *laada* as the legacy of the ancestors – that is, as knowledge and as a set of techniques, usages and customs – plays in the constitution of the social subject through the mediation of wild silk that acts as a material identity for the Marka-Dafing people [also for the Dogon of Mali (Douny 2014)].

By focusing on the material of the wild-silk wrappers, its cultural significance and agency, I explore some of ways in which women's embodiment of the silk garment in the context of public performance and as a mode of self-display and visuality contributes to the incorporation of cultural codes and to women's constitution of the self in society, in line with traditional values. I propose that the process of subjectivation in the Foucauldian sense (see Marie-Pierre Julien in this volume) occurs through the subjects' incorporation of the dynamics and properties not only of objects (Warnier 2001, 2009), such as textiles, but specifically of silk, which bestows an aura of charisma on the wearer. I shall refer to the praxic value of this material of prestige as the 'practice or actions and thus to bodily conducts' (Warnier 2007: 2–3) about silk such as in wearing the wrapper that is when the material as forming the textile and the subject are in motion (idem). In this chapter, I explore the material agency of wild silk, and in particular its property of sheen, which confers a charismatic body-envelope on women in the form of an aura. Furthermore, I examine the metacommunicative function of wild-silk wrappers that carry messages associated to linear patterns that are woven into the cloth, and that take effect visually owing to the power of the silk's sheen that legitimises the message. I propose that silk textile and aura as material and immaterial body-envelopes confer self-confidence and increase the subject's capacity for social action, bring greater social recognition and provide protection against misfortune, the evil eye and witchcraft. I focus on the role played by culturally significant materials in the shaping of these 'material subjects' owing to the agency that is attributed to the silk within the culture, and that is located in the very properties and qualities of the material itself. These properties and qualities have been uncovered by women in the course of their long experience of producing and wearing the silk. I therefore investigate the power of action of wild silk through a close examination of what is culturally defined as sheen or *daoula*, as well as of the material's role in society (Drazin and Kuechler 2015), that is, what this conceptual and material brilliance has enabled women to do socially and therefore what it means to shine in society.

Framed in a *Matière à Penser* approach to subjectivation, I attempt to show how, in the performance of a *djanjoba* that is a party or 'big event' – which in the village of Safané is organised by and dedicated exclusively to women – the process whereby the subjects 'their body-and-their objects' (Julien, Rosselin and Warnier 2009: 103) are shaped by the silk's materiality. I describe the body-technique of wearing silk textiles by wrapping the body for purposes of self-display, and hence the technique whereby women express themselves with silk (Douny 2014, Douny and Harris 2014). This study will therefore highlight modes of production of subjectivities (Warnier 1999, Julien, Rosselin and Warnier 2009, Julien 2012) by means of sensory-motor practices and through the mediation of a material of power in a double process of subject and material expression during a public event. I conclude with a consideration of Marka-Dafing heritage as a process of subjectivation and a mode of 'visuality' that I describe as the subject's ability to see and thus to have knowledge of materials, the world and society, but also as the art of 'being seen' through the wearing of this culturally significant and highly conceptualised material that is also a form of identity.

Subjectivation process and body-envelopes

For Marka-Dafing women, the wearing of wild-silk wrappers is not just a matter of pride; it is also an ethos: the essence of an enduring cultural heritage

96   Laurence Douny

that probably goes back to the sixteenth century (approximation) in localised and discrete industries in the southern region of the Mouhoun. It was
a time when the material was traded across the Sahel by Djoula and Hausa
merchants from as far away as contemporary northern Nigeria. However,
the techniques and knowledge involved in wild-silk production was probably introduced by traders from Kanem-Bornu. Hence, Marka-Dafing silk
heritage, expressed as *laada,* meaning 'what we have seen with our ancestors' or 'what our ancestors have transmitted to us' is a local concept that
entails the knowledge and techniques of turning cocoons into yarns, as well
as the socio-cultural usages and customs of wearing wild-silk wrappers. In
other words, the concept of *laada* is defined by the Marka-Dafing as the
whole set of customs and traditions that form the cultural foundation of
Marka-Dafing' society. As part of the definition of *laada*, the concept of
lambé refers to Marka-Dafing's moral observation of the rules prescribed
by the *laada*, that is, as a form of dignity, honor and respect towards the
ancestor's traditional values. The term *tigné* designates a family's heritage,
for instance, the wild-silk wrappers that are passed on through generations
from a mother to her daughters or daughters in law. In the present context,
wild-silk wrappers known as *tuntun* made of woven bands of silk and cotton dyed with indigo act as a symbol of Marka-Dafing's identity and as a
family and cultural heritage. They play a role not only in the constitution
of the subject, but also in the ways in which women present themselves in
society by harnessing the material agency of silk, as mentioned previously.
While partly assigned to the material by people, and therefore culturally
defined, the material agency of West African silk is also located in the properties and qualities of the material itself. Women harness the power of this
indigenous material that is perceived as living and active in order to achieve
social goals through creative ways of fashioning the self. In Marka-Dafing
communities, the cultivation of one's image is a complex social phenomenon that is directed outwardly and is done by aesthetically, psychologically
and metaphysically shaping the body by means of body-techniques (Mauss
1936) – for instance, the application of cosmetics and the wearing of silk to
give the body a sheen. Women's fashioning of their appearance as a technology of the subject (Warnier 2009) consists in a process of subjectivation
in which wild-silk textiles and materials that form a heritage contribute to
the shaping of the subject as the fashioning of their body-envelopes, a process learned in the course of a woman's life that is to some extent framed by
the community's social codes, rules and prohibitions that are prescribed by
their *laada.*

As Jean-Pierre Warnier suggests, the process of subjectivation takes
place through the fashioning of body-envelopes that are contiguous to the
subject – and this occurs through the mediation of materialities. In *The
Pot-King* (Warnier 2007), for example, he describes how an infant's skin is
worked on daily by energetically massaging ointment into the skin in order
to relax, galvanise and strengthen the epidermis. As can be observed in

Material shaping of women's subjectivities 97

Safané, this skin-envelope confers bodily and psychological comfort, and thus well-being on the subject, while also symbolically preventing adverse effects such as disease or witchcraft from entering the pores of the skin and weakening the infant. As an efficient action not only on the skin but also on the subject, this body-technique, in the Maussian sense, enables the consolidation of the infant's social body, since in the course of growing up the infant will interact with the outside world through its strong, healthy and glowing skin (Warnier 2007: 71). Like body ointment, a silk loincloth acts as a protective layer for the skin and the body of the subject. Moreover, by being wrapped around the body, the heavy silk cloth acts like a talisman to ward off malevolent entities by means of the sheen, which also confers social prestige by highlighting the wearer's social and economic status, and thus her power. In this regard, ointment and silk act as a material interface through which the subject interacts with and situates herself within the world. Because of their cultural significance and the various meanings that people have attached to them in particular social and historical contexts, and because of the agency, a material such as silk possesses, these materials enable subjects to do things socially.

The production and properties of sheen

The wild silk produced by the salivary glands of processionary caterpillars of the genera *Anaphe* and *Epanaphe* (Ene 1964, Peigler 1993) is crude and coarse compared to the lush silk spun by the *Bombyx mori*. Because of its natural colour, which shows as shades of light grey, beige or brown, West African silk is easily mistaken for indigenous cotton fibre kapok *(Bombax ceiba)*, or for silk-cotton *(Ceiba pentandra),* both of which are used as an alternative to silk by Marka-Dafing women when wild silk is not available. The colour of the silk is also rendered by the tannin of the leaves of trees such as of the tamarind *(Tamarindus indica)* and the doka tree *(Isoberlinia doka),* on which the caterpillars feed and from which the cocoons traders of two Marka-Dafing families based in Safané collect the silk in Côte d'Ivoire and Nigeria. In addition, the cocoons as communal nests spun by caterpillars in termite or anthills, or on the branches and trunks of trees are often tarnished by the sun, rain, dust and soil. One of the great peculiarities of wild silk, apart from its great tensile strength and endurance, is the medicinal values embedded in local beliefs systems that are associated with caterpillars and silk-related materials such as the branches on which they spin their cocoons. Thus, the protein rich insect-material is consumed to cure diabetes or to help lower high blood pressure, and the branches are smoked on the body to heal migraines and to protect against evil entities such as witchcraft. In addition, a decoction of these pieces of wood is used to purge children who have become victims of witchcraft. In a similar way, silk dust mixed with shea butter *(Vitellaria paradoxa)* is massaged into a child's skin in order to fortify it and to prevent spells and diseases provoked

98   *Laurence Douny*

by supernatural causes from entering the child's body through the pores. Hence, the interweaving of the magical and the medicinal properties of the silk shows the metaphysical complexity of this mystic insect material, which the Marka-Dafing perceive as living. Here, the material agency of wild silk or its active properties of healing and magic are components of the definition of wild silk's *daoula* or sheen (Douny 2015).

Daoula is described by the Marka-Dafing as an innate force that resides not only in people and animals but also in certain materials and substances, and hence objects. When externalised – for example, through techniques of processing and weaving – the *daoula* of wild silk is manifested in the form of an aura. It is said to 'radiate' from the material, and is amplified by bright sunlight in order to attract the eye. It immediately triggers an emotional response of appreciation or attraction in people who see the wearer of a silk garment, which the agency of the silk manifests as a charismatic envelope. In general, it is acquired by people who are concerned about their reputation, and who wish to make an impression on others and/or to obtain social networks of support. In this case, the sheen of the wild silk is a property that is doubled by an aesthetic value (Ben-Amos 1980, Rivers 2003) that confers a certain power of action on the subject, in addition to the symbolic protection against calamitous entities.

The sheen of wild silk is obtained by means of a long and painstaking process of cooking the cocoons in an alkaline solution followed by the drying, threshing, carding and spinning of the dusty fibre into yarns that are then washed and woven on a horizontal double-heddle loom along with dyed indigo cotton threads that contrast with the bands of woven silk. The production of wild silk as a bodily and sensory experience is particularly detrimental to the women's and weaver's health, as the material causes skin lesions, and its dust provokes potentially serious respiratory and ocular problems. The transformation of the material to reveal the *daoula* of the silk is an art of old women, referred to individually as *tuntun wonni ba* or 'doyenne who masters the transformation of something', in this case silk, or as *ba kerebe*. The *ba kerebe* or 'mother' of Kerebe (a village near Douroula) is a wild-silk expert who has acquired considerable knowledge about silk. The name of the wrapper 'ba kerebe doungho' that is dedicated to her due to her unique *savoir-faire* means 'the choice of mother Kerebe' whose choice is the job well done: namely, a wrapper that has been done with care. By extension, the term *ba kerebe* also designates a wrapper whose silk was produced by a woman of considerable expertise who has the ability to carefully reveal and master the intrinsic property of the material that is manifested by its sheen.

Accordingly, the production of wild silk as an embodied technique implies 'efficient body actions on the matter' (according to a formula of Mauss' [1936] developed by Leroi-Gourhan [1943] and Lemonnier [1992]) to produce silk yarns and to reveal the silk's *daoula*, which in turn acts efficiently on the subject. Throughout the production of the silk, the reciprocal action

Material shaping of women's subjectivities 99

of the material on the subject and vice versa is manifested as the material's action on the subject as it physically and psychologically affects those who produce and wear the silk as well as those who see it. The techniques of wild-silk production also become techniques of the self through which the active force of the material is released from the fibre and transferred to the subject by conferring a protective and charismatic envelope that increases one's social visibility and enables one to make a stronger impression within the community.

Shaping subjectivities: wild-silk wrappers as a material identity

In the communities of the Marka-Dafing,[1] women's wrappers are worn around the waist, leaving the left edge of the length visible. When worn by a married woman, the fabric covers the legs to the ankles and is doubled by a smaller loincloth worn beneath that descends to the knee and serves to conceal the form of the body so as to avoid attracting a man's gaze. The loincloth also restricts the body's movement by making the wearer walk at a slower pace, one that is perceived to be correct, dignified and polite. Hence, the wrapper that is formed from a large 2×1 m rectangle of cloth, and which is composed of strips of woven fabric, is worn follows specific societal rules of decency and respect. These values, which are derived from the body's praxeology show a woman's adherence to the code of usages prescribed by the *laada*.

As a customary celebration that is widespread in Mande societies, and as a part of the *laada*, the *djanjoba* or 'big event' dedicated to women is organised by the Safané women's committee – with the participation of the griots and the help of the men of the events committee – as a way of honouring Marka-Dafing women, and in particular as a celebration of youth. The *djanjoba* is a unique opportunity for women to give public expression to their discontent, but also to reconciliations and the improvement of relations within their family. For women who are unhappy in their domestic life and are overwhelmed by their suffering, a suffering known as *gami* – one that can be neither verbalised nor explained – participation in a *djanjoba* enables them to express their affliction by wearing one or several wild-silk wrappers that they alternate during the celebration that lasts from morning until late at night. At a *djandjoba*, women sing and dance in a moving line and in an astonishing body synchronicity around the public square (Figure 6.2). Some women can receive the support by the griots, who recite the history of each woman's family, and thereby emphasise their individual participation in the *djandjoba*, and comment on the beauty of their wild-silk wrappers, which represent the bravery and self-worth of these women who are also mothers, co-wives and daughters in law. Silk as a form of social prestige bestows honour and charisma on the women, who are anxious to be seen and, especially, heard, to be glorified, and thus to acquire social recognition. The sheen or *daoula* of the loincloth gives the women an aura, which in turn produces

Figure 6.2 Women wearing wild silk wrappers and matching headscarves while dancing in line at a Djanjoba in Safané in 2011.

Photograph by Salif Sawadogo.

an affect: the esteem, admiration and awe of those who see her. Hence, the *daoula* of wild silk is said to bestow a power of attraction on women, allowing them to gain notoriety, to establish and increase their power and to extend their capacity for action to the domestic sphere, in a predominantly polygamous and hierarchical society. Moreover, women are also able to acquire powers from the invisible world, which is tricked by the sheen of their cloth (Douny 2017). Wild silk's *daoula* appeals to the benevolence of the spirits that inhabit the human world, but which emanate from a tangential space. These spirits or *djinn* (a term borrowed from the Arabic language and culture) are able to help women to find a husband, to bring good fortune, to predict the future, to heal otherwise incurable diseases and to safeguard against malevolent forces and witchcraft, a common occurrence within the Marka-Dafing community with devastating social consequences. Once captured by the *daoula* or sheen, the spirits 'follow' the woman who wears the wrapper, and remain faithful to her for as long as she continues to honour them with sacrifices in the form of various material offerings made to them at specific times of the year. Thus, Marka-Dafing women increase their power of action and their notoriety through the use of wild silk, which

Material shaping of women's subjectivities 101

gives them the charisma that enables them to obtain the support of invisible entities and of people, to repel evil, to manage all of these entangled relations to their advantage, and, as a result, to shine in society.

The material expressiveness of the silk also lies in the material's agency in legitimising the messages woven into the wrappers. In fact, one of the formal characteristics of wild-silk wrappers, as in other sorts of African textiles as well, is that they serve as a form of non-verbal communication (Michelman and Eicher 1995, Beck 2000). In other words, they materialise one or more messages that cannot be verbalised directly. These include aphorisms reminding the community of its moral values, and insults and criticisms addressed to a husband, enemy or rival such as a co-wife. The idea of making the loincloths 'speak' was born of the uneasiness Marka-Dafing women felt in dealing with frictions within the polygamous domestic sphere. The wild-silk wrapper as an exclusively feminine garment allows them to assert themselves both in public and private life, and to display their power of influence via visual communication and with the support of the invisible world. Hence, performing with silk is an effective mode of 'visuality', namely, women's ability to see and engage with visible and invisible worlds. This mode of seeing, as well as of self-display or being seen, encompasses techniques of the body and of the subject by means of which moral values, social codes and status are given expression. The visual syntax of the textile as a metalanguage is created and magnified by the silk's sheen, which contrasts with strips of indigo-dyed cotton. As the main component of this syntax, wild silk legitimises one or more messages owing to its *daoula* or metaphysical force as an effective power of action, one that is culturally recognised as such within the Marka-Dafing community. In other words, the effectiveness of the message in reaching its target lies in the context of the message's exposure as well as the material – that is, the silk – support of the *daoula*. Among the most common messages is the proverb 'Sinan reme dabe', which means 'the co-wife passes through the door of the courtyard without raising her eyes', and refers to a settling of scores between two co-wives that is expressed in the silk wrapper of the woman who evicts her rival by expelling her from the homestead. The message that is woven at the request of the owner of the loincloth, who therefore produces such a wrapper for the occasion, emphasises the weakness or weaknesses of the recipient of the message. The woven message 'Ni toun ya lon', meaning 'If only I knew', expresses the psychological abuse of a woman who is a victim in her husband's family, with whom she lives. These examples show how wild-silk textiles are a means for women to release a heavy emotional burden or to cope with emotional issues and improper behaviour in the form of criticisms and insults that cannot be directly verbalised in domestic or public space without the risk of verbal escalation or, worse, the use of physical violence. In this way, wild-silk textiles materialise power relations that are implicitly negotiated through self-display and performing with the wrapper. This occurs in a society that shares a cultural heritage in which the wrapper acts

102 *Laurence Douny*

as an effective marker of social visibility by means of which Marka-Dafing women are able to give candid expression to sensitive messages. The women thereby avoid dramatic social consequences while at the same time respecting the social order, the values and the rules prescribed by the *laada* manifested in many aspects of everyday life, including in the making and wearing of wild-silk wrappers that constitute a material identity for the women and for Marka-Dafing society in general.

Conclusion

As we have seen, the process of subjectivation in which Marka-Dafing women acquire charisma and social visibility is made effective through the subject's incorporation of the properties of wild silk's *daoula*. This process emphasises the dynamic relationship between the materiality of the silk and that of the body. These relations are established through a reciprocal action of the material on the body. Through its sheen, the wrapper shapes subjectivities, and allows women to contain their emotions and to assert themselves within the domestic space and within the community. The process of subjectivation carried out by the *daoula* or sheen of the material is thus determined by the cultural, symbolic and praxic value of the garment and of the material. The materiality of the silk characterised by its visual and conceptual brilliance as an active force requires a technical transformation of the cocoons in order to be revealed. Thus, from the perspective of the subjectivation process carried out by the sheen of the wild silk, the study of Marka-Dafing textiles has allowed us to understand the agency of this prestige-conferring material: a culturally significant material that allows women to do things socially by conferring on these 'material subjects' a charismatic body-envelope that protects, assigns and reinforces women's power of action within society and with the help of the invisible world. This chapter has thus emphasised the cultural implications of a rare, living and active material whose production and usages in Marka-Dafing society form a local heritage and identity.

Acknowledgements

Part of this research was funded by the Leverhulme Trust between 2009 and 2010. I am grateful to Claude Ardouin at the British Museum who made this research possible. This chapter was partly written during a visiting fellowship (2018-2019) at the Max Planck Institute for the History of Science in Berlin, in department III, directed by Prof Schäfer. At MPIWG, I would like to acknowledge the 'posthumanist' reading group led by Mats Fridlund, Jaewan Hun and Lisa Onaga, and the 'body of animals' working group led by Lisa Onaga. It was finished at the Humboldt University in Berlin where I would like to acknowledge the research cluster Matters of Activity funded by the Deutsch Forschungsgemainschaft (DFG, German Research

Foundation) under Germany's Excellence Strategy – EXC 2025. An early draft of this paper was presented at FISO in Épinal (France) where I would like to thank the organisers, especially Ingrid Voléry and Marie-Pierre Julien and the audience for their very important feedback. Research authorisations were obtained from the CNRST in Ouagadougou, with an affiliation to Point Sud (Bamako) where I would like to thank Prof. Mamadou Diawara. Finally, I am extremely grateful to the wild-silk producers and women of Safané who participated in this research and in particular Sakira Dabe, Maminata Sanogo, Mariam Sacko and Aissata Baili and to Lossani Dayo and Salif Sawadogo for their guidance and technical assistance in the field.

Note

1. Also in the Dogons of the Tomo and Tengu regions in Mali (Douny 2014).

References

Beck, R. M. (2000), 'Aesthetics of Communication. Texts on Textiles (Leso) from the East African Coast (Swahili)', *Research in African Literatures* 31 (4): 104–24.
Ben-Amos, P. (1980), *The Art of Benin*, London: Thames & Hudson.
Douny, L. and S. Harris (2014), 'Wrapping and Unwrapping, Concepts and Approaches', in S. Harris and L. Douny (eds.), *Wrapping and Unwrapping Material Culture. Archaeological and Anthropological Perspectives*, London: Routledge, pp. 15–40.
Douny, L. (2014), 'Wild Silk Wrappers of Dogon: Wrapping and Unwrapping Material Identities', in S. Harris and L. Douny (eds.), *Wrapping & Unwrapping Material Culture: Archaeological and Anthropological Perspectives*, London: Routledge, pp. 173–192.
Douny, L. (2015), 'Wild Silk Indigo Textiles of West Africa. An Ethnography of Materials', in A. Drazin and S. Kuechler (eds.), *The Social Life of Materials. Studies in Materials & Society*, Oxford: Berghan, pp. 102–118.
Douny, L. (2017), 'Connecting Worlds Through Silk. The Cosmological Significance of Sheen in West African Talismanic Magic', *JMRW* 12 (2): 186–209.
Drazin, A. and S. Kuechler (2015), *The Social Life of Materials: Studies in Materials & Society*, London: Bloomsbury.
Ene, J. C. (1964), 'Indigenous Silk-Weaving', *Nigeria Magazine*, June: 127–36.
Hill-Thomas, G. (2012), 'Silk in the Sahel: Tuntun and Marka Faso Dan Fani in Northwestern Burkina Faso', *African Arts* 45 (2): 58–69.
Julien, M.-P. (2012), 'Sujet, subjectivation, subjectivité et sciences sociales', in J. Deniot and J. Réault (eds.), *L'odyssée du sujet*, Nantes: Les cahiers du Lestamp-Habiter Pips.
Julien, M.-P., C. Rosselin and J.-P. Warnier (2009), '"Subjectivité", "subjectivation", "sujet" : dialogue', in M.-P. Julien and C. Rosselin (eds.), *Le sujet contre les objets… tout contre. Ethnographies de cultures matérielles*, Paris: éditions du CTHS, Coll. Orientations et méthodes, pp. 111–168.

104 *Laurence Douny*

Lemonnier, P. (1992), *Elements for an Anthropology of Technology*, Ann Arbor, Michigan: Museum of Anthropology, University of Michigan.

Leroi-Gourhan, A. (1943), *L'Homme et la Matière: Évolution et Techniques*, Paris: Albin Michel.

Mauss, M. (1936), 'Les techniques du corps', *Journal de Psychologie*, 32: 271–293.

Michelman, S. O. and J. B. Eicher (1995), 'Dress and Gender in Kalabari Women's Societies', *Clothing and Textiles Research Journal*, 13 (2): 121–30.

Peigler, R. S. (1993), 'Wild Silks of the World', *American Entomologist,* 39 (3): 151–161.

Rivers, V. Z. (2003), *The Shining Cloth: Dress and Adornment That Glitters*, London: Thames & Hudson.

Sofaer, J. ed. (2008), *Material Identities,* Oxford, UK: Blackwell.

Warnier, J.-P. (1999), *Construire la culture matérielle. L'homme qui pensait avec ses doigts*, Paris: PUF, Coll. 'Sciences sociales et sociétés'.

Warnier, J.-P. (2001), 'A Praxeological Approach to Subjectivation in a Material World', *Journal of Material Culture*, 6 (1): 5–24.

Warnier, J.-P. (2007), *The Pot-King: The Body and Technologies of Power*, Boston and Leiden: Brill, African Social Studies Series.

Warnier, J.-P. (2009), 'Les technologies du sujet. Une approche ethno-philosophique', *Techniques & Culture*, 52–53, pp. 148–167.

Matter of politics

7 Politics matters:
Matière à Politique

Jean-Pierre Warnier

For several centuries, the theory of politics has been dominated by a normative, legal and philosophical approach. Since the end of WWII, several historical events have had a noticeable impact on it in various ways. Genocides, decolonisation, the rise of subaltern voices, of women, minority and civil rights movements, the collapse of the soviet world, the globalisation of financial, merchant and media fluxes, have considerably altered the political landscape. The centrality of the State in political philosophy has been dislodged under the impact of anthropological studies on a variety of non-State political systems. The normative approach characteristic of political philosophy regarding the best kind of government and Western democracy has tended to fade away under the action of critical thought. The functionalist paradigm regarding institutions deemed to have a political dimension has been successfully challenged, as well as the search for holistic self-contained political communities.

What is it that has emerged of late from a field of theoretical ruins that could amount to a renewed theory of politics? Most authors have focused on agency, without however agreeing on a single definition. Politics means power. Power rests on a capacity to act on self and others. Mainstream sociology has lined up with economic science and has taken the choice-making individual as the basic building block of political processes and institutions. In that perspective, the market could be taken as an apt metaphor of any political organisation in which individuals deal in power transactions – kinship in non-State societies, space, resources, conflicts, cooperation and coercion. This, I think, leads to a dead end.

Yet, in this chapter, in accordance with a broad perspective on agency, I will take action on self and others as a point of departure. However, I will bifurcate on the question of whose action we are talking about. The individual, the actor or the subject? Women, subaltern, labour and civil rights movements have underscored the centrality of the body and embodiment as the locus where power on self and other is exercised with maximum impact. Accordingly, Urmila Mohan and myself (2017: 375–376) have argued in favour of the subject as the best candidate for a theory of action and agency since the subject has a double status: it *is* a body and it *has* a body. It acts and is acted upon. It takes itself as the object of its own actions. It is both subjectified and subjected to others in a material world. I will not delve on this point since it is aptly developed by Laurence Douny and Urmila Mohan in the Introduction to the present edited volume, with all the relevant references to the literature. In this chapter, I only wish to apply the centrality of embodied action in a material world to the theory of politics. That is: politics matters.

Political power is not a universal substance that can be transposed as it stands from society to society. The technologies of acting on other peoples' actions obey a vast array of repertoires. It is not even sure that we can subsume them all under a common notion of political power. The reason for this state of affairs comes partly from the fact that actions on self and on others rest on a huge diversity of bodily techniques, themselves propped on complex material cultures. This statement calls for a historical and comparative sociology of politics in its bodily and material dimensions as developed in Bayart and Warnier (eds. 2004).

The burden of kingship

This approach was first brought to my attention as I was doing research in an African kingdom. In spite of his so-called 'traditional' outlook, King Ngwa'fo is a businessman and a Cameroonian politician of national stature. In 2019, he was the first Vice-President of the ruling political party, Cameroon People's Democratic Movement (CPDM) of Paul Biya. Born 1926, he graduated in agronomy at the University of Ibadan in Nigeria. In 1959, he succeeded his father on the throne of Mankon, one of the some 150 micro-kingdoms of the highlands of West Cameroon. When he was committed to take over the succession of his father, he went on a hunger strike to rid himself of the burden of an unpromising kingdom isolated in inaccessible mountains and to return to his own personal interests – agriculture, economic development and the modernisation of his country. The pressure exercised by his entourage persuaded him to oblige and to accept what Frazer rightly designated as the burden of sacred kingship.

In 1959, the year when Ngwa'fo succeeded his father, the mandated territory of Southern Cameroons under British trusteeship was making its way to political independence and was offered the choice between the federation with Nigeria or with Eastern Cameroon so far under French trusteeship. As the only university educated king, he was recruited by the British administration into the committee in charge of organising the independence plebiscite. This set his foot into national politics, never to leave it, as he himself explains in his autobiography – *Royalty and Politics. The Story of My Life* (Fo Angwafo 2009). In the 1960s, everyone thought that African kingdoms were due to wither away, relegated into insignificance by the fledging independent African States. What happened was quite the opposite. As from the 1980s, they came to the fore of the African political stage, as explained by Francis B. Nyamnjoh (2014) and by Claude-Hélène Perrot and François-Xavier Fauvelle-Aymar (eds. 2003). They were in a position to provide a scarce resource to the hegemonic alliances sustaining the young States, that is, a modicum of ancestral legitimacy and the support of their people.

Ngwa'fo is a sacred king, to the tip of his fingers, and at the same time well entrenched in the hegemonic alliance that rules the country. If not a king, then he would probably not have been a prominent politician, or else of a very different kind. His kingdom provides a magnifying lens to study contemporary African politics at a time of neoliberal globalisation. What the king does to fulfil his two faceted roles is to implement specific bodily techniques aimed at receiving ancestral substances, storing them into his bodily 'envelope' and dispensing them to his subjects while assigning them to the inner space of the kingdom, drawing boundaries and unifying the internal contents of the king body, the palace and the city into the royal body politics. The performance of such a task necessitates the implementation of specific bodily and material cultures. This is, to a large extent, a physical, bodily and material endeavour. I am not saying that speech, discourse and representations do not matter. They do. But the bodily and material techniques have to be seriously taken into consideration, not for their sign value or representations in a system of connotation and communication but for their acting value in a system of agency, that is, on the king and on his subjects providing an obvious object of ethnographic description.

Since I have already published a detailed and full-fledged account (Warnier 2007), I will only provide here a very rough sketch. Every year at the end of the agricultural cycle, the king visits the royal graveyard. He makes offerings to his ancestors. If the monarch and the notables in attendance are satisfied that the ancestors have given clear signs of acceptance, it is assumed – but never said in so many words – that the king's bodily envelope is filled with reproductive life essence bestowed on him by the ancestors. He behaves accordingly by distributing his bodily contents to his subjects: speech, breath, saliva, his semen to his numerous wives and, by proxy, with palm oil, crimson camwood powder, raffia wine and medicines. The body of the king is a container, a pot, with an envelope, apertures, contents and fluxes coming in and going out of it. The king has three material bodies: his own, the palace and the kingdom, with the same structure: an envelope and its apertures; the same functions of storage, control and dispensation; and the same contents: the ancestral life essence that inhere the bodily substances of the king, and everything that proceeds from them: children, healthy adults, crops, livestock and wealth. The king's body incorporates all the vessels and material contraptions of substances and containment: drinking cups, bags, calabashes, drums, pots, palace lodges, fences, gates, camwood powder, palm oil, raffia wine and medicines.

Territorialisation in an African frontier

Similar patterns of sacred kingship are to be found all the way from the Great Lakes of East Africa to the highlands of Western Cameroon, through

110 *Jean-Pierre Warnier*

the upper Nile valley, the Congo basin, and some areas in Nigeria. Such kingdoms are interspersed with more or less acephalous societies such as those of the Cameroon forest. Yet one can see that kingdoms and less centralised societies share a common concern with the skin, containment, contents, apertures and fluxes and that such concerns pervade the bodily and material political cultures of those societies, the difference being that, in the kingdoms, the royal body enjoys a monopoly over ancestral life-essence, as against what happens in acephalous societies in which initiation rituals turn each and every subject into a self-sufficient container of ancestral life essence.

The only reasonable explanation for this state of affairs is to be found, I believe, in the theory of the African frontier as developed by Igor Kopytoff (ed. 1987) as regards the history of king-friendly areas including the highlands of Western Cameroon, as I explained in two previous publications (Warnier 2012a, 2012b). Picking up on the notion of the American frontier developed by Frederick Jackson Turner ([1893] 1961) as a space opened up to the circulation and displacement of unmoored people and things as well as political reconfiguration, Kopytoff has extended this paradigm to Africa. Following Robin Horton (1971), he notices that chiefdoms, kingdoms and empires emerge in African history when and where such frontier situations develop, in which diverse and unrelated groups are put into contact with each other and have to come to terms and develop an overarching political organisation. Kingdoms achieve this goal by projecting themselves on the ground, drawing boundaries, separating an inside from an outside, and making sure that the body politics keeps communicating with the world at large through a number of gates that facilitate the control of the transits. It is a process of material and political territorialisation. As a matter of fact, the Mankon kingdom is made of a federation of nine exogamous clans that do not share any common ancestry and genealogy, and are supposed to have congregated together sometimes in the past. It is still a highly effective and relevant process in twenty-first-century Cameroon concerning the resources of extraversion and their appropriation by the kingdom (Figure 7.1).

The territorialisation process has a number of implications: the three bodies of the king (his own, the palace, the city) have a homologous bodily and material structure. The contents are perceived and treated as part of a system of transformation from ancestral life essence, to the bodily substances of the king, to their proxy (palm oil, camwood powder, raffia wine and medicines), to children, healthy adults, crops, livestock, money, salaries and the wealth and development items accruing to the kingdom. All these are handled and put into motion (and emotions) thanks to so many techniques of the body and material contraptions. For example, the king sprays mouthfuls of raffia wine on the surrounding crowd when dancing with his people at the annual festival; he distributes food after he has performed the offerings to his ancestors on behalf of the latter.

Figure 7.1 Territorialisation through the *ngang fo* ritual drawing the limits of the kingdom. Mankon, 2009.

Photo by Manuela Zips-Mairitsch.

These practices belong with what Michel Foucault (1994: 187–192) would consider as 'technologies of power', that is, efficacious actions on self and others. The king's spraying, or *fama* in the local language, lands on people's skin. The educated ethnographer should abstain from translating this into words such as 'benediction', 'symbol', 'ritual' and the like. A proper understanding of what it achieves can only be obtained by collecting a bunch of similar '*fama*' gestures, for example, by a grand-mother spraying her saliva on the hands of her grand-son about to leave for the university, by a carver spraying his saliva on a carved chair while handing it over to a customer who has purchased it, etc. From such a corpus of similar gestures, one may infer that *fama* is a bodily technique whereby a subject uses his/her bodily substance and projects it on the cutaneous surface of another subject or object in order to achieve a given result (Figure 7.2). Chameleons, snakes, leopards and other significant animals are said to *fama*. What effect does it achieve? It impacts the skin, for the better in the case of the king who will produce healthy and moist skins apt to contain offsprings and wealth, for the worse in the case of the chameleon who will produce a swelling of the skin, an oedema, or its destruction through leprosy, or so it is believed.

Another implication is that the king is responsible for ingesting and digesting the resources external to the kingdom, such as assimilated foreigners,

112 *Jean-Pierre Warnier*

Figure 7.2 Giving out life substances. Here, raffia wine is dispensed from the royal cup. Mankon, 2009.

Photo by Manuela Zips-Mairitsch.

NGOs, State resources, etc. Fo Ngwa'fo (2009: 32) is well aware of this process of appropriation: 'The benefits to Mankon of my active participation in politics have not only been increased political recognition and representation, but also greater socio-economic development. The developments are there for all to see, from the number of schools to medical services through businesses, pipe borne water projects and road infrastructure; there is the Congress Hall, the Airport, the motor parks, the Mankon Main Market, the Urban Council, the Mankon Museum and many other development initiatives as testimony of my active involvement in politics in the interest of Mankon'.

Politics matters 113

The appropriation and absorption process have their counterpart in expelling the 'bad things' or people from within the confines of the body politics. In the past, this excremental practice concerned mostly the witches. Nowadays, it concerns persons or institutions that have not given satisfaction. Since the king identifies with the palace and the city, his bodily envelope and that of the kingdom are one and the same. It amounts to saying that it is the king himself who produces the limit between an inside and an outside and achieves the territorialisation of the kingdom as well as the ingestion and the expulsion processes.

With urban and international migrations, the kingdom has lost many of its subjects to the outside world, as far as Central African countries, South Africa, Europe, North America and even Asia. King Ngwa'fo has tried to maintain their connections with the palace through various means: an association for Mankon elites called MACUDA (Mankon Cultural Development Association), a web site, his golden jubilee (50 years on the throne) in 2009, etc. However, what would look at face value as a futile attempt at encompassing the fragments of a kingdom blown up to pieces by the globalising forces of modernity is actually turned into an efficient inclusion process since it joins hands with an endogenous process that Francis B. Nyamnjoh (2011) calls 'bushfalling' after a popular expression (Figure 7.3).

This is a process whereby people go out of their homeland, as it were to the bush, to hunt and search for resources that can be brought back home. This process has been going on for centuries in the context of the African frontier that offers lots of opportunities for the subjects of the kingdom to venture out of its limits in order to bring back home various kinds of external resources, and first of all hunting game. Filip De Boeck (2004) has described similar patterns around the Congo-Angolan border. The outgoing hero may assume the many different shapes of the hunter, the trader, the fetish, the missionary, etc. and is therefore a mutant entity. What turns bushfalling into a powerful instrument of territorialisation is the fact that people take to it in order to fetch the resources of the global frontier. Yet, this does not make sense unless one is making every conceivable effort to bring the proceeds back home, to one's relatives, and to build a house in the village and achieve a status that, at some point, will be validated by the palace and the king. Few out-migrating Mankon people contemplate severing their kinship, physical and spiritual links with their homeland and being buried in foreign soil. The practice of royal inclusion and bushfalling are further reinforced by the politics of autochthony that have developed in Cameroon and in many parts of Africa since the early 1990s as a counter to the call for more democracy (see Warnier 2011). Accordingly, bushfalling is a means to tap the resources of the global market – mobile phone, laptop, car, clothes, fashion, globalised food, air transport, etc. – and incorporate them into one's bodily envelope Schilder-fashion (1935), and into that of the kingdom. This process of bushfalling may account partly for the fantastic growth of the town of Bamenda, the regional capital of the North-West

Figure 7.3 A 'bushfaller' seated on a motorbike, back to the kingdom with the resources of the global market. Mankon, 2009.

Photo by Manuela Zips-Mairitsch.

region, partly on Mankon territory, that counts 800,000 inhabitants in 2019, as against a mere 100,000 in the 1970s, though there is no industry and little employment opportunities on the spot.

Indeed, politics 'matters'. Yet, using a case study in Africa in support of such a claim has risen a doubt in the minds of some of my colleagues: could it be that the technologies of power implement bodily-and-material-cultures in this kingdom precisely because its king and subjects are African, as it were, close to the body, to emotions, in brief, to nature? This Orientalist bias towards what the German anthropology of the nineteenth and twentieth centuries used to call the *Naturvölker* must be squarely dismissed.

Global subjectivation through bodily and material cultures

In so-called 'modern' or 'postmodern' Western countries, the technologies of power are no less embodied than elsewhere in the world and at other times in history. Yet most social scientists, except to some extent those inspired by phenomenology, such as Pierre Bourdieu and Michel Foucault, suffer from a blind spot in this respect, for two reasons in my view. The first one is to be found in the various sociological traditions of the West for which the body and material cultures have never been legitimate objects of scholarship,

Politics matters   115

mostly because they are perceived as the insignificant, mundane logistics of daily life and not as something essential to the embodied human subject. The sociology and economics of the choice-making individual precludes an approach in terms of subjectivation through bodily and material culture. The case of anthropology is somewhat different. In the Boasian tradition of cultural anthropology, such scholars as Gregory Bateson and Margaret Mead have been sensitive to the bodily and material dimensions of culture. In Europe, by contrast, the Radcliffe-Brownian tradition of social anthropology has proved to be particularly blind to it, as has been the case with Lévi-Straussian structuralism, interested in representations of the body, but not in the body itself. A body may stink. Representations and speech do not. This is a basic difference between René Magritte's pipe and the picture of the pipe (titled as the 'Treachery of Images'), the body and its representations. Moreover, when the so-called 'material turn' occurred in the 1970s, and when 'the body' became an anthropological topic in the 1980s, they did not develop as a single integrated approach but as two independent fields of study, each of them with its specialists, seminars, publications and dedicated journals.[1] In this edited volume, we contend that the two fields of study should be collapsed into a single one. The second cause of this blind spot is to be found in what the neuro-cognitive sciences call the cognitive unconscious. That is, any human being, and even more so any sociologist, is little aware of the billions of stimuli, motions, electrical impulses in its nervous system and coordinated muscle contractions and relaxations that are needed to eat, drink, drive a car, type on one's laptop, deliver a speech in a political meeting, etc., and that all those actions shape a given lifestyle, given sorts of subjectivities and different sorts of governmentalities. Such repertoires of procedural knowledge are buried deep in our learned sensori-motor algorithms. We operate on a daily basis thanks to many acquired automatic pilots of which we have little awareness.

Consequently, we do not see that our technologies of power are embodied and materialised in every single domain of our daily life, at school, in the streets, at work, at home, in our health and leisure practices and in our consumption habits in a globalised merchant society. It could be objected that such practices belong with economics and especially consumption studies but not with politics. I wish to challenge this assumption. In Foucauldian parlance, consumption habits are a means to produce certain kinds of subjects and subjectivities, to provide them with techniques of the self whereby they will govern themselves, take themselves as the object of their own actions and, in so doing, subject themselves to some kind of sovereignty.

Jean-François Bayart ([2004] 2007: 317–404) has underlined the efficacy of the 'global techniques of the body' in producing a globalised subject.[2] The world market and all the goods and services it offers lend themselves to a process of appropriation, just as *bushfallers* go out and domesticate the resources of modernity to come back to their kingdom. We can reject both the pessimistic view of merchant globalisation inherited from the Frankfurt school, and the enchanting celebration of consumption by the so-called postmodernist ideology. What is at stake, in Weberian parlance, is the production of given lifestyles, of daily practices, of types of peoples.

Jean-François Bayart (ibid., 350) further illustrates this point with many ethnographic examples. In Turkey, the clash between laicist and Islamic democrats does not transcend material culture. One of the favourite productions of the Adalet ve Kalkinma Partisi (AKP) government of R. T. Erdogan is the Islamic female fashion, with its components, the silk *pardösü*, various kinds of scarf such as the *türban*, that originate in the merchant provision system and are domesticated and incorporated by Turkish women. Both, and other items of female dress, are submitted to local and global processes of fashion, well exemplified in the case of Iran by Alexandru Balasescu (2007), with its fashion shows, the bodily techniques of the defile, the mannequin on the catwalk and the appropriation of fashion on the clothes market. One of the most intriguing observations of Balasescu concerns the way the industrial and market provision system has been adopted in Iran with the result that ample gowns have been more and more often replaced by close-fitting garments that induce the women who have adopted them to better monitor the limits and corpulence of their own body. This has gone hand in hand with a change in aesthetic criteria of female beauty and a change in eating habits. When analysing such practices, we would certainly consider such goods for their sign value in a system of connotation but far more importantly, for their sensori-motor value in a system of agency. That is, we refer to a praxeologic paradigm rather than a semiotic one.

Yet, motor conducts in a material world as technologies of power must be set against their associated discursive practices to complement the picture. When this is done, it appears that, most of the time, there is a cognitive gap between praxis and discourse, orthopraxy and orthodoxy in any given historical context and for the same subjects. Urmila Mohan and myself (2017: 380–382) have commented on this fact already noticed by quite a few social scientists. In our opinion, this tension and even contradiction between the two kinds of repertoires has far-reaching implications regarding the dynamics of power and of consent.

Another publication (Bayart and Warnier eds. 2004) provides several case studies of the subjectivation process through bodily and material cultures in Asian and European societies, including contemporary ones. For example, François Hoarau (2004) gives a detailed ethnographic account of the bodily techniques of the customers who patronise a press and bookshop in a major and busy railway station – he himself working there as a salesman. He shows that the sensori-motor algorithms of given customers are far more predictive of what they want to purchase than the semiotics of their look. He also shows that their bodily techniques and those of the staff are often transferred from other contexts: the supermarket for the customers and the kitchen for the (female) boss. This demonstration provides him with a tool for a critical assessment of the notion of identity, in favour of an approach in terms of action and bodily conducts.

The examples I have given so far show that political subjectivation exhibits a strong historical dimension. The personal profile of Ngwa'fo, the hunger strike he initiated to avoid assuming the burden of kingship, his subsequent acceptance of it, his learning of all the monarchic bodily conducts and his political career in the Cameroon State are characteristic of a particular historical moment, that of the colonial contact with its attendant schooling system and so-called 'development' policies, the independence of former African colonies around 1960, the double process of formation of the State by social divergence and of the construction of its institutions, and of the globalisation of market, migratory and cultural fluxes throughout the twentieth century.

Similarly, the examples picked up by Jean-François Bayart and Alexandru Balacescu in Turkey and Iran are historically situated at particular moments in their political trajectory. Since they are learned and incorporated by the subjects at a given moment, bodily and material cultures have a strong historical dimension.

But is all this really political in nature? Since bodily and material culture is everywhere to be found, doesn't it dissolve politics into insignificance? Or else, in other words, if there is something that we may qualify as political, shouldn't it be clearly distinct from something that is not? I suggest that the answer to that question is to be found in what Michel Foucault calls a governmentality, that is, a historically recognisable way of producing certain kinds of subjects and of subjecting them to a sovereignty. That is, power and politics are one of the many analytical dimensions of the techniques of the body, the techniques of the self and their attendant material cultures. Other dimensions of the same may be found in religion, aesthetics and economics. This statement raises well-known definitional difficulties. I believe we can solve them at least partially by following the suggestion that was current in American anthropology in the 1970s and 1980s, that is, to adopt a processual approach rather than an essentialist and definitional one to politics, religion, etc.

Accordingly, we shall consider as political any process or action implemented to, *at the same time*, produce certain kinds of subjects and subject them to the actions of other subjects. The very process of producing different subjectivities may raise conflicts that require a resolution, either violent or negotiated. For example, in contemporary continental Europe, with international migrations and the intake of refugees, dress, sensori-motor conducts in public spaces and public transports, eating habits, smells in collective tenements may trigger conflicts of subjectivation. In the United States, the market, ownership and use of firearms is a cogent example. Back to the Mankon kingdom, we also find conflicts of subjectivation between the returning migrants who have altered their lifestyles and patterns of

118 *Jean-Pierre Warnier*

consumption (and even more so their children), and those who have stayed in the kingdom and perceive the habits of the returning migrants as offensive. Such conflicts concern musical tastes – pop, disco, variety, jazz, etc. – accessed through the media on the one hand and live local music on the other hand, with the palace trying to maintain the local standards and its power as exemplified in the kingdom of Oku studied by Nicolas Argenti (2004).

Conclusion

To conclude, as an alternative to the political sociology of the choice-making individual, a historical and comparative sociology of politics inspired by Max Weber (the daily life, the lifestyles), Marcel Mauss (the 'bio-psycho-social' techniques of the body) and Michel Foucault (the governmentality achieved by the micro technologies of the self and of power) opens up new fields of investigation into politics and into political matters. It provides an ethnographic methodology. It answers two of the three questions on which political theory has traditionally focused. Firstly, a descriptive one: what is it that constitutes a political agent, process or power? How do we identify such an object? The second debate is analytic in nature: how do we analyse, explain or interpret it? What are its essential properties? The third one assumes the heritage of political philosophy concerning the best form of political government. It is normative and implies a judgment of value. Introducing bodily-and-material culture as set against associated discursive practices provides an answer to the first and the second questions. But not to the third one which is a question that is more of a philosophical nature, though it provides all the elements that will help raise the normative question in all its relevant dimensions.

Notes

1. Such as *Body and Society*, *Journal of Material Culture*, *Corps*, etc.
2. Originally published as *Le Gouvernement du monde. Une critique politique de la globalisation*, Paris: Fayard, 2004. Translated as *Global Subjects. A Political Critique of Globalization*, Cambridge and Boston, Polity, 2007.

References

Argenti, N. (2004), 'La danse aux frontières. Les mascarades interdites des femmes et des jeunes à Oku', in J. -F. Bayart and J. -P. Warnier (eds.), *Matière à politique. Le pouvoir, les corps et les choses*, 151–180, Paris: CERI-Karthala.

Balacescu, A. (2007), *Paris Chic, Teheran Thrills. Aesthetic Bodies, Political Subjects*, Bucarest: Zeta Books.

Bayart, J. -F. ([2004] 2007), *Global Subjects. A Political Critique of Globalization*, Cambridge and Boston: Polity.

Bayart, J. -F. and J. -P. Warnier eds., (2004), *Matière à politique. Le pouvoir, les corps et les choses*. Paris: CERI-Karthala.

Politics matters 119

De Boeck, F. (2004), 'La frontière diamantifère angolaise et son héros mutant,' in J. -F. Bayart and J. -P. Warnier (eds.), *Matière à politique. Le pouvoir, les corps et les choses*, 93–128, Paris: CERI-Karthala.

Fo Angwafo S.A.N. III of Mankon (2009), *Royalty and Politics. The Story of My Life*, Mankon, Bamenda: Langaa RPCIG.

Foucault, M. (1994), *Dits et ecrits, IV, 1980-1988*, Paris: NRF Gallimard.

Hoarau, F. (2004), 'Du travail de vendeur dans un Relay d'une gare parisienne', in Bayart and Warnier (eds.), *Matière à politique. Le pouvoir, les corps et les choses*, 33–56, Paris: CERI-Karthala.

Horton, R. (1971), 'Stateless Societies in the History of West Africa', in J. R. Ade Ajayi and M. Crowder (eds.), *History of West Africa Vol. I*, 78–119, New York: Columbia University Press.

Kopytoff, I., ed. (1987), *The African Frontier: The Reproduction of Traditional African Societies*, Bloomington and Indianapolis: Indiana University Press.

Mohan, U. and J. -P. Warnier (2017), 'Editorial: Marching the Devotional Subject: The Bodily-and-Material Cultures of Religion', *Journal of Material Culture*, 22 (4): 369–384.

Nyamnjoh, F. B. (2011), 'Cameroonian Bushfalling: Negotiation of Identity and Belonging in Fiction and Ethnography', *American Ethnologist*, 38 (4): 701–713.

Nyamnjoh, F. B. (2014), 'Our Traditions are Modern, Our Modernities Traditional: Chieftaincy and Democracy in Contemporary Cameroon and Botswana,' *Modern Africa: Politics, History and Society*, 2 (2): 13–62.

Perrot, C. and F. -X. Fauvelle-Aymar eds. (2003), *Le retour des rois. Les autorités traditionnelles et l'etat en Afrique contemporaine*, Paris: Karthala.

Schilder, P. (1935)*, The Image and Appearance of the Human Body. Studies in the Constructive Energy of the Psyche*, London: Kegan Paul.

Turner, F. J. ([1893]1961), 'The Significance of the Frontier in American History', in R. A. Billingston (ed.), *Frontier and Section: Selected Essays*, 28–36, Englewood Cliffs: Prentice Hall.

Warnier, J. -P. (2007), *The Pot-King. The Body and Technologies of Power*, Leiden: Brill (African Studies Series).

Warnier, J. -P. (2011), 'Territorialization and the Politics of Autochthony', in H. Anheier and Y. R. Isar (eds.), *The Culture and Globalization Series. Heritage, Memory and Identity*, 95–104, Los Angeles and London: Sage.

Warnier, J. -P. (2012a), *Cameroon Grassfields Civilization*, Mankon: Langaa RPCIG.

Warnier, J. -P. (2012b), 'The Grassfields of Cameroon: Ancient Center or Recent Periphery?' *Africa Today*, 58 (3): 59–72.

8 Chronicles of a moral war: Ascetic subjectivation and formation of the Javanese state[1]

Romain Bertrand

Contemporary studies of 'colonial situations' have focused on the perspectives of the colonised emphasising the innumerable constraints faced by indigenous populations. However, they have put little emphasis on how the latter have used colonial constraints, or their cunning, to pursue their own path of subjectivation. With reference to the work of Michel Foucault, Gilles Deleuze (1990: 135) broadly defines the process of subjectivation as 'the individuation, particular or collective, which characterises an event'. Applied to the study of social behavior, Jacques Rancière's (1995: 59) notion of subjectivation qualifies and covers all the cognitive operations and bodily practices that allow an individual (or a group of individuals) to constitute themselves as a moral speaker. That is, to ask oneself about what one wants in a relationship of power. By belonging to a constituted social order, the individual thus becomes a political subject when s(he) expresses in action, by gesture and speech, a set of values relating to a particular conception of acting.

The problem of power in the colonial world coincides with that of material cultures through the 'control of attribution of materiality' (Warnier 2000). In the colonial situation, and especially during the racialist phase of European empires, the hierarchies of daily life were translated and constructed through *privileges of subjectivation* granted to certain social groups and denied to others in the name of laws and norms. Certain social categories have thus had the right to acquire a class of goods and to draw on an associated repertoire of gestures, postures and affects (Warnier 1999: 10–13). Other groups were not allowed to do so, on pain of sanctions. This unequal distribution of the possibilities of access to materiality proceeds either from monopolising decisions by social authorities or from structural, economic and ecological factors.

This differential allocation of materiality is never fixed once and for all. The privileges of subjectivation are the subject of incessant quarrels between competing social groups. They give rise to conflicts and wars of subjectivation (Bayart 1996a: 162), at the end of which the paths of objectification are articulated differently. Thus, the norms that regulate the political economy and the use of goods, gestures and affects trigger wars of subjectivation and

122   *Romain Bertrand*

constitute the historicity of a state of domination. It is important to pay attention to both the institutional procedures for assigning control of materiality and to the challenges that affect them.

I apply this grid of analysis to the subtle and changing relations that unite and oppose the nobility of Java – those still called *priyayi* – to other indigenous social groups, such as merchants and peasants, as well as to the various colonisers. The relationship between indigenous noble elites and foreign authorities has never been fixed once and for all by the conditions of military conquest. Quite the opposite, confrontation continued throughout the history of the Javanese empire. Domination spread gradually through the field of registers of subjectivation, 'practices of self on self' (Foucault 1982: 222–243) and the logic of acquisition and use of certain classes of goods. It is thus a question here of undertaking, through the retrodiction of a lifestyle (Veyne 1978: 194–235), the study of a trajectory of individuation: that of the *priyayi* of Java.

'Formation' of the state and the Insulinde dilemma of luxury and power

The story of the 'formation of the state' (Berman and Londale 1992: 5)[2] in Insulinde/Indonesian archipelago is that of a constant rivalry between itinerant trading communities and aristocracies powerfully tied to a territory. The states of the Straits of Malacca, like the powerful Sultanate of Malacca at the end of the fifteenth century or the Sultanate of Atjeh (Aceh) in the seventeenth century, were monarchical political systems that drew their revenue from the taxation of goods in transit. The control of the sea, its exploitation and its pacification, were necessary conditions of prosperity, because the revenues of the Royal Treasury came mainly from taxing the trade known as 'from India to India'. The latter mainly concerned spices and herbs (pepper, nutmeg, cloves, saffron, cinnamon), textile products (Chinese silk, Javanese *batik*, Malabar and Coromandel fabrics), rare woods (teak) and sometimes men (the slave trade from Macau in the seventeenth century) (Meilinck-Roelofsz 1962, Reid 1995). To gain control of the seas, the sovereigns made pacts with the fleets of Malaysian pirates, the formidable seafarers (*orang laut*) who had also created a dense network of forts (Tarling 1963).

These warehouse states, to use a standard formula, were built by capturing streams of wealth in perpetual motion. Merchants of all nationalities – Arabs, Indians, Japanese, Europeans (Portuguese, Spaniards, Dutch, French) – posed, however, a formidable political problem to the native aristocracy. For if these merchants were a source of wealth, they seldom fixed themselves at given points of trade routes. These peregrine merchants did not obey the same logic of territoriality as sovereigns and nobiliary groups, riveted to dynastic spaces. So, it was almost impossible, not only to force them by oaths of loyalty, but to impose a tax regime too restrictive, for fear of seeing them leave the city for a more hospitable port harbour. In short, the rulers had almost no control over the ship owners and crews who organised themselves into powerful corporations and free communities, providing a bridge between the world of the court and that of the port (Wilkinson 1935: 136–137).

But even more than the mobility of merchants, the aristocrats feared their progressive encrustation in the political world. The rich man, the *orang kaya* was to be kept out of palatine political life under penalty if seen claiming, in the name of his fortune, a power which could belong only to the princes and to the courtesan nobility on the one hand, and to the specialists of war on the other. In a universe that married Sufi Islamic influences and Hindu influences, the social world was divided into functional 'orders' enjoying specific rights and duties. The right of command belonged to the nobility of blood and the warriors. The religious scholars could play the role of preceptors of morality within the palaces, legitimising the reign of a dynasty. But they had no special right to the leadership of men outside their congregations.

Thus, to counter the political influence of the merchants, the Javanese rulers resorted to a whole arsenal of sumptuary laws reserving the use of certain goods to defined social categories, prohibiting any ostentatiousness to merchants. They also sparked the emergence of a nobility of the robe – the *priyayi* – more docile than the aristocracy of blood, and able to exert control over the small peasantry. The *priyayi* at once close to and distinct from aristocrats, merchants and peasants forged a regime of subjectivation through asceticism. In order to legitimise this enterprise, the *priyayi* took advantage of spiritual traditions of various origins.

Subjectivation by asceticism: the eremitic ideal of *priyayi*

In pre-colonial Javanese and Malaysian societies, money *(uang)* was very often considered unclean *(haram)*. The market *(pasar)* is a place that a noble Javanese cannot attend on pain of being defiled by the idea of gain or bad passions (Brenner 1998: 57–63). The palatine texts, chronicles, annals and poems, constantly remind us that power and prestige are not acquired by success, but derive from the birth and favour of the sovereign.

Suspicion of material success was the most widely shared thing in historic Java. There, as elsewhere, faced with a small peasantry living in precariousness, notables respected universally agreed codes of good conduct, such as the Qur'anic obligation of the mandatory charity of *zakat*. But even if the disregard for trading and individual enrichment was at the centre of a kind of moral consensus associating several social orders, the *priyayi* were unquestionably the champions of the struggle against the merchants in channelling the royal practice of asceticism. The sovereign's capacity of asceticism is attested by the existence of places in the palaces of Java devoted exclusively to the king's meditation (Woodward 1989: 199–214). In these places of abstinence, the sovereigns of Java staged their propitiatory immobility to control passions and desire by fasting and sexual solitude.[3]

124 *Romain Bertrand*

These practices of austerity placed the ruler at the antipodes of the trading world, obsessed by the accumulation of precious goods.

At the end of the nineteenth century, the aristocrats of Java, that is, the nobility of *priyayi* and the small circle of blood princes or *para bangsawan*, still lived under the regime of an antagonism between palatine virtues and bourgeois vices. The *priyayi* had in particular elaborated a very strict code of morality, organised around asceticism *(tapas)*. The practice of austerity exercises, such as food or sexual fasting, figured at the top of the empowering recipes prescribed by the texts of the Sufi literature of the Straits and the mystical literature belonging to the so-called 'renaissance' of the Surakarta court, 1790–1830. Hundreds of treatises of manners and mystical poems, preserved in the libraries of the palaces of Jogjakarta and Surakarta, open with the enumeration of practices of 'self on self' by which a *priyayi* had to overcome his impulses.

In the world of Javanese mysticism, two types of knowledge *(ngelmu)* are generally distinguished. Practical magic, which only targets the accumulation of physical power, is *kanuragan*. It is in this category that we find the Javanese martial arts *(pencak silat)* and the 'arts of the left hand', including various types of witchcraft and sorcery. The exercises of austerity are *kebatinan* knowledge, advocated by the great Javanese mystic sects. This difference between *kanuragan* and *kebatinan* is not simply a moral distinction between 'good' and 'evil' but is primarily concerned with social status intersecting the notional pair 'small people-physical body' and 'elites-mystical interiority'. *Kanuragan* is a knowledge of transfiguration which aims at the transformation of the body and appearance *(lahir)* and *kebatinan* deals with the mystical metamorphosis of the human being and interiority *(batin)*.

From the study of *Darmakoesoema*, a text attributed to Seh Djamboekarang who lived in the sixteenth century, Josef Knebel (1897: 118–127) distinguished eleven types of ascetic exercises. These different types of ascetic exercises are situated on a continuum of voluntary suffering, ranging from the simple temporary silence, assumed to keep a promise or thanks for a realised wish, to very trying techniques of mortification. Extreme forms of contrition are believed to lead to states of mystical ecstasy in which magical knowledge is acquired and the possibility of trade with the invisible spirit world *(dunia gaib, dunia kang samar)* is opened up. The ascetic forms identified by Knebel are still widely practiced in Javanese society. Regardless of their social group of reference and their degree of adherence to Islam, many Javanese people fast on the nights of *Selasa* and *Kliwon*, the days of the lunar calendar that are conducive to contact with the supernatural world. A student anxious to pass exams or a woman who wants to have a child will spend the night crouched in a sacred mausoleum, to donate the *dikir* (the 99 names of Allah recorded in the Quran) in order to imbue the mystic power of the dead. During my research visits to Jogjakarta, my main informant was *Mas* Marjdi Surjorogo, a small *priyayi* working for the Ngayogyakarta Hadiningrat house, as a palace servant *(abdi dalem)* on behalf of Sultan Hamengku Buwono X. (*Mas* is a title for male petty nobility.) I accompanied him on the evening of Selasa Kliwon to the Kota Gede Cemetery (Royal Necropolis) of Imogiri, south of Jogjakarta. Crouched between the stelae, *Mas* Marjdi recited incantations in honor of Panembahan Senopati Ingalaga – the mythical sovereign founder of the Mataram empire – or invoked the spirit of Hamengku Buwono IX. Then with infinite caution, he spread flower petals on the longitudinal tombs, before disappearing by walking backwards on his heels, hands joined at the forehead and inclined at the chest, in so-called *sembah* position. In addition to such visits, *Mas* Marjdi regularly practiced *tapa mutih*, which consists of only eating white rice for three or seven days.

The immediate effect of such devotional practices and austerity exercises is the strengthening of the moral force, the power *(kekuasaan)* that allows the individual to better overcome a social challenge. Among *priyayi*, ascetic practice is articulated in fact with a theory of power (*wahyu*: a term still used to evoke mystical knowledge, object of the spiritual quest). This theory states that the accumulation of personal power has no intrinsic limit, while the sum of power in the universe remains constant (Anderson 1990: 22–23). The power of one is always the weakness of the other. The classical Javanese texts, however, distinguish very clearly between potency *(kesakten)* and force *(kakuwatan* and *karosan)*. *Sekti* or power can also be transferred to objects *(pusaka)* and to human beings (the descendants of a demi-god or a saint). Moreover, power is acquired only for the purpose of making use of it and to acquire authority, *kuwasa* or *wewenang*. In other words, the *kesakten* which is obtained by asceticism does not, in itself, give the right to govern. Power becomes legitimate power only by virtue of the community's acceptance of its holder as master or representative. The right of command certainly derives from the codes of morality but also from practices to acquire power such as meditation in mystical places.

The *priyayi* made the ascetic repertoire of politics their collective register of subjectivation, the cornerstone of their moral identity. Their model of personality was the ascetic, sometimes in the features of the reclusive hermit in silent contemplation of divinity, sometimes under those of the itinerant moral teacher who is strengthened by many internal struggles as well as the social (oratory contests, Guillot 1981:144), and learning *ngelmu*, the 'science of reality' from peers. In contrast with the merchant who played the nobleman and with the aristocrat palatine who had dignity by birth, and even in opposition to the poor villagers, the authentic *priyayi* had the right of command only by virtue of his endurance in fasting and his intimacy with the divine. But if the ideal type of personality of the *priyayi* was indeed the *ajar* or the sage this ideal had to be adapted to the exigencies of courtesan life. The solution to this dilemma of subjectivity was to subordinate all social activities to a body of precepts of astonishing precision. This project converged with the domestication strategies of courtesan aristocracy led by the rulers of Java.

A lifestyle articulated around the rules of doing

To write a history of norms, a history of morals, it is not enough to understand life as behaviours observable empirically. It is still necessary to write the history of small arrangements with these norms, the history of personal and collective ethics. The ultimate ideal of the *priyayi* is a world of 'completeness' that is perfectly ordered *(diatur)* and harmonious. As long as he obeyed all the orders of manners, the *priyayi* could continue to frequent the orgiastic banquets of the palaces and live in luxurious mansions. The *priyayi* label, with its insistence on eating well or the duty of elegance, did not represent a denial of ascetic virtue. Instead, *priyayi* practice was a worldly transposition of the *ajar* or sage model where the measure of bounty was a substitute for fasting. The regulation of everyday life was the most important ethic and a response to the social challenges faced since *priyayi* were placed in a very unstable situation. They were involved in conflicts of subjectivation on three fronts: the 'stupid' peasants, the aristocrats refined but stuck in a dissolute life and the rich and rude merchants.

The first moral conflict pitted the *priyayi* against the peasants. The cardinal principle of 'declining status', as pointed out by Clifford Geertz (1980) about Bali, is that, after the third or fourth generation, a family of small *priyayi* returns to the fold if it has failed to renew its rank by skillful marriage strategies and subtle manipulations of genealogies. The *priyayi* feared statutory decay, the demotion towards the abhorred universe of the poor and uneducated poor people *(wong tjilik)*. The text *Sasana Sunu*, composed in 1819 by a famous court poet, Yasadipura II, draws a distinction between peasants, who are 'people of the body' *(bangsa badan)*, and *priyayi*, who are 'people of the spirit' *(bangsa ati)* (Sarman 1971, Kumar 1997: 405–411). Today, nobles continue to perceive the peasants as *masih bodoh*, 'still stupid' (Pemberton 1994: 320), that is to say, as coarse and rude beings who are imperfectly civilised.

As regards obligations, Yasadipura II attaches particular importance to the appearance of the young *priyayi* nobleman to whom he addresses his recommendations. The garment is the subject of a long series of warnings (in Chant III, stances 6–25): appropriate patterns of *batik* (a wax resist cloth) according to the wearer's rank and privileges, and the use of conventional colours. Motifs such as *parang rusak barong,* a broken sword design, were reserved for royalty (Figure 8.1) and even today, locals will avoid wearing these motifs out of respect for its sanctity and power. Such opinions come under a definition of the duty of elegance *(besus)* which insists on the necessity of keeping in mind the strategic aspect of self-presentation and how to be elegant without arousing envy or giving in to pride. As a result, *priyayi* aesthetic taste spread throughout the living environment, to the home, furniture and staff.

The second moral conflict mobilising the *priyayi* relates to the quarrel of precedence that makes them eternal enemies of the blood aristocracy. The

Chronicles of a moral war 127

Figure 8.1 K.G.P.A.A. Hamengkoe Nagara I, son of Sultan of Jogjakarta Hamengkoe Boewana VIII (r. 1931–1939), 1895, dressed in batik wrapper with *parang rusak barong* motif reserved for royalty.

Collection Nationaal Museum van Wereldculturen. Coll. no. TM- 60001458.

priyayi are civil servants engaged in enunciating the 'rules of life' that ensure social peace within the area of sovereignty *(negara)*. For them, courtiers and princes lead a dissolute life, incompatible with the dignity of those who command. One can judge the redoubled violence of this conflict at the end of the nineteenth century by reading the comment of a high-ranking *priyayi*, the regent Tjondro Negoro V of Kudus, about the court of Solo (Surakarta):

> In my opinion, the capital of the state of Surakarta does not give the impression of being a princely city because the living conditions of most Javanese are deplorable. Their houses are damaged, and there is hardly any order ... Also, many of these children go wrong ... Many are

128   *Romain Bertrand*

outlaws in smuggling cases ... The nobility of Surakarta is idle, spoiled since childhood and uneducated. (Bonneff 1986: 266–267)

The antagonism between *priyayi* and the princes of blood *(para bangsawan)* was old, consubstantial with the conditions of socio-genesis of the former. The *priyayi* had indeed been ennobled by the rulers of the Mataram empire, in the sixteenth and seventeenth centuries, to split the nobility into competing segments to prevent dissenting networks of authority. *Priyayi* were government specialists charged with managing the domains and the treasure of the sovereign, while the dynast's relatives were half warlords and half courtiers, professional dilettantes. The *priyayi* frantically envied the princes, who had the advantage over them of the hereditary transmission of offices and honors and control over the patronage of the major arts. Conversely, princes and courtiers hated these great *priyayi* families for their monopoly of administrative power.

The third moral conflict in which the *priyayi* were engaged opposed them to a handful of wealthy merchants, the *sudagar* who made their fortune in artisanal textiles. Again, a nineteenth-century document reveals the violence of lifestyles wars in colonial Insulinde. This is a satirical text composed by a court poet in 1818:

> Here again is the shame of the one who wanted to offer a wedding.
> He was a small merchant
> Mediocre fortune.
> He trained himself in the lifestyle of *priyayi*.
> [An adjutant of the Court advised him then]:
> 'Do not strive to do [your marriage] according to the *priyayi* rules'.
> The older [the merchant] intervened sweetly:
> 'I do not know yet, *adhi*,
> The true way of *priyayi*,
> And that's why I want to get closer to them.' (Brenner 1991: 68–69)

The rest of the story goes like this. *Ki sudagar* (Sir merchant) accepts the ironic advice of the *adhi* who is a *priyayi* of the palace. He calls for an assembly of nobles for his wedding. They relieve him of his money by playing games of fortune, get drunk and hunt at his expense, but give him no recognition. The lesson is clear, and after several anecdotes all ends in the ruin and humiliation of the merchant.

In order to meet this triple challenge of subjectivation, *priyayi* clung to a lifestyle on which testimonies, old photographs and even the observation of contemporary practices leave no doubt. This lifestyle is exemplified with a maniacal concern for the garment and appearance – always impeccable, perfectly adjusted, devoid of excess. It implies a perfect sensori-motor incorporation of measured gestures, facial expressions not betraying any disorderly emotion. Thus, when *Mas* Marjdi Surjorogo and I went to a market, impure place par excellence for an aristocrat, he moved with an exaggerated grace between greasy stalls, raising with one hand his *kain* (piece of cloth wrapped around the waist and legs). When we ate *nasi soto* (rice soup) sitting in the roadside trolleys, his gestures were also sluggishly calculated. *Mas* Marjdi was very resistant to contact with the 'little people' in the villages, and he constantly apologised to me for their inappropriate behaviour.

The ethnographic observation so far leaves little doubt as to the strength by which *priyayi* exacerbates the full possession of his faculties. He cultivates control, mastery and appropriation of his body, his emotions and movements. He brands himself in his body by ascetic techniques as well as by clothing, food, the discipline of the senses, tastes and disgusts. But this impulse is directed also towards the others, who are possessed, or that is to say, dispossessed of their desire. A *priyayi's* entourage is marked by his gestures, his material culture and his motor behaviours. Sexual abstinence is still considered as a testimony of inner strength: in fact, it is said that lively emotions cause the body to warm up, while sexual inactivity 'cools' it. When I met *Mas* Marjdi, he and his wife had made room for him to 'purify' himself to hasten the healing of one of his children who was suffering from a high fever.

The practice of asceticism and an exceptional lifestyle as subjectivising techniques, however, conceals a paradox. It is a diet of desire that strives to create an 'eviction of the self' but there is a certain sleight of hand that is at the heart of governmentality through asceticism. There is no painful renunciation of the enjoyment of the world, but, on the contrary, a tremendous enjoyment of influence over oneself, over others and over things. Renunciation is a 'self-technique' invested with mystical and magical meanings just like fasting or meditation. Simultaneously, the moral identity of the *priyayi* was called into question by the changes which the indigenous aristocracy brought about in the construction of the colonial state in Java.

Monetarising the colonial domain and reordering the aristocratic control of materiality attribution

Was the fear of *priyayi* vis-à-vis merchants objectively justified? Did there exist in Java, at the turn of the twentieth century, a rich indigenous bourgeoisie likely to confiscate the monopoly of moral excellence that hitherto *priyayi* held proudly? Had the old quarrel of luxury and power, which had haunted the Sultanates of the Straits of Malacca since the fifteenth century, ended in the victory of the merchants at the expense of the territorial institutions built by the palatine bureaucrats?

Between 1830 and 1870, the Insulinde became an operating colony for the Dutch and others, with large public plantations where, for a meager salary, hundreds of thousands of peasant-workers had been wrenched from their villages. The industrialisation of Java accelerated further in the second half of the century, leading to the emergence of a 'free market' of skilled indigenous

130 *Romain Bertrand*

labour. In this context, inequalities of wealth became a determining parameter of hierarchies of influence. But this fact was in flagrant contradiction with the classical Javanese aristocratic ideals, which only linked indirectly power and wealth, and qualities of command and possessions (Elson 1994).

In fact, the *priyayi* were both right and wrong to fear the rise of traders and merchants. They were wrong in the sense that, even if the available data allows us to conclude the existence of a rich urban class exerting some social influence, there is no indication that the merchant or *sudagar* had transformed into a conquering bourgeoisie, competing with aristocratic circles. On the contrary, the *sudagars*, eager to acquire social respectability, often imitated the *priyayi* lifestyle and drew their moral discourse from that of the palaces. In addition, the strength of the aristocratic prejudice against commercial activities, combined with a mercantilist policy openly hostile to indigenous entrepreneurs, prevented Javanese merchants from becoming an authentic 'capitalist class' with a different style of subjectivation.

But the *priyayi* were also right to fear the silent revolution of social structures that provoked a planned monetarisation of the colonial domain. For in a world where money inspired respect, the Islamic ethic of the 'winning sign of grace' was much more successful than the contemplative morality of the master of mysticism. The principle of talent and competence as sources of prestige eroded the classical doctrines of *priyayi*. The *priyayi* themselves, as a result of their gradual evolution towards the status of colonial officials, turned into expensive notables throughout the so-called compulsory cropping system period (1830–1870) and then during the liberal era (1870–1900). They then accumulated rapidly the riches of this world by owning luxurious mansions endowed with prodigious domesticity, statues of alabaster in their *taman* (garden) and silver candlesticks on their tables, as well as medals and wine of Burgundy (Larson 1987, Soeratman 2000).

It is not possible here to narrate in detail this slow drift of *priyayi* towards a register of subjectivation other than that of asceticism: a register of expenditure and abundance. The *priyayi* made ample use of the consumption possibilities afforded them by colonial supply systems. Thus, the legendary figure of the ascetic gradually faded at the twilight of the Empire. Today even if the mystical repertoire of politics remains relevant in Java, where it continuously informs the actions of notables and leaders (Bertrand 2001), the multiplication of action repertoires and drastic changes in city-countryside relations have relegated authority practices to the background. The mystical imagination of power now tends to be no more than a secondary, if not even secret, language of the political, whereas it was, in the eighteenth and nineteenth centuries, the publicly accepted principle of the race for honours.

Conclusion: the paradoxical articulation of *saying* and *doing*

The discussion presented in the preceding pages make it possible to posit several hypotheses on the articulation between processes of state formation and the practices and registers of subjectivation of a social elite. The case of the *priyayi* of Java, exposed by means of historical ethnography, authorises three types of questioning.

First and foremost, subjectivation by asceticism confirms that there are ways of moral individuation distinct from European liberal thought. For *priyayi*, ascetic practice is indeed a technique of subjectivation, that is, a way of recognising oneself as linked to a moral code and of posing as a subject of will/desire within a relationship of power. However, the analysis of the moral economy of volition in classical Javanese aristocratic thought suggests a specific conception of the person. The person appears simultaneously responsible for its actions on self and barred from achieving any transformative action on the world. In other words, the notion of *subject* is here disjointed from that of *agency*. The exportation of the Foucaldian approach outside the West finds its justification in this disjunction, as well as the opportunity of its clarification by the prism of comparison.

Secondly, the study of the mechanisms and procedures of the 'control of the attribution of materiality' reveals itself inseparable from an enquiry on the parameters of objectification as the incorporation of given materialities, that is to say the economic and *ecological* constraints of the practices of subjectivation – and in particular the conditions of monetarisation of a social system and the state of supply networks. It is not enough to answer the political question, 'Who has the right to acquire such types of goods and to perform such actions, and under what laws or standards?' It is necessary to consider the ecological question, 'Who has what (of what range of goods, of which repertoires of postures) at a particular moment and place to therefore legitimately objectify oneself?' This second interrogation makes it necessary to sketch a topography of the points of distribution and transit circuits of commodities under consideration, to identify and quantitatively evaluate the ebbs and flows of objects, to reconstruct the opaque flowcharts of unofficial brokers and legal intermediaries, in short, *to visualise movements*. In this perspective, power would appear to be an inciting, modifying or interruptive force of flux and no longer the organising principle of a fixed configuration of closed spaces, where permanent regimes of value prevail (Appadurai 1986: 3–63).

Third, and finally, the analytical focus on 'techniques of the self' as empowering recipes makes it necessary to elucidate local conceptions of the right to command. In other words, it seems just as dangerous to dissociate sensorimotor behaviours substantiated in materiality from the moral discourses that make the commentary, that is, to separate the *saying* from the *doing* and to postulate an adequacy between sensori-motor behaviours on the one hand and discursive practices on the other. It is doubtful that the *priyayi* actually followed the more exacting and arduous practices of asceticism that they elucidated. Yet, such masking behaviours also indicate how the Javanese government of the classical age was likely to win an adhesion, even if partial and precarious, of its subjects.

132 *Romain Bertrand*

Notes

1. This chapter was previously published in French (Bertrand 2004). It was subsequently translated into English and edited by Jean-Pierre Warnier and Urmila Mohan.
2. The distinction between state building as a conscious process of building a centralised government apparatus, and state formation as an unconscious process of spreading norms through social practice, has been at the heart of Hibou (1999) and Bayart (1996b).
3. Weber (1995: 307) defines asceticism as an 'ethic of virtuosos'.

References

Anderson, B. (1990), 'The Idea of Power in Javanese Culture', in B. Anderson *Language and Power in Indonesia. Exploring Political Cultures in Indonesia*, 17–77, Ithaca: Cornell University Press.

Appadurai, A. (1986), 'Introduction: Commodities and the Politics of Value', in A. Appadurai (ed.), *The Social Life of Things: Commodities in Cultural Perspective*, 3–63, Cambridge: Cambridge University Press.

Bayart, J. -F. (1996a), *L'illusion identitaire*, Paris: Fayard.

Bayart, J. -F. (1996b), *La greffe de l'état*, Paris: Karthala.

Berman, B. and J. Londale (1992), *Unhappy Valley. Conflict in Kenya and Africa. Vol I*, London: James Currey.

Bertrand, R. (2001), 'Ki Gendeng, a Wizard in Politics. Reflections on the Occult Dimensions of Public Space in Contemporary Indonesia', *Politix*, 14 (54): 43–73.

Bertrand, R. (2004), 'Chroniques d'une guerre morale. Subjectivation par l'ascèse et formation de l'état à Java', in J. -P. Warnier (ed.), *Matière à politique. Le pouvoir, les corps et les choses*, 57–91, Paris: CERI-Karthala.

Bonneff, M. (1986), *Pérégrinations Javanaises. Les voyages de R. M. A. Purwa Lelana*, Paris: Maison des Sciences de L'homme.

Brenner, S. (1991), 'Competing Hierarchies: Javanese Merchants and the *Priyayi* Elite in Solo, Central Java', *Indonesia*, 52: 68–69.

Brenner, S. (1998), *The Domestication of Desire. Women, Wealth and Modernity in Java*, Princeton: Princeton University Press.

Deleuze, G. (1990), *Pourparlers*. Paris: Les Éditions de Minuit.

Elson, R. E. (1994), *Village Java under the Cultivation System, 1830-1870*, Sydney: Allen and Unwin.

Foucault, M. (1982), 'Le sujet et le pouvoir', *Dits et écrits*, 4 (306): 222–243.

Guillot, C. (1981), *L'affaire Sadrach. Un essai de Christianisation à Java au 19e Siècle*, Paris: Maison des Sciences de l'Homme.

Hibou, B. (1999), *La privatisation des états*, Paris: Karthala.

Knebel, J. (1897), 'Darmakoesoema of Seh Djamboekarang. Desa-legende uit het Javaansch Medegedeeld', *Tijdschrift voor Indische Taal, Land en Volkenkunde*, 29: 118–127.

Kumar, A. (1997), *Java and Modern Europe: Ambiguous Encounters*, Richmond: Curzon Press.

Larson, G. D. (1987), *Prelude to Revolution. Palaces and Politics in Surakarta, 1912–1942*, Dordrecht: Foris Publications.

Meilinck-Roelofsz, A. P. (1962), *Asian Trade and European Influence in the Indonesian Archipelago between 1500 and About 1630*, La Haye: Martinus Nijhoff.

Pemberton, J. (1994), *On the Subject of "Java"*, Ithaca: Cornell University Press.

Rancière, J. (1995), *La mésentente. Politique et philosophie*, Paris: Galilée.

Reid, A. (1995), *Southeast Asia in the Age of Commerce, 1450–1680, Vol. 1 and 2*, Singapore: Oxford University Press.

Sarman, A. (1971), *Tinjauan Kitab Wicarakeras*, Doctoral thesis, Jogjakarta, Gajah Mada University.

Soeratman, D. (2000), *Kehidupan dunia keraton Surakarta, 1830-1939*, Yogyakarta: Yayasan Untuk Indonesia.

Tarling, N. (1963), *Piracy and Politics in the Malay World*, Melbourne: Australian National University.

Veyne, P. (1978), *Comment on écrit l'histoire*, Paris: Le Seuil.

Warnier, J. -P. (2000), 'Material Culture and Political Subjectivation', Talk at CERI, January 10–11, 2000.

Warnier, J. -P. (1999), *Construire la culture matérielle. L'homme qui pensait avec ses doigts*, Paris: Presses Universitaires de France.

Weber, M. (1995), *Economie et société. Vol. II,* Paris: Plon.

Wilkinson, R. J. (1935), 'The Malacca Sultanate', *Journal of the Malaysian Branch of the Royal Asiatic Society*, 13 (2): 136–137.

Woodward, M. (1989), *Islam in Java. Normative Piety and Mysticism in the Sultanate of Yogyakarta*, Tucson: University of Arizona Press.

Matter of religion

9 Opening and closing gestures: Weaving rituals that give and sustain life

Myriem Naji

This chapter explores the religious and cosmological dimensions surrounding the making of woven textiles in the Sirwa, southern Morocco. Not only do Sirwa dwellers conceptualise production as a living process (see Coupaye and Pitrou 2018, Gosselain 1999, Rowlands and Warnier 1993), they also seem to consider the weaving-in-the-making as a living being. By examining the words, gestures and rituals of Sirwa weavers, this paper seeks to understand the nature of this living being and the type of relationship women establish with it. This paper presents the forms this living-artefact takes and then examines weaving gestures with the view to gain some insight into emic thinking about the processes of weaving. The last part of this chapter addresses recent changes in weaving rituals and beliefs.

The theories of *Matière à Penser* (MaP) provide us, not only with a framework to explore the religious material and embodied practices of Sirwa weavers, but also with the tools to examine categories of actions that are difficult to grasp, and in particular the action of the subject on the self and the 'return' of action of materiality on the subject. The term materiality is used here to encompass the artefact-in-emergence, raw materials and tools in their dynamic interaction with the materiality of the moving, visceral, experiencing and feeling body of a subject that is ontologically incomplete without materiality (Warnier 2007).

Context

The Sirwa mountains have been inhabited for centuries by sedentarised Berber nomads who, breed sheep and goats, practice agriculture and since the 1980s have been producing large carpets for the international market. Their single heddle vertical looms are wide enough to accommodate at least two weavers, sitting side by side, who weave without a shuttle. Weaving is an exclusively female activity and the men specialise in the selling of carpets.

In addition to participant observation, semi-structured interviews with weavers about their weaving ritual practices were conducted between 2002 and 2005. Chantreau's thorough study of technical weaving operations

138 *Myriem Naji*

and rituals among Kabyle weavers in Algeria, constitutes the main source for colonial times (Morocco: 1912–1956). The striking similarity of weaving practices across the Maghreb reflects the fact that women constituted a conservative element in these societies, but also attests to the coherence and ancientness of weaving practices and beliefs in the region. The present tense is used here to refer to practices and beliefs still extant in 2005. Weaving knowledge is shared by all women, but older women normally undertake the more skilled tasks of warping and supervising the mounting of the loom; in families with a large number of daughters they may not weave at all.

Astta: linguistic clue to the nature of the weaving-in-emergence

Too often, writers investigating weaving communities in the Maghreb, use the term loom indiscriminately to translate *'astta'*, whereas weavers actually start using this term well before mounting the loom, at the warping stage. They cease to use it when they cut the woven artefact from the loom. The term *astta* therefore emphasises the artefact-as-emerging and implies the idea of a life cycle or course. In Maghrebi societies the manufacture of cloth has long been conceived as part of a seasonal transformation of crops, animals, people and things (Basset 1922, Bourdieu 1979, Servier 1962). Weaving was the female homologue of ploughing (birth of the cloth/field) and the cutting off of the cloth corresponded to harvesting (death of the cloth/field).

It is important to bear in mind that until very recently infantile/parturient mortality was very high in the Sirwa, and that up to the 1930s death through illness and war was very common. As will be further elaborated throughout

Figure 9.1 Weaver working on a *hmal* in the 'inside' of *astta,* with her little brother looking through the iron upright. Ayt Ubial village, 2002.

Photo by author.

Opening and closing gestures 139

this chapter, the unpredictability of life and divinities may have provided Sirwa communities with cognitive categories to explain technical uncertainty and problems. Maghrebi notions of life processes and life properties include ideas pertaining to life course, lifespan, life forces/substance, good health, welfare, good fortune, blessing and particularly fecundity, fertility and sexual potency. In the Sirwa, the terms *razq* and *baraka* encompass these notions of life force and blessing.

So what sort of entity was *astta*? The next two sections describe the domains it belongs to owing to its origin, form and properties: architecture and animal.

Astta as a sacred house-spirit-artefact

Despite its apparent flat surface, *astta* is perceived as a three-dimensional, enclosing space, with an interior *(aguns)*, where the weavers sit – between the wall of the room and the wall constituted by the warp-cloth stretched in front of them – and an exterior *(barra)*. Perhaps even the beams and uprights, which frame the body of the seated weaver, constitute some kind of threshold, as they are believed to have the power to hinder the vitality of people who cross them. Because of its constituent elements (wool and wood) and the way these are assembled together with ropes holding them in tension, *astta* resembles a tent, the original domestic dwelling, possibly the template for the shrines of saints and mosques. This architectural dimension of *astta* may explain why it was perceived as a house-spirit, as it shares the same properties as other house-spirits who are also constitutive parts of the house (threshold/foundation, room corners, hearth) or tools attached to the architecture of the house (grinding handmill).

House-spirits seemed to behave like domestic animals in that they needed to be cajoled into accepting the presence of foreign human and non-human beings through gifts of food. In the way that the life force of the new bride entering her house for the first time had to be protected from the 'masters' of the threshold (unless it was the threshold that was at risk), threads spun or dyed by women not belonging to the house had to receive special treatment. When a blood sacrifice was not performed (Chantreau 1941: 86), some threads were buried, as offerings, in the foundations or under the threshold of the house (ibid., 84, 86). Sacrifices could be both gifts and a form of conditional curse (*'ar*): the latter being a way of forcing the (human or non-human) gift-recipient to protect the donor (Westermarck 1926: ii551).

Jnûn behave in similar ways to house-spirits. They are, with angels, a more recent, abstract or detachable form of this entity, as they occupy rather than are a container-space. They give or take away their vitality as they choose to stay in or leave *astta*. *Jnûn* (sing. *jinn*, feminine *jinniya*) are invisible spirits, bad and good, that are always roaming around humans. They are sentient spirits that were created out of fire. Of both sexes, they procreate, are organised into societies and tribes comparable to human ones

140 *Myriem Naji*

and they have feeling and desires. Their presence during human birth and sexual intercourse, but also at death, is attributed to their taste for human substances and their enjoyment in harassing the dead. Perhaps *jnûn* are not just attracted by human bodily fluids but are actually the origin of the transformative processes of production and reproduction, whether human or technical. Rituals aiming at both warding off and coaxing *jnûn* seem to indicate that they are also present at the birth and death of *astta*. Islamic exegesis of the Coran describes angels as 'internal artisans' who transform food inside the human body and 'external artisans' who change flour into bread (Fahd 1971: 164). The confusion between angels and (good) *jnûn* stems from the fact that the former was a later apparition in Arabia (Fahd 1971).

Another linguistic clue links *astta*, the tent and women as protectors of life. The term *tazettat,* which has the same root as *astta*, designates the protection given to a person travelling in foreign land and the recompense received by the protector in exchange for his protection (Laoust 1920: 126). A person could take refuge with a woman (Westermarck 1926: i490), or a tent's owner (Westermarck 1926: i520–21), by placing himself under their protection; the shedding of human blood in their 'presence' would be a sacrilege. The verb used is another evidence of the praxeological and container-dimension of this protection: the blood of a refugee could not be shed if he 'entered in unto you' (Westermarck 1926: i543). *Astta* has also been described as a *zawit* (saint shrine) by weavers. Each villager has a least one shrine housing the body (and *baraka*) of a holy man or woman. Villagers have a contractual relationship with these saints who bestow protection and *baraka* to humans in exchange for seasonal blood sacrifices or good deeds/alms. Saints are also guardians of morality and use *jnûn,* over whom they rule, to punish humans (Westermarck 1926). Women in particular make vows to saints, often in relation to fertility. Saints are also said to have set all prescriptions surrounding the work of the wool, taboo days and the punishment of people infringing these. From them also came weaving skills, another evidence of emic beliefs associating knowledge, morality and life.

Human and non-human parallel life courses

The life course of *astta* and that of human beings seem to be closely interwoven and interdependent: the actions of women sustain its life, but the weaving activity is also good for the growth of babies during and after pregnancy. The shared experience of sitting side by side, working together at the loom, extends to angels who, like women's relatives or friends, are believed to assist weavers when they are occupied in other activities. Both women and *astta* experience liminality: whereas a woman's life is at risk during pregnancy, delivery and after birth, *astta* is said to be 'moribund-like', neither alive nor dead, throughout the technical processes preceding weaving proper. Servier (1962) mentions a case when *astta* was treated like a bride

Figure 9.2 Shed/countershed with rod lifted and lowered during the making of the hood of an *akhnif* cloak. Ayt Waghrda village, 2003.

Photo by author.

when it was carried into the house through the threshold to be put on the uprights. It is not always clear whether the talisman hung on the upper beam of *astta* (in the shape of a black magic bundle, a horseshoe, a red pepper or a knife) is there to protect it or the weavers against the evil eye.

All the rituals and proscriptions prior to and during weaving highlight the idea that the life course of *astta* should be, like the human one, continuous and uninterrupted. Similarly, no one should mention its life span for fear of shortening it. Warping and the making of the shed are the two foundation stages that should never be interrupted as they respectively determine the even spacing of the warp and its separation into two discrete sets. Normally, working the wool when a villager has died is forbidden; the only exception to this taboo concerns the warping process which cannot be interrupted. Furthermore, if the shed system was not made soon after the mounting of the loom, or if the weaving could not start straight after its completion, weavers were careful to make some (sweet) offering of food to *astta*. Flour or date stones were put in the eyes (holes) of the lower beam, because the weft is said to be the food of *astta*, and it is a sin to let *astta* feel hungry, a saying reminiscent of those heard about the dead, who should not go thirsty or hungry. The technical explanation for these taboos is that there would not be enough warp threads and they would be too spaced out. The verb used to describe this risk of the warp 'running out' or 'running away', in the sense of not being sufficient and escaping, is to exit: *'ifukh tiddi'* (the warp exits). The same verb is also used to mean ending (*astta* will be finished soon) or dying. In fact, it is believed that *astta* breathes and that its soul resides in the shed rod on account of the opening/closing movement of the shed system.

There are numerous stories about people infringing the taboo regarding interrupting the life course of *astta* before its natural term, about moving *astta* from one place to another, with a particular emphasis on its entering and exiting a house. A weaver who was asked to start the weaving of a carpet for the making of a film, decided to take it back home so as not waste the material. She soon after suffered an acute back pain, which started with the shoulder on which she carried the warp and its shed home. The explanation given was that 'it was like carrying a moribund, and anyway, who would be foolish enough to let a dead [entity] enter their house'?

In the past, Kabyle women believed that *astta* threatened those mistreating it with punishment on judgement day (Chantreau 1941). Any action threatening the efficacy of the technical process was seen as an attempt on the life of this holy entity and might be followed by a revengeful reciprocal attack on the life of the culprit or a family member. *Astta*'s power and behaviour shares similarities with that of a saint. The relationship that weavers established with it confirms it further: as long as they followed the patriarchal rules that required hard work and morality, they were rewarded by the precious help of angels, who also guaranteed the quality of their work, and ultimately their salvation.

The sacrifice of the animal-artefact

Astta also shares many attributes of sheep. As 'living artefacts', sheep (Ferret 2016), wool and *astta* are all products of human's action: a direct

Figure 9.3 Weavers working on a carpet commission. Taznakht, 2005.

Photo by author.

Opening and closing gestures 143

contact that requires little mediation through tools or very simple tools. Like the sheep, wool needs the daily and repeated care and attention of human beings on whom it depends for its sustenance. Thus, the shearing of sheep, a holy animal, did not mark the death of wool since it was harvested without killing the animals. Instead, it opened a life cycle for the wool, a living partible extension of the sheep, who grew in the domestic sphere, turned into threads and eventually into a 'human fleece', an element of architecture or furniture. The vitality and power of this living and holy material was increased by the locking and interlocking together of strands and its stretching through rotative motions to form a continuous thread. As a detached part of the living organism of several sheep, wool could reproduce: when washed (nourished?) and carded/spun (sustained?), if left in the dark for a while, it was seen to multiply on its own.

But the most explicit identification of *astta* as an animal-artefact seems to be in its ending. The death of *astta* happens with the weaving of the last weft pick, which should immediately be followed by the cutting off of the cloth. At first sight, one could argue that the end of *astta* is treated similarly to the funerals of human beings, with the recitation of the *shahada* or *basmallah* and the washing of the corpse (see use of water below). This fits in with the idea that the dead should not be kept in the house and should be buried as soon as possible, out of consideration for the deceased who suffers when his soul is hanging between life and death.

On closer inspection, however, it becomes apparent that we are not dealing with any ordinary funeral, but with a sacrificial ritual which takes on several functions. The first purpose of the ritual is prophylactic. Before proceeding to cutting, weavers throw some salt at the warp, or dip the beating comb in salted water and beat the last weft with it, or lick the comb and hold it upside down when they beat the weft. Salt wards off the jnûn but using a tool in the wrong manner is supposed to reverse a process and can be interpreted as a ritual of expulsion (of evil influences). Furthermore, a common practice thirty years ago was to accompany the cutting off of the cloth with a phrase listing the negative forces that weavers wished be freed from: 'Remove the teeth of the jackal [to protect sheep/goat] and the women from the youth' [so they marry quick]; 'I cut the foe, the envious, the gossips'. A more recent one is: 'I cut the diseases, I cut the expenses'. Thus, by sympathetic magic, the gesture of cutting, is also one of removing negative influences in women's life, a rite of separation inherent in death.

Another complementary function of this ritual is the absorption of the sacredness of the victim by gestures that both involve a contact with the sacred and a show of respect. Whereas today weavers tend to cut in one go from right to left, in the past, women cut off seven sections in the warp still attached to the beam (like the seven paradises), and each time touched these openings with the forefinger of their right hand and took it to their lips (as both salutation and prayer) dedicating each 'door' to the women who helped during the weaving and the angels (Chantreau 1941: 90). In the Sirwa, they

144 *Myriem Naji*

pronounce the first words of the *fatiha* prayer or 'paradise' and *'razq'* at each opening. By sympathetic magic, they open the door to good things and say a prayer on the threshold of the other world.

A few decades ago women did not cut the warp threads with a tool made of iron (a defiling material for holiness) and made a point of using their bare hand instead, saying: 'I do you good by breaking you with my hands'. Here again, we find this idea that *astta* is a divinity and an intercessor who will recompense in the other world good deeds made in this world. In fact, the 'killing' of *astta* in the mind of women may have been thought as a female homologue of the ram sacrifice of the Aîd Kbîr. The analogies between *astta* and the sacrificed ram, go well beyond the fact that they both relate to the same animal. It has been amply demonstrated that sacrifice in Islam is polysemic (Bonte 1999, see also Mahdi 1999 and Rachik 1990). Against the hypothesis of the sacrifice of *astta* as sheep-artefact, this ritual could be said to belong to the category of harvest sacrifice. It could be argued, however, that weaving rituals by their richness and complexity cannot be limited solely to agricultural sacrifices. Moreover, being performed secretly, this particular feminine ritual was not exposed to the scrutiny of male criticism and religious orthodoxy.

If we look at the way *astta* and the ram-victim (see Brisebarre 1999, Hammoudi 1993) are treated during their 'lifetime' before the ultimate sacrifice, they both enter the domestic and feminine space and share the family life during the period of time when they grow to completion. They are both humanised and sacralised. They are fed and cared for by women, they are respected and protected against the evil eye. Nothing should be mentioned about their lifespan as this could shorten it and hinder it.

The sacrificial practices seem to be conspicuously similar:

The sacrificed sheep is supposed to know its own death and destiny (which is that of a martyr who will access paradise). Because of this awareness, the victim should not be shown the knife, and its pain should be minimised: its throat has to be slit in one stroke and women often give it a treat of food and salt to ease death.

The sacrificed ram has a role of psychopump (conductor of the soul of the dead) following the word of the prophet that Muslims should fatten up the victims that they offer God because they will ride them when they enter paradise (Westermarck 1926: ii152). We have seen that many words and practices convey this idea that *astta* may intercede for the weavers in the other world. Whereas the male sacrificer would identify his body with that of the Aîd Kbîr's victim (Doutté 1909: 467, citing Garcin de Tassy 1874: 228), weavers used to say as they gave the last beating with some salted water: 'I water you in this world, water us in the other' (Basset 1922: 156, Laoust-Chantreau 1990: 90). Among the Ulad Bu-aziz, the same saying was said by men before they sacrificed the ram (Westermarck 1926: ii117).

Furthermore, the fear that *astta* may take revenge on a human life is a common feeling in instances where a divinity is killed or its life is threatened, but it is also reminiscent of the Ismaelian model (Bonte 1999) where Ibrahim sacrifices the ram instead of his son. As they cut off the weaving, weavers say: 'I take your life but not mine, or that of the one on his/her way'. Taking a life without any blood sacrifice in exchange, women need to take such precautions. The prohibition on men's presence in the house during this ritual is explained by the risk that they may walk in unknowingly during the cutting off process and thus put their life (sexual potency) at risk. If an (unmarried) woman enters as they cut *astta* off, she is supposed to say: 'I enter knowingly and it is your life I take, not mine', and at the same time, she is supposed to hit the beam or *astta* with anything she can lay her hand on (stone, shoe, etc.). This is a ritual of expulsion of the evil by throwing something at it (Doutté 1905: 101). Thus, there is a clear analogy between the life of *astta* exiting and a human being putting their life at risk by entering at the same moment.

In taking the life of *astta*, women are performing a religious act, a necessary and unavoidable sacrifice that concludes the process of growing life. The killing of the ram leads to the restoration of the victim in a different state; it is part of a yearly cycle of revival of the pact of alliance with God (Bonte 1999, Virolle 2001: 48). With *astta*, especially when it was produced once a year, there was this idea of a life cycle finishing which opened the possibility of the use of a finished object, foldable, wearable, no longer stretched on its support, no longer between life and death. The ram does not experience a definite death, but moves to another life (Virolle 2001). *Astta* too experiences a second birth as a cloth (Chantreau 1941: 79).

A materiality of closure and aperture

One dimension of the materiality of weaving is that it lends itself to be thought of as a space-container that invites gestures and actions of opening/closing and entering/exiting and acts back on weavers. This in turn informs and influences emic thinking about technical processes.

The activity of weaving involves body movements between two spaces, the front and back, but also transitionally: from right to left and vice versa. This is reflected in the verbs used by weavers when they give instructions to learners, whether to make the brocading motifs or the selvage: Open! Close! Come back! Return! Bring together! Throw! [to the back].

Whilst the loom keeps the warp threads in tension, the heddle controls the opening of the shed and the easy passage of the weft in the shed and countershed. As the weaver introduces her hand in the shed in order to pull a weft thread from right to left, then from left to right, she uses the weight of her body to widen the gap. She forgets herself in that thread which becomes the driving force of her movements and her thoughts. Where does the thread start, the hand finish? She becomes the weft thread, anticipates its progression through the shed even before her other hand has come to receive it. Her eyes are already on the next weft pick as she lifts the rod to change the shed.

146 *Myriem Naji*

Figure 9.4 Weaver working on the latest carpet trend. Ayt Ubial village, 2011.

Photo by author.

She follows the thread with her eyes, or is it the eyes who pull the thread in the right direction? With the rhythmic lifting and lowering of the heddle rod, she is both weft and warp, vertical and horizontal, back and front, she is the shed opening and closing. She beats the weft down with her 2-kilo comb with enough force to ensure the even density of the cloth. In fact, the beating is arguably another closing gesture, thus reinforcing (locking) the closure effected by the passing of the weft.

Who enters whom? Who closes and binds whom? Who acts on whom? This becomes blurred in the mind of the practitioner, for whom the materiality of *astta* is not exterior to her body but is incorporated in her bodily schemata as she manipulates it and is transformed by it. The contact with the woollen threads, the wooden beam, the beating comb is not one-directional but also involves the reciprocal action of *astta* on the weaver. Repeated and alternate gestures of opening and closing are a characteristic of the weaving process. These are complemented by the action of passing, crossing and going between. Warnier (2007: 284) has analysed the ontology of the subject/object praxeological relationship as a 'constant shifting between grasp and letting go, embodiment and disembodiment ...'. This description of the human engagement with materiality seems to correspond with the primary gestures of weaving: opening/entering, closing/exiting, that Sirwa people tend to link with living processes. Interestingly, homologous absorption/expulsion processes are at play during rituals of blood sacrifices, when saints and spirits exteriorise/give their life essence, but also interiorise/absorb humans' badness/sins (Westermarck 1926: i475).

Material practices around opening/closing constitute the basis of unconscious and metaphorical thinking about life and death: the successive addition of layers of wool, and their beating down which involves a closure, implies growth, life generation and is associated with the idea of entering and birth. One could oppose these gestures to those of opening, cutting, exiting and the idea of death. Such binary models, however, do not account for the gestures of weaving. These bodily movements are instead complementary: they are transitive in that they all contain an element of the other in their very processual dimension, which involves the crossing or passing from one space to another: to enter a space one has to exit another, to open a door, it had to be closed; life is followed by death, which is also the source of life.

Disenchantment, discipline and change

As a result of the combined effect of women's access to education and new technologies and the intensification of production in a neoliberal economy, girls started to challenge their mothers' and grand-mothers' beliefs and practices. Younger generations tend to think that it is their own will, their actions and those of their coworkers, independently from those of angels, that determine technical success. This disenchantment appeared once at the sarcastic remark made by a weaver when her cousin explained to me that angels assisted weavers when they were asleep: 'If only this was true!'

Today weavers seem more concerned about the judgement of other women, their harshest critics, than about upsetting the spirits/divinity. Some women pride themselves in their self-discipline and have contempt for those who are more relaxed about their work. They will criticise the families who divide the technical sequences preceding weaving over several days instead of starting early in the morning in order to manage to weave a few weft picks before the evening. Similarly, after cutting off the cloth from the loom, those who put care in their work will not wait to sweep the area where the loom stood and put away its elements.

Mullatna Fatima, daughter of the Prophet Mohammed, whom weavers strive to emulate, seems to have replaced the village saint. Rachida, an educated woman from Taznakht, remembers that when she started blaming whoever had invented *astta* she was criticised for being blasphemous. Fatima is said to be the origin of *astta*, she is the first woman to have woven, and has therefore invented weaving.

148 *Myriem Naji*

Weaving production has become so disciplinary, so constraining, that weavers see their work as a sacrifice of their labour, time, health and beauty. Ijja Samoh, a Znaga singer, used the term *jihad* to describe the work of *astta*, thus using a charged religious term to express this idea of the self-discipline that Foucault terms 'techniques of the self' (Foucault 1984, Mahmood 2005, Mohan and Warnier 2017, Naji 2009) where one works on one's own resistance (body and mind) to the constraints of materiality (pain, energy) to improve and better oneself. The very gestures of weaving are seen as a form of prayer: several weavers mentioned that they pronounce the *basmallah* or *shahada* (profession of faith) with each weft passed, thus hoping to reach a certain state of grace. This is reflected in some of their sayings: 'Each weft we give you are *hasanât*'; 'We add to you, O *astta*, leave the door open to blessings/good fortune *(razq)*'; *hasanât* or *a'mâl*, are charitable acts, meritorious alms. The work that weavers perform on themselves by giving themselves entirely to the task, whole heartedly, with care and devotion, is implied in the notion of *hasanât*. Virtue in itself may be recognised socially, but there is another motivation: the belief (in divine justice) that moral action will be recompensed by a positive outcome in their future life and will eventually lead to salvation. Some women mention retribution *(ajûr)* both during the weaving process and at the solemn moment of the cutting off of the cloth.

Conclusion

This exploration of the rituals and gestures performed by weavers has allowed us to gain some insight into Sirwa weavers' past perception and experience of the making process and the artefact-in-the-making. Container-space-spirit, animal-spirit, divine entity similar to the village saint, *astta*'s polymorphism suggests several overlapping diachronic conceptions, some elements of which remain whilst others have receded. Life sustainer, judge and punisher, *astta* seemed to combine many of the attributes of a divinity. On the other hand, like the sheep, it depended on humans for its continuation, hence its ambivalent characteristics: familiar, intimate but also feared; powerful but vulnerable. It is a betwixt entity with the power to confer life and take it away. It belongs to and shifts between several realms: the human and the non-human, the pastoral and the domestic, the visible and the spiritual, the dead and the living.

Far from being subversive, women's religious practices around weaving are acts of worship that parallel those of men, and although they take place in the domestic rather than the public religious space, they share the same features: prayer, sacrifice and moral behaviour. Through working the wool, women transformed themselves materially into strong and determined women, applying their effort, skills and energy day after day, hour after hour to produce textiles that helped reproduce their families.

References

Basset, H. (1922), 'Les Rites de la laine à Rabat', *Hesperis II*, 139–160.

Bonte, P. (1999), 'Sacrifice en Islam: Textes et contextes', in P. Bonte, A. -M. Brisebarre and A. Gokalp (eds.), *Sacrifices en Islam: Espaces et temps d'un rituel*, 21–61, Paris: CNRS.

Bourdieu, P. ([1963, 1972] 1979), *Algeria 1960: Essay*, translated by Richard Nice, Cambridge: Cambridge University Press.

Brisebarre, A. -M. (1999), 'La fête du sacrifice: Le rituel ibrâhîmien dans l'islam contemporain', in P. Bonte, A. -M. Brisebarre and A. Gokalp (eds.), *Sacrifices en Islam: Espaces et temps d'un rituel*, 93–121, Paris: CNRS.

Chantreau, G. (1941), 'Le tissage sur métier de haute lisse à Aït Hichem et dans le Haut-Sebaou', *Revue Africaine*, 85: 78–116, 212–229.

Coupaye, L. and P. Pitrou, (2018), 'Introduction: The Interweaving of Vital and Technical Processes in Oceania', *Oceania*, 88 (1): 2–12.

Doutté, E. (1905), *Merrâkech., fasc. 1*, Paris: Comité du Maroc.

Doutté, E. (1909 [1984]), *Magie et religion dans l'Afrique du Nord*, Alger: Jourdan.

Fahd, T. (1971), 'Anges, démons et djinns en Islam', in D. Meeksed (eds.), *Génies, anges et démons: Egypte, Babylone, Israel, Islam, Peuples altaïques, Inde, Birmanie, Asie du Sud-Est, Tibet, Chine*, 155–214, Paris: Editions du Seuil.

Ferret, C. (2016), 'Outils vivants? De la manipulation des animaux', *Les actes de colloques du musée du quai Branly Jacques Chirac* [En ligne], 6, 2016 (accessed 27.01.2020), http://journals.openedition.org/actesbranly/658

Foucault, M. (1979 [1984]), *A History of Sexuality. Vol. 2, The Use of Pleasure*, translated by R. Hurley, Harmondsworth: Penguin Books.

Garcin de Tassy, G. H. (1874), *L'islamisme, d'après le Coran*, Paris: Maisonneuve.

Gosselain, O (1999), 'In Pots We Trust: The Processing of Clay and Symbols in Sub-Saharan Africa, *Journal of Material Culture*, 4 (2): 205–230.

Hammoudi, M. ([1988] 1993), *The Victim and Its Masks*, Chicago: University of Chicago Press.

Laoust, H. (1920), *Mots et choses berbères*, Paris: Seuil.

Laoust-chantreau, G. (1990), *Kabylie, coté femmes: La vie féminine à Ait Hichem, 1937-1939. Notes D'ethnographie*, Aix en Provence: IRENAM & Edisud.

Mahdi, M. (1999), *Pasteurs de l'Atlas, production pastorale, droits et rituels*, Casablanca, Fondation Konrad Adenauer.

Mahmood, S. (2005), *The Politics of Piety: The Islamic Revival and the Feminist Subject*, Princeton: Princeton University Press.

Mohan, U. and J. -P. Warnier (2017), 'Editorial: Marching the Devotional Subject: The Bodily-and-Material Culture of Religion', *Journal of Material Culture*, 22 (4): 369–384.

Naji, M. (2009), 'Gender and Materiality in the Making: The Manufacture of Sirwan Femininities Through Weaving in Southern Morocco', *Journal of Material Culture*, 14 (1): 47–73.

Rachik, H. (1990), *Sacré et sacrifice dans le Haut Atlas,* Casablanca: Afrique-Orient.

Rowlands, M. and J. -P. Warnier, (1993), 'The Magical Production of Iron in the Cameroon Grassfields', in T. Shaw, P. Sinclair, B. Andah and A. Okpoko (eds.), *The Archaeology of Africa. Food, Metals and Towns*, 512–550, London: Routledge.

150   *Myriem Naji*

Servier, J. (1962), *Les portes de l'année: Rites et symboles, l'Algérie dans la tradition méditerranéenne*, Paris: Laffont.

Virolle, M. (2001), *Rituels algeriens*, Paris: Karthala.

Warnier, J. -P. (2007), *The Pot-King: The Body and Technologies of Power*, Leiden: Brill.

Westermarck, E. (1926), *Ritual and Belief in Morocco*, London: Macmillan and Co.

10 Devotion on the home altar as 'efficacious intimacy' in a Hindu group

Urmila Mohan

Introduction

Interest in the lived experience of Hinduism can been related to redress for the way non-scriptural and, consequently, embodied and material ways of knowing and transmitting beliefs were marginalised during the nineteenth century by early Indologists (Narayanan 2003: 516). For nineteenth-century religion scholars, such as Max Müller (1823–1900 CE), the sacred was located not only along an evolutionary scale of religious thought and practice but also via what may be termed more broadly a 'surface-depth ontology' (Miller 1994)[1] with an emphasis on inner reality as spiritual essence. In keeping with perceptions of sacredness developed by Protestant Europeans in the nineteenth century, Müller incorporated a Christian goal of inward spiritual development into his studies of India and searched for an authenticity that was to be found in text and the knowledge of Brahmins. He placed Hinduism on a scale of human religious evolution from the visible to the invisible, and from the material to the spiritual (Waghorne 1994: 89), seeking to create 'a purified form of Hinduism devoid of its images and idolatrous tendencies' (Sugirtharajah 2003: 60).

In a British colonial context, this intellectual legacy of early Indologists also influenced Indian self-perceptions, provoking the self-conscious articulation of a Hindu reformist and sectarian identity by religious leaders in the nineteenth and twentieth centuries. Part of this response was the codification and rationalisation of Hindu thought in the form of sacred texts *(shastra)* or exegesis of existing texts.[2] This systematisation also influenced the practices of contemporary Hindu groups including the global International Society for Krishna Consciousness, or ISKCON. Simultaneously, with notable exceptions (such as Holdrege 2015 and Waghorne, Cutler and Narayanan eds. 1985), scholars of Hinduism have tended to relate practice to *shastra* rather than *how* devotees rely on the non-discursive efficacy of materials and actions. Using reflections from my study of clothing in ISKCON (Mohan 2019) and the way objecthood is related to subjecthood (Mohan 2018), this chapter emphasises the realm of the bodily *and* material, surface and depth, to contest the long-lasting and still prevalent emphasis on inner essences

152 *Urmila Mohan*

as seats of Hindu spirituality and religiosity. Although limited to a specific sect of Vaishnavism that glorifies the Vedas (an ancient form of Sanskrit sacred literature) as well as other forms of *Shastra*,[3] my study employs a praxeological and phenomenological lens to explore altar worship and deity dress pattern-making in the homes of lay devotees as activities that make devotional subjects.

The state of being a believer or a member of the faith requires not just intellectual comprehension but constant social and cultural work on bodies-and-materials, accessed by the anthropologist through direct participant observation and documented with media such as photography and video. Too often the role of materials in the anthropology of religion as well as religious studies is explored without due consideration of people's procedural knowledge, or knowing *how* to do something. While it is clear that the dimension of procedural knowledge belongs with the study of the feeling, affective body (Morgan 2010: 4), the *Matière à Religion* (MaR) approach gives us a toolkit that helps us focus on processes of (dis)incorporation of objects as they transform and subjectify/subjectivate the Maussian 'whole person' into a 'believer', 'devotee', 'worshipper', etc. (Mohan and Warnier 2017). In noting that 'the bodily-and-material culture of religion is not the same as its representation through verbal description, guidelines and norms' (ibid., 371), the notion of technique and procedural knowledge as something 'propped' on material culture becomes central to the conception of religious or, in this case, devotional subjecthood.

Techniques have been regarded as elementary, efficacious actions upon matter (Lemonnier 1992: 4, following Leroi-Gourhan 1943, 1945) and a technique is 'an action which is effective and traditional' (Mauss [1936] 2006: 82). Mauss' ([1909] 2003: 54) definition of technique is similar to his definition of religious rites, referring to the latter as 'efficacious traditional actions, which have bearing on things that are called sacred'. Both techniques and religious rites are traditional actions with effects, but the latter pertains specifically to the sacred and/or transcendental. Further, Mauss claims that 'a rite has a real material efficacy' (ibid., 51) and the power of the ritual is not derived from prescription alone[4]. While a technique simply refers to a certain manner of doing things, the issue is complicated in the context of religious belief, where a technique is considered to have an otherworldly effect by acting upon an invisible entity, or sacred force (see Mohan 2016, 2017). One can observe and analyse the work done by objects, aesthetics and senses and their effects on people and objects (Warnier 2007, 2009), but also keep in mind that, for the devotee, performative acts draw upon the original ontological efficacy of a God, deity or other supreme entity/power. A religious framework, for our purposes, is therefore a combination of bodily techniques propped against given material cultures, as well as the sovereign power (Foucault 1982) of the divine which transforms individuals into subject-devotees.

This chapter uses ethnographic data from the ISKCON Chandrodaya temple, in Mayapur, West Bengal, India. ISKCON is a neo-Brahmanical, Hindu, missionising group and a sect of Gaudiya or Bengali Vaishnavism:

Vaishnavs are those who worship Vishnu, one of the main three deities in the Hindu pantheon apart from Brahma and Shiva, and Gaudiya Vaishnavs elevate the worship of the medieval saint and mystic Chaitanya as an incarnation of Krishna, in turn a form of Vishnu. The organisation's philosophy is popularly known as 'Krishna Consciousness', referring to a message of salvation through *bhakti* (devotional love) and *sewa* (service) to the deity Krishna. ISKCON is unconventional in converting foreigners and non-Hindus into the uppermost tier of the caste system as Brahmins. It has done so by reviving the traditional Hindu caste system as *varnashram dharma* – the religio-moral categorisation of persons according to their qualities and propensities. Positive transformation in a devotional context is the progressive refinement of oneself at the particulate level by using substances in 'right eating, right marriage, and other right exchanges and actions' (Marriott and Inden 1977: 233). Thus, ISKCON has emphasised the power of personalised, transformative devotion and simultaneously, created its own standardised orthopraxy.

In Hindu devotion, religious, affective and aesthetic experience cannot be separated. Devotees are aware of the spiritual-sensory value of the actions they perform on the sentient deity image *(murti),* hoping that deity service *(murti sewa)* will create efficacious feelings of love, empathy and trust. From an anthropological perspective, the deity's agency arises from external human actions of dressing, feeding and bathing the deities and the belief that the deity figure is a social 'other'. Through the 'abduction of agency' (Gell 1998: 132),[5] the deity is imparted a mind and intentionality, and becomes someone with whom the devotee can form a relationship.[6] Devotional attitudes and states are produced in the play between forces that devotees exert upon themselves and others, as well as forces exerted upon them by their gurus, the community and the sentient deity whose personhood is 'distributed' (ibid., 116–121) through associated objects and actions. By combining this notion of agency with MaR's ideas, devotion in ISKCON can be explored as 'efficacious intimacy' (Mohan 2019: 70) or a specific type of subjectivating process.

Gaudiya Vaishnav scriptures that pertain to deity worship provide general guidelines about how the deity is to be dressed[7] but do not address the situated need for, or processes of, innovation within deity care. Further, worship at home is less codified and restricted than in the temple. Thus, this chapter attempts to explore the question of *how* devotees transform themselves as specific, Krishna-conscious subjects within home deity care.

Performing relationships on a home altar

The setting

Mayapur is the global spiritual headquarters of ISKCON. It falls within the Nadia district of West Bengal, a three-and-a-half-hour drive north from the state capital of Kolkata. The tributaries of the sacred Ganges form a shifting

154   *Urmila Mohan*

boundary around Mayapur that ultimately feeds into the Hooghly River. Historically, Bengali Vaishnavs were monastic, and monks would study with a guru and then break away to form their own order. But, ISKCON has consolidated its identity in the twentieth century, both in relation to Bengali Vaishnav sects and Indian *bhakti* in general.

Founded by A. C. Bhaktivedanta Prabhupada in New York in 1966, ISKCON's growth was initially propelled by its success in the United States, UK and Europe, later expanding to other parts of the world. The group has now established itself in India, with at least sixty temples in urban and rural areas, and temple-affiliated services such as preaching and other programs in homes, schools and colleges. ISKCON welcomes non-Indians as well as non-Hindus. Upon conversion through initiation into the group, the new member indicates allegiance to his or her guru, takes on a devotional name, accepts a set of prayer beads from the guru, and vows to chant on them daily while following the four regulative principles: no gambling, meat, illicit sex or intoxicants. Initiated devotees, both Indian and non-Indian, are given traditional Sanskrit names and the last name Das, if male, or Dasi, if female. Both these terms mean 'servant' in Sanskrit, indicating their fealty to Krishna. If desired by the devotee, a second initiation is believed to convert the subject into a Brahman, the highest in the Hindu caste system, enabling him or her to perform liturgical procedures and practices.

The growth of the faith community in Mayapur can be attributed both to the more stable presence of families, students and trainee priests, as well as a transitory population of pilgrims and tourists. This small town has become an idealised destination both for families from the West, and those from other parts of India who wish to raise their children in a seemingly authentic, Vedic manner away from the distractions of materialism. Life revolves around a schedule of daily worship rituals called *darshan,* the exchange of embodied gaze between devotee and deity. A global and local network of people and resources sustains Mayapur, and this dynamic has significantly shaped the culture of the town into an international neighbourhood as well as a sacred place *(dham).*

ISKCON's emphasis on learning and preaching through scripture, publications and book distribution means that nearly every literate devotee has a collection of religious books in their home with which they have familiarised themselves. Knowledge of the scriptures is also gleaned by attending, or listening to, talks by spiritual leaders and gurus. Publications that are frequently invoked in religious discourse and print form include the founder Prabhupada's (1986) purports on the sacred text *Bhagavad Gita*, as well as writings of the medieval saint Chaitanya[8] and his associates. However, it is in spaces, such as the home, and the home altar, where one can learn *how* members of the faith community use materials for transformative, devotional purposes. The following sections include observations of a few different home altars of devotees who reside in Mayapur, and discuss how formal and sensory elements of deity care enable moods and relationships of efficacious intimacy.

Case study: Snehalata

I became acquainted with Snehalata, a European devotee,[9] and her family due to their involvement in the various projects in the temple's sewing room, and I was often invited to their home. Snehalata was in her fifties when I met her. Influenced by the mood of the early 1970s and the hippies, she had travelled twice to India as a young woman in her twenties, and her visits to pilgrimage sites in northern India had led her to a spiritual life. There she met her husband, who was also a traveler and, at that time, part of a Shivite (Shiva worshiping) group in India. They returned to Europe for their wedding, and subsequently their first child was born. Snehalata's husband taught yoga classes, and as they were struggling, they found support with the ISKCON devotees in Europe. With their help, and a family gift of money, they were able to return to India. Once back in India, the couple became ISKCON initiates and travelled between ISKCON centres in India and Europe. The couple later separated, and when I met her Snehalata lived in Mayapur with her two daughters, supporting herself by teaching German, translating German works into English, and occasionally creating objects, such as devotional board games, when she needed money for visas and flight tickets. A devotee friend covered her rent, and the rest came from Snehalata's two eldest sons, who lived and worked in ISKCON centres abroad.

The deities formed the physical centre of Snehalata's home and were positioned prominently on an altar in the living room. Upon entering the apartment, visitors and inhabitants first greeted the deities by bowing in front of them and then proceeded to go inside. The residents of the house took care not only to include the deities in any new activities, but also to give them preference by serving them food before others, offering them any new purchases, such as incense, games and food, before they were used, and by bathing and dressing them regularly. (At another devotee's house, I once commented on the delicious smell of lunch that was yet to be offered to the deity. Since savouring the food mentally or verbally is also considered a form of consumption, my acquaintance sprinkled some holy water on the food to decontaminate it before offering it to the deity. A stricter devotee might have discarded the food.) While traveling with Snehalata's daughters, Lakshmi and Kavita, in the coastal temple town of Puri, I observed that they continued this practice of according Krishna preference in the hotel room we shared, taking care to place their deities on a shelf and making offerings of whatever they purchased at the market, whether vegetables, bread, or a tin of cheese.

Snehalata followed a routine of bathing and dressing the deities every ekadasi, a fast that takes place every fortnight, but there were times when this was postponed. Unlike the formality and discipline of temple worship, there was no fixed time when home worship activities took place, and it was based on the family's convenience. Normally, the deities were 'put to sleep' in beds assembled from shelves and tiny wooden cots, along with pillows and bedding. If everyone in the family was travelling, the family would arrange for friends to take care of the deities. If this was not possible, the deities were packed in their box and 'awakened' when they returned. Over the months of January to April 2013, the altar increased almost a third in size in order to accommodate the deities of neighbours and friends. In early January, a devotee couple that was leaving on a journey entrusted the family with their large Radha-Krishna murtis (deity images) and shilas.[10] Snehalata was on a pilgrimage in Vrindavan at that time, and the friends did not trust her daughters to care for them – a fact that irked the younger one since she had been doing this for a long time – and so when I saw the deities in the apartment (Figure 10.1), they were 'asleep' or placed in a partial state of incorporation.

The murtis were displayed nestled in their steel suitcase with the lid open. Since it was cold, they were also wrapped in knitted shawls. When Snehalata returned a week later, the murtis were fully installed with matching white and green outfits, and placed in the corner of the altar. The shilas were placed on crocheted doilies and soft cloths on two brass plates, and displayed on a small stool next to the altar. Over the next month, I would see the friends' large Radha-Krishna murtis and shilas intermittently on and off the altar when they travelled to Mayapur. A tulasi (basil) plant

Figure 10.1 Radha-Krishna deities 'asleep' in a box next to Snehalata's altar. Mayapur, January 2013.

Photo by author.

had also been brought indoors from the balcony, and a new spot had been created for it on one side of the altar, with the plaque of the goddess Vrinda Devi placed in front of it.

A month later, the altar had grown and changed significantly. It now spread horizontally, and occupied about a third of the living room. The eldest son, Achyuta, lived abroad and had visited Mayapur for his brother Neelachal's wedding. He had added a wooden plank to extend the base, and the deities from the altar of Chaitanya Rasa, a neighbour and family friend, had been incorporated. Chaitanya Rasa and her husband were considered part of Snehalata's family since she was a childhood friend of Achyuta from their time in the northern Indian town of Vrindavan. Having recently given birth, Chaitanya Rasa could not take care of her own deities and had left her numerous tiny deities on Snehalata's altar, where Kavita and Lakshmi helped take care of them.

Processes of bathing and dressing the deities

It was around 8:40 a.m. on the Saturday morning of *dwadasi* in April 2013.[11] Since Snehalata had been busy cleaning the walls and the altar on *ekadasi*, or Friday,[12] the bathing and dressing of the deities had been postponed to the following day. All the elements of the altar, including the photographs, had been 'put to sleep' overnight and were being 'woken up'. Space was a precious commodity on the altar now that the Radha-Krishna *murtis* and plates of black Vishnu *shilas* had been re-incorporated. A Prabhupada deity from another devotee that was too large to be included on the altar had been provided its own stool on one side of the altar. I noticed that the *tulasi* plant was sick with a white spider infestation, and the family was praying that 'she' recovered – the plant being considered an embodiment of a goddess.

The process of waking the various deities began with Snehalata lifting each one gently off its small pillow and – since there was no place anywhere else – putting them temporarily on the altar before the bath. Snehalata then performed the *achamana* ritual, the sipping of water for self-purifying purposes, with her right hand while ringing a bell with her left, chanting mantras. She brought a large brass bowl filled with water and placed it on the altar, also mixing in a *tulasi* leaf and a spoonful of the *achamana* water to purify it. Placing a clean cloth on her lap and dipping another cloth in the water, she undressed and then wiped the family's wooden deities of Jagannath, Baladev and Subadhra. Handling the deities firmly but gently and resting their backs on her palms, she began by wiping their heads and arms and then moved down their bodies. After the bath, the deities were placed on a small stool to be dried and dressed. Snehalata took the various stone *shilas* from the altar and rubbed them with Well's Almond Oil that she made a point of showing me, explaining that it was good for babies' skin. She massaged the oil into the stones to give them a gentle sheen, then placed them in the bowl of water. She then used a conch from the altar to

158 Urmila Mohan

pour water onto the *shilas* with her right hand, ringing the bell with her left hand as she did so. The conch and bell were then wiped and returned to their original positions.

By now the wooden deities had dried, and Lakshmi, who worked as an acupuncture assistant, had returned home from an early morning visit to a patient. Kavita was outside the house, helping with a project in the temple. Lakshmi sat down on the floor next to her mother and began to help dress the deities. She explained that, since it was getting warmer, they would be dressed in summer clothing and light jewellery. Snehalata massaged the brass deities with yoghurt from a cup and, unprompted, told me that yoghurt was also used in cosmetics since it was good for the skin. Similar to the way a baby is massaged, she started with the head of the deity and worked her way down to the feet, taking care to rub the yoghurt into the crevices. She then washed the deities in a bowl of water and passed them on to Lakshmi for dressing. Framed photos were merely wiped with a damp cloth.

A devotee's connection to Krishna is made real by 'taking shelter' with a guru from the appropriate Vaishnav lineage, or *parampara*. Such a relationship is believed to be eternal, transcending even death. Devotees believe that revered gurus are both teachers and saints, and consider items that were in contact with their bodies to be sanctified. One of the prized items on Snehalata's altar was a box with flowers from her guru's *pushpa samadhi* – a monument where the flowers from her guru's body were interred. Photos of her guru were also on the altar. As they worked, Snehalata and Lakshmi listened to her guru's address on a compact disc, and slowly and methodically completed the process of bathing and dressing the deities, *shilas* and photos. The guru's voice was loud as he fervently exhorted in English, 'The lap of *maya* [illusion] is so comfortable. Why are you sleeping in the lap of *maya*?' I found his voice disconcertingly vehement, and as if reading my mind, Snehalata assured me that despite his tone, he could also be gentle and compassionate.

In speaking about the deities, the family had no hesitation in identifying items as 'belonging' to someone, implying a relationship of ownership between that artifact and a specific member of the family. Yet, it was unclear to me whether it was the devotee who belonged to the deity, or vice versa. Krishna was their 'master' to whom they had surrendered completely, to the extent that Snehalata did not have a steady income and relied on assistance from her elder sons and other devotees. She attributed this help to Krishna, and was firm in her belief that her devotion – conceived as total submission to the deity – was being reciprocated.

Case study: Padma and Haladini

Padma was a Russian devotee in her early fifties. She had trained as a dress designer in Russia, and supported herself by undertaking deity decoration commissions for various temples in India. Padma's conversion narrative was related initially to her childhood sensory and emotive experience of Indian cinema, color, dance, costume and later her encounter with *ISKCON* illustrations, especially popular images of the child Krishna with his mother Yashoda, found in many preaching texts, posters and storybooks. Padma also referred to the 'line', or the longitudinal axis that runs through India and central Russia, as a physical connection between her childhood home and the home that she had found in Mayapur. For Padma, this line was not simply a coincidence but an actual physical and metaphysical link between her past and present that both predicted and explained her path as a Krishna devotee.

I first met Padma in her tiny flat on the Mayapur campus that measured about 120 sq. ft., and consisted of a single room, a small balcony and an attached bathroom. I was struck by the fact that her entire home had been turned into a shrine. As I entered, a table to the left served as an altar for a figure of Prabhupada, with paraphernalia that included his own small Radha-Krishna deities. A built-in shelving system to the right had been converted into a storage space for Padma's luggage, and a bedroom for the Prabhupada figure (Figure 10.2). On the farthest side of the room was another altar for a set of dancing Gaur-Nitai deities and their various companions, which included miniature animals and toys. Each deity had been provided various objects to populate a scaled-down world of their own. Prabhupada had his own miniature copy of the Gita, a pen, a glass,

Figure 10.2 Padma's shelf converted into a bedroom for Prabhupada. Mayapur, 2012.

Photo by author.

160   *Urmila Mohan*

a working lamp, a pair of slippers and spectacles. His bedroom consisted of a shelf that had been repainted and decorated with a tiny bed, working floor lamp, ceiling lamp, wardrobe, cabinet and rug. Inside the cabinet was a set of miniature utensils. The walls of this tiny room were painted green and gold, while the bedding and pillows were a matching shade of green – the same as the rest of Padma's small apartment.

Padma was not upset when I called her room a 'dollhouse'. Quite the opposite: she was proud of the diminutive size of the home she had made for her deities. 'Whatever I am doing now was the same in childhood', she said. 'I was stitching everything for dolls, like socks, shoes everything. When my mother came to Mayapur three years ago, she commented that it was same as when I was small. But now I am doing it for a real person. That was training for this'. Along with creating and enhancing the miniature worlds of her deities, it seemed that Padma's own human-scaled one had been correspondingly compacted. Padma told me that the happiest time in her life had been when a fire burned her belongings in an ashram (a spiritual retreat) in Europe, leaving her only with the clothes on her back and a set of prayer beads. Padma's deities were now her prized possessions. Her ability to create a style of delicacy, youthfulness and lightness had become her signature as an artist. Since she could make tiny, custom garments for deities, often less than a foot in height, it meant that she was sometimes asked to make garments for other devotees' home deities.

Making a pattern for a deity garment

It was around 8:00 a.m. on a cool morning in November 2012, and Padma had been invited to the home of Haladini, a French devotee, to make a blouse pattern for her twelve-inch-tall Krishna deity. Haladini's devotion was expressed in her desire to make the clothing fit properly. She'd thought about what would look appropriate on the small deity, as well as her own ability, or lack of it, to use her fingers to drape the garment. This concern with what looked 'natural' was also evident in the way she dressed her own Radha and Krishna deities: she chose fabrics that would drape and flow realistically on small forms, and used appropriately sized and styled accessories such as earrings, necklaces, bracelets and crowns. She showed me some of the deities' garments, and I was impressed with the fit of the clothing and how various elements, such as ruffles, had been scaled down to suit the deities, making the figure more compelling.

Haladini had chosen Padma to make the shirt pattern since she could not do 'tiny' work. Padma agreed to do so without payment, since Haladini was a senior devotee who had served for many decades in ISKCON. I had formed a relationship with Haladini during my time in the temple's sewing room, and was allowed to observe. As I began to record the process with a video camera, Padma commented that it must be Krishna's 'kindness' that I was being given access to such an intimate event, while cautioning

Home altar as 'efficacious intimacy' 161

me to avoid her face and only shoot actions over her shoulder. She set up a small work area at a table near the window with some thin white cloth, A4 sized paper and initially tried using a pencil to mark the fabric, but later switched to a ballpoint pen. Haladini picked up the Krishna deity from the altar, placed him on the table and proceeded to remove his clothes, including his *kaupina* (undergarment). Padma remained immersed in thought for a few seconds before beginning, silently fingering the white cotton fabric. Haladini watched Padma as she was lost in contemplation and asked her, 'Who do you ask for things like that? When you need to do something that's difficult?' Padma responded, 'I am asking Krishna to give me intelligence'.

Making a pattern for the front of the shirt was difficult because Krishna's right hand was attached with a strip of marble to his chest. Haladini suggested that they could make a *bagalbandhi* (a shirt that ties on the side), and gestured toward her own torso to indicate the draping. Padma pinched tiny balls out of Blu-tack and pressed them onto the deity's smooth marble torso. Then she cut oblong pieces of the cotton and carefully patted them on the *murti*. She consulted with Haladini about where to draw the seams and, once they had agreed, used the ballpoint pen to mark out the seams. She was very slow and precise in her movements and, as she told Haladini, tried to get as exact a fit as possible by repeatedly moving, flattening, patting and folding the fabric to match the contours of the *murti's* form. Padma continued to work her way through the front, back and the sleeves of the shirt pattern (Figure 10.3).

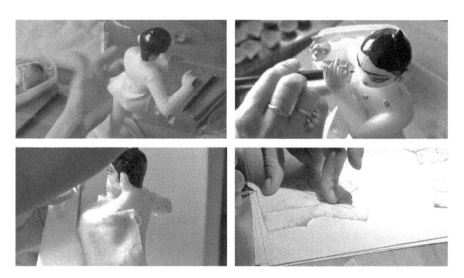

Figure 10.3 Padma making a shirt pattern for Haladini's home deity. Mayapur, 2012.

Stills from video by author.

162 Urmila Mohan

Nearly two hours passed before Padma had completed the fabric version of the pattern and started tracing/transferring it onto a sheet of A4 paper. She placed the cut pieces of fabric on the paper and carefully traced their outlines, playing with the paper pieces and trying to fit them together, much like pieces of a jigsaw puzzle. The paper pattern was not a replica of the fabric pattern, but a translation, since she also used the transfer process to make decisions about where the final seam-lines should be placed. For example, while tracing the pattern on paper, Padma joined the back of the shirt pattern to a section of the front and made it one whole piece. This was necessary because unlike garment mannequins, the *murtis* are small, carved and cannot be disassembled or bent, and so the dress pattern must accommodate the deity's stiffness.

Interest in dressing home deities was not restricted to devotees in Mayapur. I saw Haladini viewing a home deity worship site on Facebook that was populated by entries from ISKCON devotees all over the world. People were sharing images of their home deities, new clothing, jewellery and tutorials on how to make these items. Some also discussed real-life problems – for example, how they dealt with the demands of having home deities while serving in the temple, or how to involve young children in home worship. Haladini had not met them but was touched by the camaraderie on the site, and was contemplating posting some images of her own home deities, overcoming her usual concerns over privacy. Listening to her speak, I realised that her community consisted of physical and virtual relationships with like-minded people who were passionate about serving their home deities.

Conclusion: devotion as a practice of 'efficacious intimacy'

Practices of right living and a host of other decisions regarding material choices and actions shape non-Indian devotees as Hindu Brahmins. Matter is not separated from spirit, and neither is the feeling body differentiated from the spiritual body, produced through an orientation toward, and a consciousness of, the deity Krishna as both a divine and spiritual entity. Practices, such as caring for the deities, performing ritual ablutions before worship, chanting/listening to mantras, etc., are important because they are believed to be efficacious. They are considered to have a real material and spiritual effect by transforming peoples' nature and situating them vis-à-vis Krishna, pleasing him, and, thereby, shaping their soteriological destiny. Simultaneously, there is room for experimentation with *how* to care for the deities and elicit potent, relational states within the paradigm of *bhakti*. Indeed, without this space it is unclear how a devotee would ever form a truly subjective bond with the deity.

Devotional attitudes and behaviours are produced in the bodily-and-material play between actions that devotees perform upon themselves and others, as well as forces exerted upon them – a form of efficacious connectivity and intimacy. Certainly, home as an ethnographic space invokes domestic affinities through the ease with which children and women accessed the altar, and the nurturing maternal attitudes demonstrated by Snehalata, Padma and Haladini towards their home deities. But it is by comparing a corpus of gestures, the handling of deity figures in bathing and pattern-making, that we understand how the *murtis* became an intimate part of the family. Patting, handling, and pressing were common actions, and touch enabled physical and emotional intimacy. Simultaneously, the women's daily practices differed in the precise nature and goal of their activities, indicating how they situated themselves in a relational network of objects (*murtis,* worship paraphernalia, compact disc, fabric, paper, Blu-tack) and subjects (priests, gurus and other devotees).

Practices of pattern-making and bathing may not be thought of as religious but, framed by our initial MaR approach, are deemed as such since they help subjectify devotees to the sovereign, omnipresence of Krishna. The ISKCON devotee is fully aware that the deity and its multiple forms on the altar do not show signs of animation. Simultaneously, the deity's very passivity and 'need' to be cared for through bathing, feeding and dressing becomes an indication of divine sentience. Deity figures, through their stillness, force devotees to bend and move around them, further reinforcing the idea of divine causality – that everything takes place due to Krishna and his various manifestations. This also extends to entities in the vicinity such as the presence of the researcher and her camera. For instance, Padma attributed my presence at the pattern-making session to Krishna's 'kindness' rather than Haladini's relationship with me or, indeed, my efforts, since ultimate agency and intentionality came from the deity. This is one example of how ISKCON devotees enact 'Krishna consciousness', situating themselves and their altars, as well as non-devotees, within a knowledge of the world as theophany.

While distinguished by autobiographical details, divine agency was also incorporated through devotees' life experiences of struggle and succour. Snehalata was convinced that it was due to her total submission to Krishna, after losing the support of her husband, that she was able to live on the Mayapur campus and raise her daughters. Loss also amplified devotion, for instance, when Padma regarded the fire that destroyed her belongings as a sign that what really mattered were her deities. Devotionality across these various instances was framed as an issue of recognising the presence of Krishna, performing certain actions, developing intimacy and demonstrating appropriate attitudes so as to be fully transformed and subjectified to the divine.

Notes

1. This term is invoked in the context of Trinidadian clothing style where what is on the body's surface is given much importance as an indication of the true self. Miller contrasts this approach with a cultural mindset where what is important and real is believed to lie in some deep interior while what is on the surface is considered to be ephemeral and shallow.

164   *Urmila Mohan*

2. Characteristically the authoritative product of Brahmin authors, *shastra*, had never enjoyed mass appeal in India, since it largely seemed disconnected from the activities of the world. In a modern Hindu reform context, *shastra* became a distinctly self-consciously doctrinal and ideological modality of religious propagation.
3. Here I highlight the reformist emphasis on the Vedas as prescriptive, doctrinal text. Performative uses of texts might be said to exist even within ISKCON through the example of chanting mantras.
4. The manner in which Mauss ([1909] 2003: 48) discusses religion and prayer in ancient India, ranging from the spoken mantra to inner mystical thought, demands further study into how his ideas related to those of Indologists, such as Max Müller (1823–1900), who placed Hindu practices on a scale of human religious evolution from the visible to the invisible, and from the material to the spiritual.
5. ISKCON deity figures, with their naturalistic human features, also lend themselves to this abduction and attribution of a mind to the deity figure.
6. For definitions of external and internal agency, see Gell (1998: 134). Also see Morgan (2018: 188, n. 33) where he observes that Gell used the idea of 'distributed personhood' and its various agencies as a way of thinking about idolatry and how images come to life.
7. See the chart for deity embellishment or *prasadhana* in De (1961: 187).
8. The medieval Gaudiya Vaishnav saint Chaitanya is worshiped in ISKCON as an incarnation of Krishna.
9. All names of people, countries of origin and languages are pseudonymised.
10. A *shila* is a term used to refer to ammonite fossils or stones that are considered embodiments of gods and goddesses.
11. *Dwadasi* is the 12th lunar day of the *shukla* (bright) or *krishna* (dark) fortnight of every lunar month in the Hindu calendar.
12. *Ekadasi* is the 11th lunar day of the *shukla* (bright) or *krishna* (dark) fortnight of every lunar month in the Hindu calendar. It is considered a spiritually auspicious day that devotees observe by fasting.

References

De, S. K. (1961), *Early History of the Vaisnava Faith and Movement in Bengal: From Sanskrit and Bengali Sources*, Calcutta: Firma KLM Private Limited.

Foucault, M. (1982), 'The Subject and Power', *Critical Inquiry*, 8 (4): 777–95.

Gell, A. (1998), *Art and Agency: An Anthropological Theory*, Oxford: Clarendon.

Holdrege, B. (2015), *Bhakti and Embodiment: Fashioning Divine Bodies and Devotional Bodies in Krsna Bhakti*, Milton Park: Routledge.

Lemonnier, P. (1992), *Elements for an Anthropology of Technology*, Ann Arbor: University of Michigan.

Leroi-Gourhan, A. (1945), *Milieu et techniques. Évolution et techniques, II*, Paris: Albin Michel, Paris.

Leroi-Gourhan, A. (1943), *L'homme et la matière. Évolution et techniques, I*, Paris: Albin Michel.

Marriott, M. and R. Inden (1977), 'Toward an Ethnosociology of South Asian Caste Systems', in K. David (ed.), *The New Wind: Changing Identities in South Asia*, 227–238, The Hague: Mouton Publishers.

Mauss, M. ([1909] 2003), *On Prayer*, S. Leslie transl. and W. S. F. Pickering, ed., New York: Berghahn Books.

Mauss, M. (1936 [2006]), 'Les techniques du corps', *Journal de psychologie*, 32: 271–93. Translated by B. Brewster and reproduced in M. Mauss, Techniques, Technology and Civilisation (edited and introduced by N. Schlanger), 77–95, Oxford: Berghahn books.

Meyer, B., D. Morgan, C. Paine and B. Plate (2010), 'The Origin and Mission of Material Religion', *Religion*, 40: 207–211.

Miller, D. (1994), 'Style and Ontology', in J. Friedman (ed.), *Consumption and Identity*, 71–96, Oxfordshire: Taylor and Francis.

Mohan, U. (2016), 'From Prayer Beads to the Mechanical Counter: The Negotiation of Chanting Practices within a Hindu Group', *Archives de Sciences Sociales des Religions*, 174: 191–212.

Mohan, U. (2017), 'Clothing as a Technology of Enchantment: Gaze and Glaze in Hindu Garments', *Magic, Ritual, and Witchcraft*, 12 (2): 225–244.

Mohan, U. (2018), 'Objecthood', in H. Callan (ed.), *The International Encyclopedia of Anthropology*, Wiley Online Library, doi: 10.1002/9781118924396.wbiea2155.

Mohan, U. (2019), *Clothing as Devotion in Contemporary Hinduism*, Brill Research Perspectives E-Books Online. Leiden: Brill. [DOI:10.1163/9789004419131]

Mohan, U. and J. -P. Warnier (2017), 'Editorial: Marching the Devotional Subject: The Bodily-and-Material Cultures of Religion', *Journal of Material Culture*, 22 (4): 369–384.

Morgan, D. (2010), 'Introduction', in D. Morgan (ed.), *Religion and Material Culture: The Matter of Belief*, 1–18, London: Routledge.

Morgan, D. (2018), *Images at Work: The Material Culture of Enchantment*, New York: Oxford University Press.

Narayanan, V. (2003), 'Embodied Cosmologies: Sights of Piety, Sites of Power', *Journal of the American Academy of Religion*, 71 (3): 495–520.

Prabhupada, A. C. (1986), *The Bhagavad Gita as It is*, Los Angeles: Bhaktivedanta Book Trust.

Sugirtharajah, S. (2003), 'Max Muller: Mobilizing Texts and Managing Hinduism', in S. Sugirtharajah, *Imagining Hinduism: A Postcolonial Perspective*, 38–73, London and New York: Routledge.

Waghorne, J. P. (1994), *The Raja's Magic Clothes: Re-visioning Kingship and Divinity in England's India*, University Park: Pennsylvania State University Press.

Waghorne, J. P., N. Cutler and V. Narayanan, eds. (1985). *Gods of Flesh, Gods of Stone: The Embodiment of Divinity in India*, New York: Columbia University Press.

Warnier, J. -P. (2007), *The Pot-king: The Body and Technologies of Power*, Leiden: Brill.

Warnier, J. -P. (2009), 'Technology as Efficacious Action on Objects... and Subjects', *Journal of Material Culture*, 14 (4): 459–470.

Matter of knowledge

11 Anthropology of knowledge transmission beyond dichotomies: Learning and subjectivation among watchmakers in Switzerland

Hervé Munz

Introduction

Over the last 30 years, human sciences, particularly anthropology's representatives, have highlighted the sociocultural anchorage and relativist dimension of dichotomous thought exemplified in dualisms such as nature/culture (Descola 2005), human/non-human (Latour and Woolgar 1979, Callon 1986, Haraway 1991), body/mind (Ingold 2000, Marchand 2001) and social/technical (Akrich 1987). Those sets of works have undoubtedly revealed the unnecessary aspect of dichotomous thought and the arbitrariness of its distribution in systems of categorisation, classification and taxonomy. However, when approaching the sociocultural study of knowledge construction and circulation, some scholars tend to reproduce and strengthen similar kinds of thought. Indeed, some researchers still observe, describe, analyse and classify forms of knowledge and their transmission process through the prism of dichotomous categories, occasionally even rigid opposites, such as theory/practice, cognition/action, intellectual/manual, propositional/procedural, abstract/concrete, formal/informal, manifest/tacit, explicit/implicit, declared/undeclared. One example of such a stance may be found in the *Anthropology and the Cognitive Challenge* of Maurice Bloch, an author who is yet usually careful on the reductionist bias through which we think others think (see Bloch 1998). In his recent book, Bloch (2012: 192–193) introduces the seminal works of Jack Goody (1977) and Jean Lave and Etienne Wenger (1991) with these words: 'These anthropologists (...) were struck by the lack of explicit teaching in this way of transferring knowledge and the discouragement of the learner asking questions of the master. This method of transfer of practical knowledge is quite unlike the method used in school contexts. It is expected that, somehow, through hanging around expert craftsmen such as weavers, learning occurs through a process that Lave and Wenger call legitimate peripheral participation. Knowledge seems to *seep* into the apprentice, but it takes a very long time to do so'.

170 *Hervé Munz*

Challenging the dichotomous approach of knowledge transmission

When referring to the topics of trade acquisition, job training or occupational identity, some of these researchers (Jorion and Delbos 1984, Chevallier and Chiva 1991, Lévine and Develay 2003, Bloch 2012) differentiate academic from vocational forms of knowledge and the correlative ways through which they are learnt and passed on. According to them, academic and vocational forms of knowledge differ in nature, and take place, respectively, in educational spaces such as schools or vocational training settings, and in occupational spaces such as companies. This differentiation of knowledge forms regarding the spaces where they take place allows them to differentiate and contrast vocational knowledge from academic, by enumerating a number of its features that will be analysed in the first section.

Beyond those oppositions, what if such a dichotomous categorisation of knowledge and learning could be destabilised by focusing on the example of a vocational activity such as watchmaking (Munz 2017, 2019). Grounded in four years of fieldwork carried out in the Swiss watchmaking world (Munz 2016), this chapter is theoretically framed in the non-dichotomous ecology of knowledge promoted by the works of *Matière à Penser* (MaP) representatives (Warnier 1999, Julien and Warnier eds. 1999, Julien and Rosselin-Bareille eds. 2005, 2009, Jeanjean 2006, Julien 2006, Roustan 2007, Rosselin-Bareille 2015).

In combining the insights of the heterogenic field of anthropology of objects and techniques (Marchand 2001, 2008, Geslin 2002, 2017, Harris ed. 2007), and Michel Foucault's reflections on the links between power, materiality and subjectivation (Foucault 1975, 1976, 1977, 1981, 1982), MaP representatives (Julien and Rosselin-Bareille 2003, Bayart and Warnier 2004, Julien 2009, 2014, Rosselin-Bareille 2017) emphasise the importance of artefacts and the body in the shaping of human knowledge and interactions. They reinvigorate, regarding specific sociocultural and historical situations, the ways material culture is theorised in the formation of subjectivity and skills, and in the framing of individuals' and groups' logics of action. Above all, they systematically reverse the traditional question of anthropology of techniques: the concern is not only to ask, 'What do human individuals and collectives do to matter?' but to wonder, 'What does matter do to subjectivity and social belonging?' and 'How are matter and actions on matter means of subjectivation?'

The material formation of vocational identification: the case of Swiss watchmakers

Therefore, the MaP approach offers a relevant frame to underline that technical objects occupy a central position in the transmission and the learning of vocational knowledge and related subjectivity. This material way to consider the formation of vocational identification allows us to characterise

Anthropology of knowledge transmission 171

learning not as a mechanical reproduction but as a processual set of dynamic actions. Based on this approach, this chapter aims to criticise and challenge the dichotomous typology of knowledge transmission that exists in human sciences. The chapter attempts to demonstrate accordingly that the learning of a vocation cannot be relevantly described by the dichotomy academic knowledge/vocational knowledge, based on a strong contrast between school and work contexts. More specifically, this chapter examines how the study of watchmakers' craft learning and practice through the prisms of materiality and corporeality gives a better understanding of what is effectively a knowledge *in the making.*

Besides, Swiss watchmakers and their skills offer an interesting study case that deals with the issue of discontinuity and emphasises the ambivalence of the traditional status associated to a knowledge. While brands, tourist guides and even some museums entertain the fiction that contemporary watchmaking in Switzerland descended in a direct line from the famous urban workshops that first began producing watches in the Geneva region in the early seventeenth century, the watch industry was in fact profoundly transformed by the economic crisis that swept through the market in the 1970s. In the early 1980s, the Swiss watch industry progressively reemerged on the international stage by shifting its production toward high-value-added mechanical products. This rebirth was supported by the organisational restructuring of its production system and the use of one key concept, namely heritage (Munz 2017). Mobilising a rhetoric of continuity, heritage has progressively become, over the period from 1975 to the present day, the key notion through which the Swiss mechanical watch has changed its status from that of an object that had been made obsolete by the unsurpassable chronometric superiority of quartz technologies to that of a luxurious, precious and technically prestigious item. However, today, many watchmakers and craftspeople look with suspicion at the notion of heritage (Munz 2016). They have not forgotten that Swiss mechanical watchmaking, and their craft along with it, had a dynamic rebirth based on heritage, framed by luxury, but they now also see heritage as the cause for the level of success that justified the automation of the luxury sector and their own progressive marginalisation. Ironically, it is heritage itself, the very resource that previously protected them and allowed the conservation of their knowledge through reappropriation, that now threatens them.

Methodologically, this paper draws on my empirical research as interested in the embodied dimensions of watchmaking knowledge and in the importance of artefacts in its implementation. I studied how this vocational knowledge was learnt, carried out and passed on in apprenticeship[1] and daily activities of multiple practitioners in training institutions and industrial firms. I led around three hundred interviews with craftspeople and watch industry stakeholders, and conducted observations during some events (multi-scale companies visits, professional fairs and trade shows).

172   *Hervé Munz*

Besides, I conducted, in parallel, participant observation in two vocational schools (sometimes as a trainee), and in the occupational workshop of an elite independent small-scale watchmaking firm.

On the basis of the data collected in these surveys, this chapter has two sections that elaborate a critique of dichotomous meanings associated with the transmission of vocational knowledge. The first section focuses on the organisation of watchmaking practice in Switzerland, and offers further descriptions of learning processes that dissolve the apparent opposition between academic transmission as theoretical and explicit and vocational as practical and implicit. It is worth noting that the initial vocational training program in Switzerland is located both in public schools and private firms. This implies a permanent didactic dialogue between these two practice areas and boils down to specific learning experiences among craftspeople. In order to fit with national vocational training standards, firm-based watchmaking apprenticeship requires a high degree of explication and formalisation. Thus, the craft knowledge that apprentices acquire in these settings tends to be explicit. In addition, by examining the everyday life of the small-scale workshop and the multiple interactions that occur there between watchmakers and their surroundings, it appears that interaction is constant between practitioners, along with a whole set of material resources and artefacts where propositional or declarative knowledge is codified as much as is procedural knowledge.

The second section of the chapter will refer to the experiences I had as a trainee at the workbench in two technical colleges. I will underline that even in places officially dedicated to the teaching of craft, formalisation and explication are far from being the only way that watchmaking knowledge is passed on. Transmission can happen without the actor's intention; learning occurs through informal or tacit processes, where the impact is hard to determine or its relevance is recognised retroactively by the stakeholders. Sociotechnical features of the craft are also transmitted via uncodified means, and can sometimes remain unsaid or even veiled or concealed. In this respect, the school-based vocational training milieu must be investigated with an awareness of the blurred side of educational or didactic relationships, explicitly qualified as tutoring.

The transmission and appropriation of watchmaker's knowledge

In their understanding of occupational knowledge and its circulation, over the last 40 years, many anthropologists have embraced dichotomous classifications. Since the 1980s, the works produced by ethnologists of craft and knowledge (including Jorion and Delbos 1984, Chevallier and Chiva 1991) made three major assertions: vocational knowledge is diffuse and its technical aspect is inseparable from a larger set of sociocultural elements; it is integrated, informal and rarely explicit; and it is diametrically opposed to academic knowledge.

In *La transmission des savoirs*, Jorion and Delbos (1984) list, for example, a certain number of characteristics that distinguish vocational knowledge from academic knowledge. In the view of these authors, vocational knowledge is totally embodied and rarely formalised in discourse. It is based on a singular case and lacks any theoretical ambition. It is focused on 'what works here and now' and is completely recreated in every practitioner's knowledge-generation through a long process of personal identification.

Learning beyond dichotomies

Following the publication of some of these works, Sigaut (1991: 33) wrote that 'the opposition between (initial vocational) learning (in firms) and school' is much more porous and less distinct than what the human sciences and ethnology had admitted up to that point. In the article 'L'apprentissage vu par les ethnologues: un stéréotype?', he showed how some researchers had presented caricatured versions of learning situations, systematically opposing the vocational context with the academic context, mainly because they often understood the vocations not through direct observation but through the accounts of aged informers.

In what follows, I extend Sigaut's critique in different ways by pointing out that the watchmaking apprenticeship in Switzerland does not satisfy such a division in any way. First, since the second half of the nineteenth century, watchmaking training necessarily occurs in school institutions. The historical singularities of the organisation of this training have led to it being given a central place in schools and vocational centres. All of the publicly recognised and certified curriculum are at least in part accomplished there. Properly speaking, apprenticeships never only take place in a company. Watchmaking apprentices in the dual program (which represents slightly more than one-third of students, with the remaining two-thirds completing all of their training at school) have theory courses and final exams at school.

In addition, for nearly 10 years, the initial training has been increasingly geared towards the dual program. This involves significant coordination efforts between the firms, the umbrella organisation, school establishments and the Swiss Confederation and the cantons so that the content of the practical teaching provided to young people in companies is strictly the same as what is offered to their counterparts based at school. In order to train, firms usually appoint one of their watchmakers to become an 'apprenticeship master' (which involves passing federal training or taking specific courses) and develop training material describing their products and explaining the techniques involved in their fabrication. This is not a world governed by secrets and the informal.

Second, the independent workshop in Geneva where I conducted my observations provided me with another way to extend Sigaut's critique. In their activities, the workers engaged there routinely consulted a whole set of object resources that contained propositional and procedural knowledge (Figure 11.1).

The continuous learning of these already-trained people occurred throughout practice via encoded teachings that were appropriated and adapted to the action (dimension and tolerance tables, binders with industry standards, diagrams and mathematical formulas, procedure instructions, review cards that summarise the steps to take, various memory aids, etc.). Qualified craftspeople are thus involved in a continuous learning process that requires the use of artefacts, where formalised knowledge is inscribed, appropriated and adjusted in response to ongoing actions.

More globally, the transfer of a vocation does not occur only where the actors believe they work. It would be incorrect to think that in locations reserved for transmission such as schools, the circulation of vocational knowledge had only one explicit meaning. Even in these spaces, informal modes of communication accompany the practices that pass on more standardised skills. The vocation is also, and perhaps even more so, communicated through that which is not mainstream or codified. It is not the subject of realisations or systematic reflection, and a large amount of knowledge that results from learning situations remains undeniably implicit. Watchmaking training at school requires that attention be paid to the small asides of the pedagogical or didactic interactions that are explicitly qualified as 'transmission'.

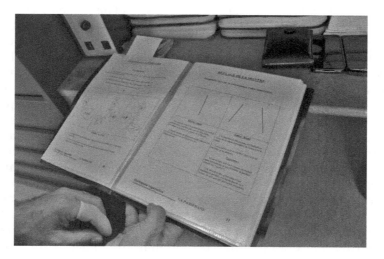

Figure 11.1 A junior watchmaker named Richard introduces me to the documents (functioning figures, graphics and charts, descriptions of tasks and instructions for procedures) he uses while attempting to time a mechanical watch. Geneva, 2013.

Photo by author.

Dichotomy reconsidered: initial vocational training at school

The pedagogy of concealment

The idea that making watchmaking knowledge explicit is a condition of its transmission can also be criticised according to the practices of concealing/revealing that take place, for didactic purposes, in certain vocational schools. During my ethnography of apprenticeship (2010-2014), I regularly witnessed specific tactics through which certain teachers intended to teach the 'mechanical sense' to their students. These tactics are not secrets properly speaking. They are not strictly an example of information withholding, but rather a case of leveraging a lack of clarity or obfuscation in the relationship that apprentices have with each piece of knowledge, information, technique or gesture. The description of these strategies makes it possible to re-evaluate the approach of certain anthropologists such as Fabre (2008) who, in his general thinking on knowledge transmission, opposes two models: pedagogy, based on an imperative of transparency, which organises instruction and training in school, and initiation, which places particular emphasis on secrets and is more concerned with the world of practice and the world of work.

In Switzerland, the school institutions that teach watchmaking training employ a hybrid type of transmission that demonstrates the porous nature between the pedagogy and initiation paradigms. Learning the vocation in a school does not entirely fall under either paradigm. It is not based exclusively on the principle of demonstrating the appropriate gestures to be imitated and repeated. According to some teachers, imitation has obvious limitations, because it does not allow apprentices to develop their 'mechanical sense' that requires incorporating a strong principle of autonomy.

'Mechanical sense' is the expression used by trainers to describe what they attempt to impart to their apprentices. This is more of a 'way of knowing' (Harris ed. 2007) than an accumulation of 'forms of knowledge'. More so than in holding propositional knowledge or specific procedural knowledge, the watchmaker's 'mechanical sense' translates into both an art of 'resourcefulness' and manual[2] 'correction'[3] of its components. This also materialises in an ability to make their own tools and to recreate, if needed, the integral parts of the movement (whether they are missing, damaged or broken) as well as an aptitude for the identification and resolution of various problems. For many watchmakers, analytical skills appear more central than the question of the practical mastery of techniques in the definition of quality work (Munz 2016: 176–180). The keywords in this line of thinking are attention, autonomy and adjustment.[4]

Therefore, the presumed pedagogical transparency is removed. The model of the 'demonstration' is substituted for one that encourages 'resourcefulness'. The latter model complicates the obligation of revealing how to proceed, which seems so tied to pedagogy and through which learning in a school setting is often understood. Some instructors admit that in order to transmit better, they sometimes withhold access to certain 'tricks' of the trade by keeping silent or not providing any relevant information to students. Thus, the acquisition of vocational knowledge is partly shaped by a didactic approach that leads teachers to conceal their knowledge.

In Switzerland, I carried out two years of participant observation in vocational schools where I sometimes took part to lessons as an apprentice. In one of those schools, I was welcome in the workshop of Joe, a 25-year-old Swiss watchmaker that trained a classroom of 12 apprentices, around 15 to 17 years old. In these settings, the apprentices are therefore engaged in exploring, 'How do I do this?' through other routes. It is not, properly speaking, a professional secret, as it is not intended to mean 'the total prevention of access to knowledge', but a temporary masking of it. These practices of concealing never definitively restrict this access, but distinguish it in time to 'encourage the apprentices to observe'. For example, through calculated silence, Joe intended to create an environment that was conducive to instilling 'visual expertise' in his students (Figure 11.2). This strategy of calculated silence originated from the desire to influence the students' actions by requiring them to acquire a capacity to identify and solve a wide range of problems without recourse to the instructor. They must learn to build their resources 'by themselves' using formalised procedures, existing or not, and to implement their own work methodologies by documenting the problems they encountered in their logbook.

Figure 11.2 Trainees acquiring 'by themselves' visual expertise at the workshop of a vocational training school in the Swiss Jura region, 2012.

Photo by author.

In this model, communication in the workshop is not severed. The economics of speech is merely organised around another framework. The desire to transmit is not excluded from the process of concealing. Concealment is, on the contrary, one of its modalities. Its objective is to optimise technical learning and ingrain students with a system of values where independence is paramount. The objective of the transfer is not only concerned with the content of the knowledge or dexterity, but above all with incorporating an obligation to 'figure it out'. What is transmitted is a principle of autonomy in the work. In this regard, learning is sometimes experienced, as much from the side of the teachers as the apprentices, as a battle. These moments of didactic 'anti-pedagogy' create frameworks of experience that build exposure to the trade. Still, these methods require time and are not well suited to instances of stress and urgency, which are numerous throughout the school year, when an instructor must 'stall' and apprentices must 'advance'.

Ultimately, the school institution related to vocational training and the pedagogical model of transmission that it embodies are not ideal sites of transparency. The institution remains interlaced with logics of concealment, strategies of masking information or withholding solutions. However, these practices have a limited duration and the intensity with which they are maintained depends on the time that the teachers have available to explore a course module. The practices are tests that are as much means of perpetuating the trade and making apprentices into 'experts' of watchmaking.

Certain forms of watchmaking education in school are not systematically the subject of discussions, even if they are conscious and reflected. What is transmitted is not always explicit, or even able to be explained. In a certain number of cases, the transfer of skills and the values that underlie those skills are achieved through forms of concealment: its effectiveness is derived from the temporary silencing of certain hints or techniques that are connected with the craft. The skills are therefore acquired in these partial inversions of visibility. The principle of transparency and formalisation valued by a certain ideology of pedagogy conflicts with everything that, in the circulation of the watchmaking 'mechanical sense', is not revealed and emerges from *'savoir-taire'* (knowing when to remain silent) (Zempléni 1996, Munz 2016).

Objects as central transmission vectors

The anthropocentrism inherent to a certain meaning of transmission that occurs immediately, from human to human, should also be critiqued. The human figure of the master who breaks down technical procedures for his followers to better communicate them is not central to the transmission of knowledge. Artefacts are important vectors for the preservation of watchmaking gestures and knowledge. In training, the apprentices acquire their knowledge through the mediation of artefacts and sometimes without even direct intervention or support from people.

178 *Hervé Munz*

Following Latour (2007: 88) who criticises phenomenologists for attributing an 'excessive weight [to] human sources of action', it seems that the circulation of the 'mechanical sense' cannot only be considered by focusing on the interactions between teachers and students. These interactions are framed, experienced, accompanied and extended by several artefacts (components and watch movements, tools, machines, equipment, workspaces, workshop layout, etc.). The bodies of the practitioners (for example eyes, hands, backs, elbows) are so often equipped with tools that when some practitioners speak of 'manual operations' (as opposed to 'automatic operations') they naturally include the hands and a very large number of objects, even conventional machines, in this formula. In training activities, teachers translate technique into material that can be taught in many formats. Given the small size of the watch pieces, the microscopic scale at which operations are carried out, and the precision required for such dimensions to be respected, the use of didactic objects to visually enlarge the work is common. These demonstrative explanations given by teachers are often integrated into pedagogical materials and objects, which makes the craft more visible and accessible for apprentices.

Incidentally, the 'correct gestures' and appropriate techniques are rarely presented as established models that will subsequently be repeated. Most of the time, they are derived from the relation that aspiring practitioners establish with the objects that define their field of action and shape their interventions on watch movements. It is through the domestication of hand tools and the regular manipulation of watchmaking components that young practitioners appropriate vocational gestures. Furthermore, if those gestures are transmitted in watchmaking schools from one cohort of apprentices to the next, it is, in part, because identical material is provided to students and they are trained on the same objects, with the same tools, in similar environments. By circulating in this way, these artefacts promote the recreation of similar uses and the learning of physical references that must lead to satisfying the same technical objectives. The techniques of the body outlined in this way form 'objectified' repertoires whose gradual sharing allows for the emergence of watchmaking subjects and a sense of belonging to the trade. The construction of the vocational identification of watchmakers only develops through an intimate dialogue between different forms of materiality.

One of the first observations that alerted me to the importance of the mediation of objects in watchmaking education occurred in the second-year class taught by Iannis. The students were learning about timing.[5] By attending more than a month of his lessons, I observed that the teacher did not often correct the apprentices by returning to specific questions of postures or gestures to realise. The differences between the results obtained by the students and the prescribed exercise standards were often the subject of terse comments that translated into formulas as follows: 'spiral not centred', 'spiral not quite flat ... it's going back to nine o'clock', 'balance problem', 'height problem', 'there, you are too rude, the spiral is concealed' (Figure 11.3).

Without batting an eye, the students would return to their places and get back to work adjusting their balance-spirals with their tweezers and pegwood.[6] What needed to be modified to reach the result was not mentioned and at no time was there a correction that elaborated the correct gestures to be made. Iannis had given the instructions and demonstrated the operations to undertake succinctly during the first course of the module and since then had contented himself with awaiting students at his office equipped with a video camera and a projection screen to enlarge the image of the components. Similarly, the teacher rarely corrected students when they were making their interventions on the detached pieces. He assessed the work by considering the entire process without having directly observed it, but reading it on the balance-spiral. He had not necessarily watched what had been done, but he could nevertheless see it.

In this way, he corrected the methodology of the students by judging it by the results and encouraging them to try the task again if necessary. In this case, their work was assessed and corrected based on the result legible on the small objects. The objects were spaces that recorded the apprentices' activity, which was only assessed through their 'trace'. Iannis evaluated the quality of this trace embodied on the material and invited the students to

Figure 11.3 Trainees working silently at their benches at the workshop of a vocational training school in the Swiss Jura region, 2012.

Photo by author.

180 *Hervé Munz*

correct the course of their actions until their work satisfied the standard upheld within his gaze and objectified on the instruction sheet. This was a process of learning at the centre of which the balances and spirals mediated and punctuated many of the interactions that took place between the teacher and his class.

In the same register, several accounts from watchmakers testify to the fact that learning the trade sometimes only occurs 'through the object', through its didactic authority, without the presence or supervision of an instructor being required. At various times, teachers also told me about their first years of training and their first occupational experiences by underscoring the importance of all the works of reparation and restoration of antique pieces that they carried out 'to acquire the skills'. In such contexts, the vocation is often learned not directly from a master or the imitation of a third party, but 'face to face' with the greatest possible number of timepieces (wristwatches, pocket watches, clocks, pendulum, etc.) that showcase different issues to identify, diagnose and solve.

Re-mapping typologies of knowledge transmission

The strong opposition between academic and vocational knowledge seems to be irrelevant to acquiring knowledge. What many scholars have identified as distinct types of knowledge fail to adequately describe the watchmaking craft. Based on that, it is worthwhile to underline that this disparity is more related to broader political and economic contexts than to the nature of knowledge. The distinction between vocational knowledge and scholarly knowledge proposed by, among others, Bloch (2012) and Jorion and Delbos (1984), has nothing to do with a natural difference between the two types of knowledge. It is related to an arbitrary distinction in the English and French institutional contexts where there is a strong separation between vocational and academic learning. The meaning that learning takes on based on national contexts has a major influence on the way in which anthropologists have developed their classification of knowledge to date. This is a major issue because the distinction between practical knowledge and academic knowledge is a regularly used motif in socio-anthropological studies. However, in the case of Swiss watchmaking, this distinction does not apply, which strongly nuances a part of the results of the above-mentioned research.

In sum, the learning of a vocation, regardless of the school-based or the work-based contexts in which it takes place, does not at all satisfy the dichotomous classification through which vocational knowledge is usually considered. Everything that happens in practice cannot be understood through simplistic dichotomous oppositions. A scientific approach that systematically associates the academic context with formal knowledge and the vocational context with informal skills is reductive and not very relevant. However, it is also not a question of denying the differences between vocational training and work as two kinds of situations of practice, and the types

Anthropology of knowledge transmission 181

of knowledge that are mobilised there, but rather of not opposing them, so as to understand how their differences are distributed socially and spatially and are reorganised in a dynamic way depending on the moving contexts and frontiers.

Notes

1. In Switzerland, the apprenticeship is the first step on the vocational path that all individuals who want to learn a trade take after finishing the required schooling around age 15. Because of the dual-track orientation of the Swiss vocational education and training system, which is historically rooted with socio-political transformations that took place in the second half of the nineteenth century (Munz 2016, Bonoli 2017), today the apprenticeship involves attending a school institution *by definition.* Depending on the chosen trade, an apprentice must either conduct her/his apprenticeship in a public vocational training school 'full-time' (for the theoretical and practical aspects of the curriculum) or in 'dual-track mode' (theoretical courses at school and practical workshops in firms).
2. In watchmaking vocabulary, the formula 'by hand' refers to a hand holding a tool, whether the tool is a screwdriver, tweezers, a file, an engine lathe or a milling machine.
3. Term employed by watchmakers to designate the principle that consists of removing some material from the components of the movement of a watch during its assembly.
4. Term referring to the adaptation, manually or with hand tools, of the arrangement of the components of the movement during their assembly.
5. Adjustment technique of the regulating organs of a mechanical watch that ensures it functions.
6. Round stick of wood used by watchmakers for cleaning holes, leaves of pinions, etc. (see Berner 1961).

References

Akrich, M., (1987), 'Comment décrire les objets techniques?', *Techniques & Culture*, 9: 49–64.

Bayart, J. -F. and J. -P. Warnier (2004), *Matière à politique. Le pouvoir, les corps et les choses*, Paris: CERI-Karthala.

Berner, G. -A. (1961), *Illustrated Professional Dictionary of Horology,* (online) http://www.fhs.ch/berner/?l=en, date last accessed 25 July 2019.

Bloch, M. (1998), *How We Think They Think: Anthropological Approaches to Cognition, Memory, and Literacy,* Boulder: Westview Press.

Bloch, M. (2012), *Anthropology and the Cognitive Challenge*, Cambridge: Cambridge University Press.

Bonoli, L., (2017), 'An Ambiguous Identity: The Figure of the Apprentice From the XIX Century Up to Today in Switzerland', in F. Marhuenda (ed.), *Vocational Education beyond Skill Formation. VET between Civic, Industrial and Market Tensions*, 31–49, Bern: Peter Lang.

Callon M., (1986), 'Éléments pour une sociologie de la traduction: La domestication des coquilles Saint-Jacques et des marins pêcheurs en baie de Saint- Brieuc', *L'année sociologique*, 36: 169–2008.

182 *Hervé Munz*

Chevallier, D. and I. Chiva (1991), 'L'introuvable objet de la transmission', in D. Chevallier and I. Chiva (eds.), *Savoir faire et pouvoir transmettre: Transmission et apprentissage des savoir-faire et des techniques*, 1–11, Paris: Éditions de la Maison des Sciences de l'Homme.

Descola, P. (2005), *Beyond Nature and Culture*, Chicago: University of Chicago.

Fabre, D. (2008), 'A propos de la forme scolaire de transmission', paper presented at the *Séminaire du Laboratoire d'anthropologie et d'histoire de l'institution de la culture (LAHIC): L'institution de la culture*, 2007–2008, 24 January 2008, Paris: LAHIC.

Foucault, M. (1975), *Surveiller et punir. Naissance de la prison*, Paris: Gallimard.

Foucault, M. (1976), *Histoire de la sexualité I: La Volonté de savoir*, Paris: Gallimard.

Foucault, M. (1977), 'Pouvoirs et stratégies (interview with J. Rancière)', *Les révoltes logiques*, 4: 89–97.

Foucault, M. (1981), 'Les mailles du pouvoir', in M. Foucault, *Dits et écrits IV*, 182–194, Paris: Gallimard.

Foucault, M. (1982), 'The Subject and Power', in H. Dreyfus and P. Rabinow (eds.), *Michel Foucault: Beyond Structuralism and Hermeneutics*, 208–26, Chicago: The University of Chicago Press.

Geslin, P. (2002), *L'apprentissage des mondes, une anthropologie appliquée aux transferts de technologies*, Toulouse: Octarès Editions, Éditions de la Maison des Sciences de l'Homme.

Geslin, P., ed. (2017), *Inside Anthropotechnology, User and Culture Centered Experience*, London: Wiley.

Goody, J. (1977), *The Domestication of the Savage Mind*, Cambridge: Cambridge University Press.

Haraway, D., (1991), 'Science, Technology, and Socialist-Feminism in the Late Twentieth Century', in *Simians, Cyborgs and Women: The Reinvention of Nature*, 149–181, New York: Routledge.

Harris, M., ed. (2007), *Ways of Knowing: Anthropological Approaches to Crafting Experience and Knowledge*, New York and Oxford: Berghahn Books.

Ingold, T. (2000), *The Perception of the Environment: Essays on Livelihood, Dwelling and Skill*, London: Routledge.

Jeanjean, A. (2006), *Basses oeuvre: Une ethnologie du travail dans les égouts*, Paris: Éditions du CTHS.

Jorion, P. and G. Delbos (1984), *La Transmission des savoirs*, Paris: Éditions de la Maison des Sciences de l'Homme.

Julien, M. -P. (2006), 'Techniques du corps,' in B. Andrieu (ed.), *Dictionnaire du corps*, 45–55, Paris: Éditions du CNRS.

Julien, M. -P. (2009), "Subjectivité', 'subjectivation', 'sujet': dialogue,' in M. -P. Julien and C. Rosselin-Bareille (eds.), *Le sujet contre les objets… tout contre. Ethnographies de cultures matérielles*, 111–168, Paris: Éditions du CTHS.

Julien, M. -P. (2014), 'Techniques corporelles, culture matérielle et identifications en situations', in M. Durand, D. Hauw and G. Poizat (eds.), *Apprendre les techniques corporelles*, 20–45, Paris: Presses Universitaires de France.

Julien, M. -P. and C. Rosselin-Bareille (2003), 'C'est en laquant qu'on devient laqueur. De l'efficacité du geste à l'action sur soi', *Techniques & Culture*, 40. http://tc.revues.org/1454 (accessed September 17, 2016).

Julien, M. -P. and C. Rosselin-Bareille (2005), *La culture matérielle*, Paris: La Découverte.

Anthropology of knowledge transmission 183

Julien, M. -P. and C. Rosselin-Bareille, eds. (2009), *Le sujet contre les objets... tout contre: ethnographies de cultures matérielles*, Paris: Éditions du CTHS.

Julien, M. -P. and J. -P. Warnier, eds. (1999), *Approches de la culture matérielle. corps à corps avec l'objet,* Paris: L'Harmattan.

Latour, B. and S. Woolgar (1979), *Laboratory Life: The Social Construction of Scientific Facts*, Beverly Hills: Sage Publications.

Latour, B. (2007), 'Une sociologie sans objet, remarques sur l'interobjectivité', in O. Debary, and L. Turgeon (eds.), *Objets et mémoires*, 37–58, Paris: Éditions de la Maison des Sciences de l'Homme.

Lave, J. and E. Wenger (1991), *Situated Learning: Legitimate Peripheral Participation.* Cambridge [England] and New York: Cambridge University Press.

Lévine, J. and M. Develay (2003), *Pour une anthropologie des savoirs scolaires: de la désappartenance à la réappartenance*, ESF: Issy-les-Moulineaux.

Marchand, T. H. J. (2001), *Minaret Building and Apprenticeship in Yemen*, Richmond: Curzon.

Marchand, T. H. J. (2008), 'Muscles, Morals and Mind: Craft Apprenticeship and the Formation of Person,' *British Journal of Educational Studies*, 56 (3): 245–71.

Munz, H. (2019), 'Keeping Them 'Swiss': The Transfer and Appropriation of Techniques for Luxury Watch Repair in Hong Kong,' in F. Martínez and P. Laviolette (eds.), *Material Mediations Series*, Special Issue on 'Repair, Brokenness and Breakthrough. Ethnographic Responses', 201–224, London and New York: Berghahn Books.

Munz, H. (2017), 'Crafting Time, Making Luxury: Heritage Regime and Artisan Revival in the Swiss Watches Industry (1975-2015),' in P. -Y. Donzé and F. Rika (eds.), *Global Luxury: Organizational Change and Emerging Markets in the Luxury Industry Since the 1970s*, 197–218, New York: Palgrave Macmillan.

Munz, H. (2016), *La transmission en jeu: Apprendre, pratiquer, patrimonialiser l'horlogerie en Suisse*, Neuchâtel: Éditions Alphil.

Rosselin-Bareille, C. (2015), 'Scaphandriers non autonomes à l'épreuve des matières. culture matérielle, sensations et culture motrice,' in M. Schirrer (ed.), *S'immerger en apnée: Cultures motrices et symboliques aquatiques*, 105–120, Paris: L'Harmattan.

Rosselin-Bareille, C. (2017), 'Matières à former-conformer-transformer', *Socioanthropologie*, 35: 9–22.

Roustan, M. (2007), *Sous l'emprise des objets? Culture matérielle et autonomie*, Paris: L'Harmattan.

Sigaut, F. (1991), 'L'apprentissage vu par les ethnologues, un stéréotype?' in D. Chevallier and I. Chiva (eds.), *Savoir faire et pouvoir transmettre: Transmission et apprentissage des savoir-faire et des techniques*, 33–42, Paris: Éditions de la Maison des Sciences de l'Homme.

Warnier, J. -P. (1999), *Construire la culture matérielle: L'homme qui pensait avec ses doigts*, Paris: Presses Universitaires de France.

Zempléni, A. (1996), 'Savoir taire: Du secret et de l'intrusion ethnologique dans la vie des autres', *Gradhiva*, 20: 23–43.

12 The enskilled subject: Two paths to becoming a skilled person among the Paiwan indigenous people of Taiwan

Geoffrey Gowlland

Introduction: *pulima* and *shifu*

The Paiwan are one of now 16 officially recognised indigenous peoples of Taiwan. Indigenous people in Taiwan are Austronesian speakers, and descendants of populations that inhabited the island prior to waves of European, Japanese and Chinese colonisation, and settlement of ethnic Chinese populations starting in the sixteenth century. During my fieldwork among the Paiwan, I became interested in the revitalisation of indigenous crafts, connected to a broader movement of promotion of indigenous rights and identities. The Paiwan term *pulima* was often used to refer to those people engaged in these revitalisation practices: literally translated as 'many hands', it has long been used to refer to a skilled or talented person (man or woman) who is proficient at a range of manual tasks. The term is now associated with 'traditional' Paiwan skilled practices, in particular the craft forms that define Paiwan identity: wood and slate carving, glass bead making and pottery, among other practices. *Pulima* is a term that both identifies a skilled practitioner, and has acquired particular meaning in the context of revitalisation of Paiwan culture.

The word *shifu* is another term used to identify a skilled person, but with different implications. *Shifu* is not a Paiwan word, but a Mandarin Chinese term of address for trades-persons who have acquired a specialised set of skills, similar to the original meaning of the English term of address 'master'. In the mountain settlements of the Paiwan and other indigenous people, *shifu* refers to those people, mostly if not exclusively men, who acquired work-based knowledge during migrant work in the cities of Taiwan, and in particular in the construction industry. Among the indigenous mountain populations of Taiwan, migration to the cities started in earnest in the 1970s, driven both by limited sources of income in the mountains (new environmental policies imposed restrictions on the logging industry, which employed many indigenous people until then), and by an economic boom in the country. Migrant workers returned to their settlements at the weekends and for holidays with new knowledge and skills, and put them into practice in their village. Signs of this building knowledge can be seen in the Paiwan

186   *Geoffrey Gowlland*

mountain settlement I discuss in this chapter, in the form notably of cement, brick and mortar and concrete constructions. These materials, together with the skills and knowledge necessary to handle them, were imported. The term *shifu* then contrasts with *pulima*: it generally refers not to those people who are skilled in Paiwan vernacular building techniques or crafts, but those who acquired their building knowledge in the culturally foreign towns and cities of the Taiwanese plains.

I introduce this chapter with these two terms, *pulima* and *shifu*, to set a framework for a reflection on skilled practice, informed by the ideas of the research collective Matière à Penser (MaP), and centred on the subject, understood both as a person with a subjectivity (having a point-of-view, and experience) and being a subject in relations of power (Julien et al. 2009b; Douny and Mohan, Introduction to this volume). I propose that the concept of 'skilled subject', with 'subject' having this dual meaning, can be useful in addressing an apparent disconnect in the anthropological literature on crafts and other skilled practices. One strand of research has explored the experiential dimension of making things with skills: scholars such as Tim Ingold, Greg Downey or Lambros Malafouris discuss craft practices to explore philosophical issues relating to mind, the material world, and the enskilled body (e.g., Downey 2005, Malafouris 2008, Ingold 2010, 2012). Another strand of research on crafts addresses the politics of crafts, including issues of authenticity, legitimacy, or the politics of access to skills (e.g., Moeran 1997, Chibnik 2003). At times, accounts of craft practices alternate between these two perspectives of the experiential dimension of making things with skills, and the socio-political 'contexts' in which craftspersons work. In this chapter, I address skilled practices from the perspective of the skilled subject, in other words, both an enskilled person and one who is subject within relations of power. This offers a framework of analysis that can encompass these two strands of the literature. *Pulima* and *shifu* are interesting terms for such an investigation in that they do not refer to a skilled activity, or material form resulting from skilled practice, but to skilled persons. These are both enskilled persons, and subjects within specific relations of power, in this case between indigenous people, the ethnic Chinese majority population, and the state in Taiwan. Before discussing the case study, in the next section I provide a short critical discussion of ethnographic methods applied to the study of skills, and point to the interest of a focus on enskilled subjects. In the subsequent sections, I turn to a discussion of the contrasts between *shifu* and *pulima* as enskilled subjects, and the relationship between their material practices and relations of power.

Enskilment and subjectivity gap

It is common sense that the experience of skilled practice is personal and subjective, one only has experiential access to one's own practice. We have a sense of ownership of the practice, in the way neuropsychologist Antonio

Damasio speaks of feelings in general: feelings are not simply about sensing the world around us, but relating those feelings to a sense of self which make the experiences uniquely our own (Damasio 2010: 185). However much we describe and analyse skilled practice, the information we gather about it is qualitatively different from the thing described: 'what we get in the end is a sum of knowledge, not a skill' as Sigaut (1993: 107) points out about academic efforts to discuss skills. Trevor Marchand (2003) similarly argues that the role of the anthropologist investigating skilled practice is not to describe the content of knowledge – an impossible task given that it is qualitatively different to the words used to describe it – but its (cognitive) nature. One might develop descriptions of, for instance, the *chaînes opératoire*, or sequence of procedures, of skilled material practices (Lemonnier 2006), but these are descriptions of a process, and not of the nature of the skilled performance itself. Carl Knappett (2011) thinks of the *chaîne opératoire* as a scale of analysis distinct from the engaged, skilled and creative encounters with tools and materials: from the creative and open-ended skilled practice (with reference to Ingold 2007, 2010), we can zoom out to describe the necessary process for the completion of a task, but we cannot hold in the same analytical focus both the prescribed (and describable, to some extent) process of making (the *chaîne opératoire*), and the creative engagement of the maker with tools and materials. For Knappett, it is interesting to consider the tensions between these two scales of analysis, the open-ended and creative processes that have the power to change prescribed procedures, or the prescribed procedures that restrict what is creatively available to the maker.

Ethnographers researching practices such as crafts, sports or music, have had to be particularly explicit about issues of methods because of this lack of available tools to describe engaged skilled practice. If other people's experiences of making are not directly accessible to the ethnographer nor translatable, we cannot rely on the traditional data of ethnography, namely the words of our interlocutors. This does not mean of course that we ignore their words, but we need to reflect on the way in which words relate to practice, not as a direct translation of the experiences of making but as verbal elaborations (Bloch 1991). Anthropologists might become apprentices in the field as a method to gain first-hand knowledge of the experience of learning and making. This 'apprenticeship as method' (Coy 1989, Downey et al. 2015) does not solve the issue of accessibility of another's experience, but it can complement interview and observation data with insights into tacit knowledge and experiences of making. But apprenticeship as method can bring its own set of issues to the research: there is a risk of confusing one's own experiences of acquiring skills and knowledge with the experiences of other skilled practitioners or learners. Rebecca Prentice (2008) offers a telling critical account of her experience of learning to be a seamstress as part of a research on Trinidad's garment industry. During fieldwork, she realised that her enjoyable experience of learning was at odds with the experiences of her interlocutors, who were sewing not as a hobby but as workers in an

188 *Geoffrey Gowlland*

economically precarious situation. As anthropologists, we might assume that our experiences of making brings us closer to those of other skilled person, yet we might be missing to account for the significance of life trajectories: in what context were the skills acquired (as part of a hobby, or necessary for earning a wage), and what kind of (political) subject was formed through enskilment? There is a subjectivity gap (Warnier 2011) between the experiences of the ethnographer and of our interlocutors, that shared practice as part of apprenticeship as method deceptively appears to bridge. We need to acknowledge this subjectivity gap as part of the methods we bring to the study of skilled practices. Our theories of skilled practice also need to acknowledge the inseparability of experiences of practice, and subjects in relations of power.

In Knappett's definition of two scales of analysis of material culture practices mentioned above, he imagines the engaged, creative work of the craftsperson as asocial, and by implication apolitical. For Knappett, it is by zooming out from this engaged practice that one gets a sense of the social. By starting with the enskilled subject, we can approach skilled practices as social and political at the core: the enskilled person has a subjectivity, a feeling of ownership in the experience of making, and is a subject of relations of power that both shape, and are shaped by their practice. In the terms *pulima* and *shifu,* the implied dimension of skills is not separate from the (political) subjects that they refer to.

Another note on methods before presenting the empirical research. During fieldwork, I learnt to carve slate, and on a couple of occasions, participated in building activities using bricks, mortar and concrete. This provides me with limited exposure to the practised work of my interlocutors in the field. Another approach provides me with further insights into the skilled work of the *shifu* and *pulima.* I am inspired again by the work of the MaP collective, and in particular an article by Jean-Pierre Warnier (2011), who argues that by looking at and handling items of material culture, we can enter into a dialogue of sorts with previous users of these items. The things that are produced by *shifu* and *pulima* are extensions of their subjectivities: their creative work as well as who they are as particular subjects. Although not bridging the subjectivity gap, Warnier suggests that through material culture, we can gain clues about other people's subjectivities. I turn my attention now to some of these material forms: the houses and tombs of a Paiwan mountain settlement.

Transforming a village: *shifu*

The skilled practice of the *shifu,* those villagers who migrated to the cities and found work as construction workers, is visible throughout the Paiwan settlement of Paridrayan. The vernacular architectural form of the Paiwan houses is built using slate and wooden beams, with different floor plans depending on the status of the family. Slate is an abundant material in the mountainous lands of the Paiwan. Paiwan houses are built using different kinds of slate, categorised as male or female depending on hardness: the harder male slate is used for walls, the female slate, softer and lighter, is used for the roof. Female slate is also appropriate for carving due to its relative softness. The first time I heard a Paiwan person referred to as *shifu* was when an interlocutor was talking about his house, which was built in the vernacular style, with slate and wooden beams, but some of the slate walls had been covered with cement. My interlocutor explained that his uncle had become a *shifu* in the 1970s, he was a migrant to the cities and became a construction worker there. When the uncle returned to the village, he brought a new material, cement, and new building knowledge that enabled him to cover the slate walls of the house. In the village, we can see other combinations of slate and cement. For instance, some houses in the settlement have one wall built with brick and mortar, with concrete columns holding up a slate roof; the other walls are built using slate (as in Figure 12.1). Another example is a house in the vernacular style that has been covered in tiles using mortar. Some houses appear to have been built entirely of slate and wood, yet cement has been used strategically to fill in gaps in the slate walls. Most of the more recent houses are built of concrete,

Figure 12.1 House combining slate with brick-and-mortar wall and concrete columns. The dilapidated appearance is the result of the torrential rains that accompanied typhoon Morakot in 2009. Paridrayan, 2013.

Photo by the author.

190 *Geoffrey Gowlland*

and do not resemble the vernacular style, but rather houses one might see throughout the Taiwanese towns and cities.

In these houses that include cement and concrete, one might see loss of tradition, and imposition of 'modern' building forms onto indigenous people – and indeed, below I will discuss the relationship between cement and processes of assimilation. Yet in these built forms, I see also evidence of the creativity of the *shifu* return migrant workers, their experiments with new materials. The different built forms and material combinations in the village demonstrate the problem solving and creative work in using foreign materials and techniques and adapting them to existing structures of their village according to need, convenience and aesthetics. At first, the *shifu* did not just reproduce the buildings they were employed to build in the plains, but engaged with the possibilities afforded by cement, mortar, concrete, and ceramic tiles. Cement, combined with aggregates to form mortar or concrete, is plastic, it can adapt to the nooks and crannies of existing structures. Concrete might be the iconic material of modernity, but as historian of architecture Adrian Forty (2013: 14–15) suggests, it can be considered a craft material because of this plasticity and because it requires at least basic skills to handle it. The *shifu* were also responding to issues of availability of materials: slate, in particular the larger slabs used for the front walls of houses, albeit plentiful in the mountain environment, is difficult to transport from the riverbeds where it is found, and extraction is regulated by environmental policies; brick-and-mortar front walls became a way to solve these issues. Even the two or three storey concrete buildings are the result of creative solutions to the issue of limited land on the mountain plateau they are built upon. In the village cemetery, we see a similar transformation of built forms: early graves built with slabs of slate gave way to grave chambers constructed with bricks and mortar, with cement floors and sealed with tile-covered concrete (Figure 12.2).

This creative transformation of the village was happening at a particular moment in the history of relations between indigenous people and the Taiwanese state. The participation of the Paiwan in migrant work itself has its roots in state assimilation efforts. Participation of the Austronesian populations in the market economy as labourers, notably in the logging industry, was imposed as a tool of assimilation by the Japanese colonisers (at the time of their presence in Taiwan from 1895 to 1945) (Ching 2001: 135–137). In the 1970s, the Taiwanese economy was booming and in need of labour, whilst environmental policies limited employment opportunities in the logging industry. The Austronesian populations found work in the cities, often taking the most demanding and dangerous jobs, notably in the building industry. At that time, Taiwan was under martial law (1949–1987), and the Kuomintang government was imposing policies to Sinicise the population,[1] and assimilate the Austronesians. In the early 1950s, a government policy was introduced to 'improve' the conditions of the 'mountain dwellers' (not yet recognised as 'indigenous') (Chi 2016: 268–269). Its aims were

The enskilled subject 191

Figure 12.2 Building a grave with bricks and mortar. The floor will later be partially covered with concrete. Paridrayan, 2013.

Photo by the author.

to promote the use of Mandarin Chinese to the detriment of Austronesian languages, 'improve' clothing, diets, housing and the general condition of daily life, and 'reform' folklore and customs by prohibiting 'superstitious' beliefs and other 'backward' practices. The policy promoted ideas about cleanliness, hygiene and order (Yang 2001: 51–52), requiring people to wash often and keep the interior of houses tidy and swept clean. As part of these policies, in Paiwan settlements, local state officials destroyed the wood and slate carvings that were the signs of power of the chieftain families (Chiang 1993: 157) – artefacts made by *pulima* persons.

The imported materials of cement, bricks and concrete were not imposed as construction materials, but the properties of these materials were apt to be used in the context of assimilation policies: they were useful in adapting

192 *Geoffrey Gowlland*

to the image of modernity and civilisation that was promoted by the state, notably in terms of house hygiene. Cement and tiles created smooth, uniform surfaces, contrasting with the jagged surfaces of slate, and the nooks and crannies that slate walls and flooring create. The creative work of the *shifu* was then also, and at the same time, a creative work to shape who the Paiwan people were in relation to the majority population and the state. This creative work shaped not only the aesthetics of built surfaces, but also how houses were experienced. The walls of slate houses are porous, the air passes through the gaps of the dry stone walls, and slate has certain thermal qualities that prevent houses from overheating in summer. Imported materials in contrast – cement, mortar, concrete, tiles – create impermeable envelopes that prevent the air from passing except through windows, and the interiors of concrete houses can get stifling on hotter days. The subjective experience of the house was transformed with the work of the *shifu*, and this subjective experience was at the same time a transformation of the Paiwan subject in relations of power, in the midst of heavy-handed assimilationist policies.

(Re)New(ed) subjectivities: *pulima*

I started the chapter with a contrast between two terms denoting skilled persons, *pulima* and *shifu*. I have looked at the meaning of being *shifu*, a return migrant worker, someone who acquired skills in a foreign place, and used these skills and knowledge to transform the material environment of the Paiwan settlement. In this section, I want to take a closer look at people who are recognised in the settlement as *pulima*. Again, one can consider this term against a historical backdrop. *Pulima* people are integral part of Paiwan culture, persons recognised (including by chieftains who acknowledge the work of *pulima* with gifts) for their talents in many domains requiring the work of the hands. The term could be translated as a 'talent', but it is not the individualistic talent of Western creativity (Leach 1998, Hughes-Freeland 2005) since *pulima* originates in ancestral power. But the term has taken on new meanings in the context of revitalisation of Paiwan culture and the Taiwanese indigenous movement that gained momentum in the late 1990s. A number of successes of this movement lead to the recognition of Austronesian speakers as indigenous peoples in the mid-1990s, which included the recognition of collective rights, and the reversal of assimilationist policies.

The revitalisation of craft practices played a defining role in the indigenous movement. One of Paridrayan's natives, Sakuliu Pavavalung, became the most revered of indigenous artists on Taiwan. He was the son of a *pulima* person known for his building knowledge and fine carvings. As a child, at the time of assimilation and Sinicisation policies, Sakuliu was a model pupil, winning Chinese calligraphy competitions; he went on to start a career as a civil servant. In part due to his experience as an anthropologist's research assistant in his own village (Sakuliu was selected in part for his good spoken and written Chinese), he became interested in the history and culture of his people, at a time when the Paiwan, as all other Austronesians in Taiwan, were considered culturally backwards and in need of civilising. Talking to elders, he gathered knowledge about Paiwan material culture. He decided to revive the production of pottery that the Paiwan had abandoned centuries earlier, learnt to carve wood and slate, and eventually became an authority on Paiwan culture, and an indigenous activist. He taught craft skills to village youths, many of whom are now artisans and artists recognised nationally and in some cases internationally, and his approach to revitalisation and teaching of indigenous crafts has been replicated around Taiwan. Through his practice, Sakuliu transformed himself from an example of accomplished state Sinicisation efforts to a major force in Taiwan's indigenous movement.

In contrast to the knowledge of the *shifu* relating to foreign materials, the practices of *pulima* are largely grounded in knowledge of the mountains and its material resources, and of the practices and crafts of the past. This has not prevented some to experiment with imported materials too, for instance in creating metal sculptures or experimenting with combining concrete and local materials in buildings. After all, to be *pulima* is to be skilled in many domains, and have the knowledge to work with many materials.

The Paiwan might not draw the same contrast as I am between *shifu* and *pulima*. A *shifu*, someone who has specialised skills acquired in the construction industry, might also be recognised as *pulima*. But these two terms capture contrasts between forms of knowledge, practices and materials. I suggested in the previous section that the *shifu* were engaged through their skilled work in the transformation of what it means to be Paiwan, responding to state promoted ideals of modernity. Paiwan artists and artisans participating in the revitalisation of crafts are engaged in another phase of this transformation: figuring out what it means to live as indigenous people in a settler society now that they are recognised as indigenous and after the end of state assimilation efforts.

To add to the discussion on the creative work of the *pulima*, I could talk about my own experience of learning to carve slate and wood from Cemelesai Takivalit, one of the many talented artists of Paridrayan. In the short period of learning and practising, I learnt to respond to different kinds of hardness of wood, learnt about the particular resistance of the material when the carving knife encounters the knots in wood, or how slate reacts when it is chipped away in a carving. Ingold's (2010) descriptions of the work of craft could help me characterise this practice: materials have a particular textility that is felt through the tools and into the fingers. The act of carving is open-ended, one cannot impose pre-defined form but rather creatively engage with the materials. But my relation to these materials is different from that of my teacher, and not only because he is more experienced than I am. He learnt to carve at a time when he was seeing Paiwan practices and material forms being replaced by imported ones. He became dedicated to his practice at a time when it was expected that young people, and especially men, move out of the settlement to engage in wage labour, and he had to endure the disapprobation of other villagers. His sense of slate as a material was acquired from working with, and living in the midst of, this material, and emerged through a particular life trajectory.

I mentioned how the cement and concrete structures built by the *shifu* transformed the experience of house interiors, shaping the subjectivities of villagers, both how they experienced the village and situating them within the power relations of assimilation. As part of revitalisation efforts, *pulima* persons reintroduced carved images, and promoted once more the use of slate, for instance to rebuild dry-stone walls and paths. The flank of the mountain alongside the road leading to the village has for instance been decorated with dozens of slate carvings, firmly indicating that this is an indigenous Paiwan village (Figure 12.3), and reintroducing a Paiwan aesthetic that contrasts with the aesthetics of imported materials still visible in many buildings in the village.

In 2010, in the aftermath of the previous year's typhoon Morakot that caused much damage to the village of Paridrayan and the road leading to it, villagers were offered the possibility to move to a new settlement closer to the plains. In that new environment, the houses that were built with the

Figure 12.3 Slate carving near the village of Paridrayan, representing the 100-pacer snake, considered the 'friend' of the Paiwan people, 2013.

Photo by the author.

financing of a non-governmental organisation bore little resemblance to Paiwan vernacular housing, despite villagers asking to use slate as a building material. In the years after the displacement, resident artists have contributed to shape the village to make it more their own, notably integrating slate in existing structures, and in the form of carvings. In this new environment too, the *pulima* are engaged in creative work to shape the daily experiences of villagers. Through their creative work, and to use a concept defined by James Clifford (2001), they *articulate* the tension between the desire for resilience as indigenous people in Taiwan, and the need to adapt to the realities of living in a settler society (in other words, their subject positions) (Gowlland 2020). The creative work of building can then be thought of as creative engagement with what it means to be Paiwan at different periods, in the 1970s or more recently: whether to accept the necessity of assimilation, or to be resilient to such pressures. The village is an extension of Paiwan skilled subjects, it grows through the skilled work of the *pulima* and *shifu*, and in material forms we can see layers of work that hint at changing creative engagements with building materials, changing ways of experiencing the built environment and changing relations of power.

Conclusion

In my research on the Paiwan, I found it difficult to single out the creative practices I encountered from the politics of assimilation and of indigenous cultural revitalisation and activism. Paiwan people coming to skilled practice are already certain kinds of subject as indigenous people living in a settler society, and in a state of becoming subjects through skilled practice as they negotiate the terms of this subject position. Starting with the enskilled subject provides a framework in which there is no need to artificially separate these two aspects of the lives of skilled practitioners, namely the practice and experience of making, and the political 'context' of the practice. The terms *pulima* and *shifu* were relevant to this discussion on enskilment because they refer to the political subjects who are engaged in skilled practice.

The concept of the enskilled subject has several implications for research. First, it brings us to acknowledge the subjectivity gap between ethnographer engaged in skilled practice and skilled interlocutors, and the different life trajectories that shape respective experiences of creative work. This implies that we cannot assume a politically neutral skilled practice or practitioner, or universal bodily experience of practice distinct from life trajectories and subject positions. In turn, we have to acknowledge the inseparable twin meanings of 'subjectivity' in creative practice, the experience of making, and the position of the maker in relations of power.

The literature on enskilment qualifies the concept of enskilled subject: skilled practice is creative and open-ended (Hallam and Ingold 2007). There is a distinction to be made between creativity and habituation. One of the

196   *Geoffrey Gowlland*

principles of the MaP approach is that items of material culture become consequential in mediating relations of power when they become second-nature and part of our habitual gestures (Julien et al. 2009a; Douny and Mohan, Introduction to this volume). There is room for creativity within this theoretical framework. The focus on creativity highlights moments of attentive engagement with materials in contrast to 'distracted' habituation (Taussig 1991). A reflection on what it means to be engaged with materials in processes of making invites an attention to open-ended processes of subjectivation. The *shifu* and the *pulima* each have been involved in the transformation of subjectivities: through creative engagements with local or new materials, they shaped villagers' experience of the built environment, and shaped their own subject positions and those of fellow villagers. They contributed to the transformation of Paiwan people into modern subjects as promoted by the state, or alternatively enabled resilience in Paiwan ways of living and identity. The idea of the enskilled subject allows us to recognise and embrace the subjectivity gap that is necessarily part of our investigations into creative practices.

Acknowledgements

This article is based on fieldwork activities supported in part by a Taiwan Fellowship, awarded in 2012 by the Ministry of Foreign Affairs, Republic of China, and a Postdoctoral Fellowship awarded by the Cultural History Museum, University of Oslo (2014–2017). I am thankful to my Paiwan interlocutors who welcomed me during my stay in Taiwan and were available to talk about their lives and culture.

Note

1. The policies of Sinicisation applied also to the ethnic Chinese native populations: Mandarin Chinese, a foreign language also to the Taiwanese Chinese, was imposed, and history and geography of mainland China was taught in schools throughout Taiwan.

References

Bloch, M. (1991), 'Language, Anthropology and Cognitive Science', *Man*, 26 (2): 183–198.

Chi, C.-C. (2016), 'Indigenous Movements and Multicultural Taiwan', in Schubert, Gunter (ed.), *Routledge Handbook of Contemporary Taiwan*, pp. 268–279, London: Routledge.

Chiang, B. (1993), *House and Social Hierarchy of the Paiwan*, Philadelphia: University of Pennsylvania.

Chibnik, M. (2003), *Crafting Tradition: The Making and Marketing of Oaxacan Wood Carvings*, Austin: University of Texas Press.

Ching, L. T. S. (2001), *Becoming 'Japanese'*, Berkeley, Calif: University of California Press.

Clifford, J. (2001), 'Indigenous Articulations', *The Contemporary Pacific*, 13 (2): 467–490.

Coy, M. (1989), 'From Theory', in *Apprenticeship: From Theory to Method and Back Again*, pp. 1–11, Albany, N.Y: State University of New York Press.

Damasio, A. (2010), *Self Comes to Mind: Constructing the Conscious Brain*, New York: Pantheon.

Downey, G. et al. (2015), 'Apprenticeship as Method: Embodied Learning in Ethnographic Practice', *Qualitative Research*, 15 (2): 183–200.

Downey, G. (2005), *Learning Capoeira: Lessons in Cunning From an Afro-Brazilian Art*, Oxford: Oxford University Press.

Forty, A. (2013), *Concrete and Culture: A Material History*, London: Reaktion Books.

Gowlland, G. (2020), 'The Materials of Indigeneity: Slate and Cement in a Taiwanese Indigenous (Paiwan) Mountain Settlement', *JRAI*, 26 (1): 126–145.

Hallam, E. and T. Ingold (2007), 'Creativity and Cultural Improvisation: An Introduction', in Ingold, Tim and Elizabeth Hallam (eds.), *Creativity and Cultural Improvisation*, pp. 1–24, Oxford: Berg.

Hughes-Freeland, F. (2005), 'Tradition and the Individual Talent': T.S. Eliot for Anthropologists', *Cambridge Anthropology*, 25 (2): 20–35.

Ingold, T. (2007), *Lines: A Brief History*, London: Routledge.

Ingold, T. (2010), 'The Textility of Making', *Cambridge Journal of Economics*, 34 (1): 91–102.

Ingold, T. (2012), 'Toward an Ecology of Materials', *Annual Review of Anthropology*, 41 (1): 427–442.

Julien, M.-P. et al. (2009a), 'Pour une anthropologie du matériel', in Julien, Marie-Pierre & Céline Rosselin (eds.), *Le sujet contre les objets… tout contre : Ethnographies de cultures matérielles*, pp. 85–110, Paris: CTHS.

Julien, M.-P. et al. (2009b), '"Subjectivité", "subjectivation", "sujet": dialogue', in Julien, Marie-Pierre and Céline Rosselin (eds.), *Le sujet contre les objets… tout contre : Ethnographies de cultures matérielles*, pp. 111–168, Paris: CTHS.

Knappett, C. (2011), 'Networks of Objects, Meshworks of Things', in Ingold, Tim (ed.), *Redrawing Anthropology: Materials, Movements, Lines*, pp. 45–63, Farnham: Ashgate..

Leach, J. (1998), 'Where Does Creativity Reside? Imagining Places on the Rai Coast of Papua New Guinea', *Cambridge Anthropology*, 20 (1/2): 16–21.

Lemonnier, P. (2004), 'Mythiques chaînes opératoires', *Techniques & Culture, Revue semestrielle d'anthropologie des techniques*, 43–44: 25–43

Malafouris, L. (2008), 'At the Potter's Wheel : An Argument for Material Agency', in Lambros Malafouris and Carl Knappett (eds.), *Material Agency*, pp. 19–36, New York, NY: Springer US.

Marchand, T. (2003), 'A Possible Explanation for the Lack of Explanation; Or "Why the Master Builder Can't Explain What He Knows": Introducing Informational Atomism Against a "Definitional" Definition of Concepts', in Bicker, Alan et al. (eds.), *Negotiating Local Knowledge: Power and Identity in Development*, pp. 30–50, London: Pluto Press.

Moeran, B. (1997), *Folk Art Potters of Japan: Beyond an Anthropology of Aesthetics*, Richmond: Curzon.

Prentice, R. (2008), 'Knowledge, Skill, and the Inculcation of the Anthropologist: Reflections on Learning to Sew in the Field', *Anthropology of Work Review*, 29 (3): 54–61.

Sigaut, F. (1993), 'Learning, Teaching, and Apprenticeship', *New Literary History*, 24 (1): 105–114.

Taussig, M. (1991), 'Tactility and Distraction', *Cultural Anthropology*, 6 (2): 147–153.

Warnier, J.-P. (2011), 'Bodily/Material Culture and the Fighter's Subjectivity', *Journal of Material Culture*, 16 (4): 359–375.

Yang, S.-Y. (2001), *Coping with Marginality: The Bunun in Contemporary Taiwan*. PhD thesis. London School of Economics and Political Science. Available from: http://etheses.lse.ac.uk/1631/1/U155956.pdf (last accessed 11 October 2017).

13 Afterword

Matter(s) of material culture

Nathan Schlanger

A solid bedrock

What is striking in equal measure, reaching towards the end this volume, are the diversity and the coherence of its contributions. The 'fieldworks' or 'terrains' explored by the authors reach far and wide, both geographically and thematically. Besides France (and Switzerland), they range from North and Sub-Saharan Africa to the Indian sub-continent and the islands of the Far East, and from the lingering odours surrounding municipal divers and waste managers to the rarefied atmosphere of Parisian museums, from the transmission of skills among Swiss watchmakers to the swapping of shirts among suburban teenagers. Inbetween we encounter, weavers of spirited fabrics, wearers of charismatic silks, dressers of altar deities and upholders of royal powers. In a broad spectrum spanning from behaviourism to phenomenology, the contributions we have just read, and more generally the *Matière à Penser* (MaP) approach they exemplify, are all situated far closer to the latter pole. To be sure, a range of 'objective' measures are at hand, epistemologically and methodologically speaking, including field enquiries, participant observation, pseudonymised interviews and apprenticeship immersion, as variously attested in the chapters by Céline Rosselin-Bareille, Marie-Pierre Julien, Urmila Mohan, Hervé Munz or Geoffrey Gowlland. Granted that, these are quite manifestly subjects – and more specifically subjects-in-becoming, acting, with and on their bodies, with and on things – that occupy here pride of place.

Put otherwise, the chapters across this volume convey a diversified and stimulating array of material culture-aided introspections, whereby subjects – be they scavengers, believers, craftspeople or dressed-up kids (and grown-ups) – performatively incorporate the material world into their beings. Alongside Marcel Mauss' famous *homme total*, fleshed out already in the inter-war years as a fusion of physiological, psychological and social realms (as recalled in the introductory chapter by Laurence Douny and Urmila Mohan), the thread linking most contributions together resides in their phenomenological reliance, so to speak, on material culture, lived and thought-with. Rather than being reduced to the mere provision of

200   *Nathan Schlanger*

subsistence needs, or elevated into a scaffold on which to suspend symbolic meanings, this category is posited here as an ontological and epistemological bedrock on which to rest and to build.

This is not to say that uniformity of purpose is attained or indeed sought for. Some contributors readily consider material culture in the plural, as in Jean-Pierre Warnier's statement that 'actions on self and on others rest on a huge diversity of bodily techniques, themselves propped on complex material cultures' (see also Mohan and others): are we then to infer as many and as equally diverse 'material cultures' as there are bodily techniques? And how, to give a further example, are we to square much touted notions of agentivity or even affordance – let alone the Maussian insight whereby things given can capture and convey something of their givers – with Mélanie Roustan's assertion, à propos museum collections, that 'a material culture approach "in praxis" implies that objects have no essence; rather they are embodied by actions' – as if unable to bear or to evoke anything, left to stand on their own? It may well be, furthermore, that 'material culture, materials, objects and the divers co-define themselves together' as Céline Rosselin-Bareille sums up her discussion of the tacit strategies of public works divers – what purpose, however, might be served by considering 'threads, ropes, straps, pipes, tape rolls of various colours, tire tubes, pieces of wood, plywood, polystyrene, metal .... [as being] the *material culture* that is recovered at the end of a (...) worksite'?

So, much like waste products and such odds-and-ends, also the meanings and functions ascribed to 'material culture' seem to come in haphazard heaps rather than coherent series. What sense can we get, across these examples, of what could be meant by 'material culture'? Of what does the expression serve as a synonym or an extension? How might these usages differ from other strands of 'material culture studies', notably as invigorated over the past three decades or so through the so-called 'material turn', henceforth surging throughout the humanities and the social sciences? Encouraged by Douny and Mohan's introductory exhortation whereby 'in this book, the theoretical and analytical concepts developed in a specific milieu are used by MaP *'by considering the history of ideas that precedes them',* I will dedicate the coming pages to a historical overview of this so central and yet so often taken for granted notion of 'material culture'. Such an overview will necessarily be brief, and merely touch upon a selected range of theoretical and historiographic considerations, mainly in the Anglo-Saxon and the French traditions. In the process, some light will hopefully be shed on the so essential links postulated here between subjects, bodies and the cultural materials which they make, and of which they are made.

Historiographic retroprojections

The point is not, it should be evident, to normalise any attested fluctuations or discrepancies in the uses and meanings of 'material culture'. It is rather to

Afterword   201

acknowledge this variability, across time and space and research traditions, and then further examine some of its causes and consequences. After all, as we embrace 'material culture' as a theory-friendly panacea, as a MaP par excellence, we might also recall some of the challenges it has encountered, and occasioned, through the history of its usages. A range of publications dealing generically with 'material culture' are of course available – to those mentioned by Douny and Mohan (in their introductory chapter) can be added Buchli (ed. 2002) and Hicks and Beaudry (2010). Granted the relevance and diversity of these works, there still remains much to explore from a critical historical standpoint about 'material culture', as a concept and as a category.

The first challenge to overcome is historiographic, in view of some widespread but rather unwarranted retrospections. The prevailing impression is that 'material culture' has been around forever, as a straightforward and constitutive fixture of post-enlightenment anthropological enquiry. Evolutionist and Victorian anthropology in particular, together with early twentieth-century culture-historical diffusionism, – the whole often lumped together as the 'museum age' – are repeatedly portrayed as the 'heydays' of material culture studies, which then occupied both conceptual and institutional centre stage. As D. Miller put it a while ago, 'At that period of the nineteenth century when the discipline of anthropology was coming into being, material culture studies represented the very core of this emergent social science (e.g., Haddon 1895, Tylor 1881)' (Miller 1987: 110). There is no doubting that early anthropologists and museum curators dedicated much efforts to the collection, documentation and study of a vast array of things …but not, so it happens, 'material culture', insofar as this generic, evocative and all-encompassing notion was simply not available for these founding fathers to conceptualise, explore and convey their interests. In an otherwise compelling article, T. Schlereth may note that 'an early scholarly use of the term "material culture" was by the nineteenth-century anthropologist, A. Lane-Fox Pitt-Rivers' (Schlereth 1985: 1). Yet, even his provision of a specific page number will not conjure any 'material culture' in Pitt-Rivers' work, certainly not as a notion with which to subsume and cohere, as we would expect of it today, the rather rambling presentation of his collection:

> [Part I. Physical anthropology]. Part II. The weapons of existing savages. Part III. Miscellaneous arts of modern savages, including pottery and substitutes for pottery; modes of navigation, clothing, textile fabrics, and weaving; personal ornament; realistic art; conventionalized art; ornamentation; tools; household furniture; musical instruments; idols and religious emblems; specimens of the written character of races; horse furniture; money and substitute for money; firearms; sundry smaller classes of objects, such as mirrors, spoons, combs, games and a collection of implements of modern savages, arranged to illustrate the mode of hafting stone implements. Part IV refers to the prehistoric series (…) (Pitt Rivers 1906 [1874]: 1).

202　*Nathan Schlanger*

Notwithstanding its historical shortcomings (see similar postulates in Pfaffenberger 1992: 491–495, Schatzberg 2018, Stocking 1995: 3, 105 passim), the retrospective attribution of 'material culture' to its alleged Golden Age is not without disciplinary implications – some no doubt welcomed by current practitioners. For one, the idea instilled here is that 'material culture' is somehow an inherent, permanent, natural category. No surprise therefore, despite several decades of decline – attributed to changing fieldwork practices (i.e., taking notes rather than objects) and to the rise of university teaching, by the likes of Boas, Malinowski or Lévi-Strauss – that this category can be expected now to re-emerge with renewed conceptual vigour and intellectual relevance. Together with that, this narrative implicitly maintains 'material culture' within the academic sphere, as a neutral, unmarked field of erudite internalist considerations – rather than as a category inherently replete with 'danger', as Mauss once put it, a category that, very much like anthropology at large, is fully embroiled within wider economic, political, imperial and indeed post-colonial debates (see Fowles 2016, Schlanger 2012).

'Culture' and 'material'

In the United States, the final decades of the nineteenth century saw the Washington-based *Bureau of American Ethnology* dedicating much attention to indigenous processes of production and consumption, notably as a means to redeem and to resettle those rapidly vanishing 'Indians'. In contrast, the 'new' discipline soon to take over asserted rather that 'the interests of anthropological science requires ... that those line of human activity that do *not* find expression in material objects – namely language, thought, customs and, I may add, anthropomorphic measurements – be investigated thoroughly and carefully', as Franz Boas decisively argued to S. Langley in 1902 (quoted in Hinsley 1981, see Schlanger 1999). Nevertheless, paradoxically, it was very much on Boas' watch, so to speak, that the expression 'material culture' first gained its anthropological foothold. Admittedly, some early twentieth-century uses harked back to the evolutionist preoccupations of Tylor and Morgan. When the British authors of *The Material Culture and Social Institutions of the Simpler Peoples - An Essay in Correlation* (Hobhouse, Wheeler and Ginsberg 1915 – one of the earliest books with such a title) focussed on 'material culture', being 'the control by man over nature as reflected in the arts of life', this was effectively because it represented a tangible, widespread and significant indicator of the inexorable march of progress (ibid. 1915: 5–6).

Notwithstanding such an 'incremental marker' conception, 'material culture' first secured its visibility and relevance as category within an encompassing classificatory framework (attested, for example, in early issues of *American Anthropology*, or the 1905 Jessup expedition), alongside the likes of 'mental culture', 'religious culture' and 'social culture'. As we know, these

Afterword 203

other headings soon merged and fused into 'culture' *tout court*, thus placing this concept – of which Boas remains the quintessential hero – at the forefront. Even if we skip over its innumerable definitions, we need to specify the kind of 'culture' that is on the cards for 'material culture' to be plausible and useful, in post-evolutionist times. Firstly, such a 'culture' is set to be *universal*, common to and constitutive of humanity as a whole – an understanding which, by the way, leaves in suspense not only our *pre-sapiens* prehistoric ancestors, but also the eventual occurrence of 'culture', let alone of 'material culture', among so-called non-humans, be they animals, actants or other cyborgs (McGrew 1992, Haraway 1989). Moreover, the 'culture' sought here appears also to be *particularistic* and relativistic, insofar as it displays from group to group (communities, societies, ethnicities and the like) differences which, however systematic and accountable they may be, there is neither theoretical need or ethical justification to rank and to judge.

Yet, even in this broad acceptation, 'material culture' led no easy life throughout the twentieth century, often viewed with suspicion by the very same scholars who made of 'culture' the grail of anthropology. Thus, Alfred Kroeber, considering material and non-material culture, noted that 'The literal difference is of course obvious: physical objects as against institutions and ideas. But do they stand for something basically different? Do they function with significant difference in culture? The answer seems No'. After all, he disconcertingly added, 'What counts is not the physical axe or coat or wheat but the idea of them, the knowledge how to produce and use them, their place in life'. (Kroeber 1948: 295). Likewise, Cornelius Osgood could assert that 'material culture' was a contradiction in terms, since the real cultural entities are the conceptual norms or patterns, and not their particular expression (see Bidney 1944). And when, a generation later, George Kubler made of the 'history of things' the leitmotif of his celebrated *The Shape of Time*, this was deliberately to substitute it against 'the bristling ugliness of "material culture" [, used] by anthropologists to distinguish ideas, or "mental culture", from artifacts' (Kubler 1962: 9).

Thus, whereas numerous scholars nowadays, from across disciplines and traditions, readily consider the expression 'material culture' as a useful pleonasm to get their exegesis going – including, of course, contributors to this volume, focussing as they do on the interface between materiality and subject-in-becoming – the concept has also been tasked and dismissed as an oxymoron, crushed under its 'material' weight. Besides and beyond the *ontological* properties of materials (physical, tangible, emanating from nature) and their *epistemological* virtues (objective, measurable, factual), these are mostly their *interpretative* or frankly ideological connotations that seem to stir up trouble. As we saw above, strands of more or less vulgar Victorian materialism have tended to persist and resurface. Notably in archaeology, they appear as acknowledged functionalist or determinist prioritising of subsistence needs and adaptive strategies, unless they are taken as instances of a 'methodological materialism' which restricts explanatory powers to securely

204 *Nathan Schlanger*

and 'etically' graspable evidence (Harris 1968). As the sole survivor of a classificatory system initially willed to encompass all the segments of cultural 'totality', 'material culture' ended up, for some, as a heretic gauntlet to the primacy of the 'non-material'. What this analysis also highlights is the essentially idealist, psychologising orientation of large swaths of Anglo-American theoretical anthropology for much of the century – in fact, well into the above mentioned 'material turn' attempts in the 1980s and 1990s to bring the social and symbolic 'life of things' to the fore. And, still today, when some items or others are labelled as 'material culture' – be they Pitt-Rivers' erstwhile collectible 'spoons, combs, games', or, closer home, the 'straps, pipes, tape rolls of various colours' amassed by Rosselin-Bareille's divers – this is very often in order to recover in them, beyond their dire materiality or utilitarian vocation, some symbolic and ideal supplement of soul.

Meanwhile, French civilisation

Until the last decades of the twentieth century, 'material culture' has had a rather subdued presence in francophone lands, with different historical and scientific configurations at play, as well as diverse appreciations of the notions of 'material' and of 'culture'. With their sociological propensities honed by Comte and Durkheim, many French scholars have taken issue with the concept of 'culture', especially in its more traditional or para-anthropological sense of acquired refinement and aesthetic sensibility, a distinctive *bildung* attained by self-acclaimed 'cultured' individuals, and by extension, communities and even nations, and then disseminated as distinct 'traits' or 'forms' across time and space. To this idealist culture-historical conception, often cast as 'Germanic', has been systematically opposed a satisfyingly enlightened notion of 'civilisation', as a collectively elaborated, cross-social and large-scale undertaking, both rational and universal in scope, and readily grounded in tangible material and infrastructural achievements. Tellingly, one of the earliest French books featuring the Boasian version of 'material culture', by Americanist Alfred Métraux, was entitled *La civilisation matérielle des tribus tupi-guarani* (1928). By that time, Mauss had joined forces with *Annales* school and *Revue de synthèse* historians to critique the expansionist idealism of his *Kuturkreise* protagonists, and to champion instead a sociologically-oriented concept of 'civilisation'. Just as there are no peoples without civilisation, he had long argued, so have they all their *civilisations matérielles* – a concept that reached its pinnacle, in the singular or the plural, with the post World War II *longue durée* of historian Fernand Braudel (see Bert 2009, Bénéton 1975, Braudel 1979, Mauss 1930).

Better even than *civilisation matérielle*, the commonly used *'vie matérielle'* confirms a definite lack of inhibition towards materialism, at least in its theoretical guises. Some might have shied at its ideological connotations, and Durkheim for one, when tasked with historical materialism, hastily abandoned his initial inquiries into the 'material' and 'moral densities' of industrial societies, in favour of a 'primitive' religious superstructure compatible with secular republican morality (Schlanger 2012). Others however felt no such inhibitions: alongside avant-garde artistic movements such as the *'bas matérialisme'* of Georges Bataille, several of their anthropological and museological accomplices also proved attuned to this perspective, including Marcel Mauss and Paul Rivet. The ethnographic exhaustivity they called for in their teachings at the *Institut d'ethnologie* (which they co-founded with L. Lévy-Bruhl in 1925) clearly echoed epistemological ambitions, but their repeated appeal to fieldworkers to observe, gather and document all possible materials also sprang from genuine theoretical concerns. Mauss' writings and teachings on the topic are quite clear (see Mauss 2006, 2012), as are the *Summary Instructions for the Collectors of Ethnographic Objects* (attributed to Mauss's influence) issued by the *Musée d'ethnographie* at the occasion of the 1931 Dakar-Djibouti expedition:

> A collection of ethnographic objects is neither a collection of curiosities, nor of oeuvres d'art. The object is nothing but a witness, which should be envisaged in function of the information it provides regarding a given civilisation, and not following its aesthetic value. We must therefore become used to collect all kinds of objects and get rid of two prejudices, the prejudice of *the purity of style* [– 'All is mixture, product of disparate influences, result of multiple factors (...) We should in no way reject an object in the pretext that it is 'impure'. Even marked by European influence, an indigenous object must be collected' –] and the prejudice of *rarity* [– 'The most common objects are those who teach us most on a civilisation. A tin can, for example, characterises better our societies that the most sumptuous jewel or the rarest stamp. We should therefore have no fear to collect even the humblest or most despised things' –]. (Anonymous 1931: 8–9, emphasis added, my translation).

What seems to be here within reach (and see Rivet 1929 for similar exhortations to reach the *'aspects moyens'* of material civilisations), through this plethora of mundane objects, with their admixtures, their imperfections and their signs of use all systematically documented and researched, was the 'life of society' as a whole, including its ordinary, average, common or popular aspects (*sensu* pertaining to the people) – these all-too-often invisible masses that remain so notoriously elusive as objects of anthropological, historical and archaeological inquiry (see notably, Bourgeois et al. eds. 2018, Miller 2017, Pesez 1978, Roche 1997). Incidentally, given that the founding intention underlying these ethnographic collections was to reach beyond any pre-imposed art-historical and aesthetic vistas – and also, despite some shared documentary practices, away from the trait- and style- approach of the diffusionist school – it is surely an ironic regression to see so many items ending up (for now, at least) translocated into a Parisian museum bent on parading the 'fine arts' of the Others.

206 *Nathan Schlanger*

Be it is as it may, there is clearly in these sundry object lessons a potential for questioning and destabilising some entrenched aesthetic and socio-political orders. All the more so, as recalled here by Gowlland, Bertrand and Warnier, that the skilled practices involved in making and using them remain political to the core. So, in some cases, as indicated above, the naming of some items as 'material culture' is meant to elevate them, as it were, into the realm of semiotic and symbolic meanings. In other cases, however, applied to a different array of items – be they museum objects whose avatars are pursued here by Roustan, or Greek red-on-black pots studied by radical classical scholars in 1970s Italy and Germany – this designation of 'material culture' rather serves to bring them down from their ethereal Olympus and back into the nitty-gritties of material sciences and production processes, not to forget contentious divisions of labour and insidious tactics of consumption.

What is more, besides challenging the purity of styles and underpinning the politics of skills, another field of research has opened up with these modest paraphernalia of daily life – around the 'techniques of the body'. Just as the body was the first and most natural instrument of each human being, as Mauss argued in his famous presidential address to the society of psychology, so there existed in his view techniques of the body with instruments, as well as without (Mauss 1936, and see Bert 2012, Schlanger 2019). These *habitus*-substantiating objects included African wooden stools used as pillows to sleep on, or Moroccan leather slippers worn with astounding dexterity, and also those English-issued digging spades which Mauss and his comrades had found so awkward to handle in the trenches of the First World War – this relentless fieldwork of modernity. Such a perspective requires no further justification here, since the idea that the body encompasses objects through actions is so well established among all MaP contributors. It is worth recalling, however, that an early adherent to this approach was André-Georges Haudricourt, one of Mauss' most original students. As an agronomist, linguist and ethnographer, Haudricourt undertook a range of studies on the human motor, on ploughing, harnessing, animal husbandry and plant domestication, including, as he titled his 1948 paper, on 'The Relations Between Habitual Gestures, the Shape of Clothing, and the Manner of Carrying Charges' (see Haudricourt 1987, 2010, Sigaut 1987). As it happened, Haudricourt elaborated his contribution without much concern (to my knowledge) for the constitution of subjectivity, let alone appeals to any notion of 'material culture'. Not only was Haudricourt resolutely in the camp of 'civilisation' against 'culture' (pers. com., and see Bert 2009), he was also, within the distinctive research tradition he contributed to create, an ardent promoter of *'La technologie, science humaine'*.

To end with technology

So, we can perhaps now turn to consider, in rounding up this far too rapid overview, the relations between the notions 'material culture' (until recently

Afterword 207

fairly marginal, in France) and a seemingly dominant 'technology'. Are these terms convergent or complementary, with one focusing on production, and the other on consumption? Do they occupy the same scientific and intellectual space ('materiality'?), and render the same disciplinary services? French perspectives on technology, since the days of Mauss, of Haudricourt and indeed of André Leroi-Gourhan, Mauss' other famous follower in this field of research, are undoubtedly well known. Technology is the social and human science that studies techniques, understood as 'traditional efficient acts' (to recall Mauss' formulation), as 'the productive forces' (following Haudricourt), or as 'the means by which humans act on their environment' (as Leroi-Gourhan put it, and see a range of appraisals in Coupaye and Douny 2009, Digard 1979, Loeve and Deldicque 2018, Segalen and Bromberger eds. 1996, Sigaut 1994, 2013, Vatin 2004). So, notwithstanding some inconsistencies due in part to over-globalised linguistic and scientific drift, *'technologie'* has long been used not as a qualifier of industrialised modernity (e.g., fishing techniques vs. nuclear technology), but as a logos or discourse on its subject matter. This meaning, as a matter of fact, rejoins and substantially overlaps with that of 'material culture *studies*' – itself a well-accepted Anglo-Saxon designation, though probably not dating earlier than the 1980s, and no doubt conceived or adopted on the wake of the then emerging 'cultural studies', 'visual studies' and the like.

This is not to say that ambiguity and room for manoeuvre have not prevailed between 'techniques' and *'technologie',* some of it quite productive and useful. The notion of *'technologie primitive'* can be mentioned in this respect, applied as it was in interwar ethnological writings to indigenous industries and arts as well as to their study. This leeway extended with the newer term of *'technologie comparée',* an implicitly decolonised appellation characteristic of the eponymous research laboratory at the *musée de l'Homme.* The relatively recent designation of *'anthropologie des techniques',* with its disciplinary specification, is even more straightforward in its application across the board, to both 'us' moderns and 'the others' (cf. Lemonnier 1992, Cresswell 1996). On the other hand, the term *'technologie culturelle'* may well rekindle the above encountered quandaries involving redundancy and non-sequitur. What would a technology be (here *sensu* techniques, in fact) that is not cultural? Natural? 'Technical'? Can techniques be conceived (or indeed studied) without or outside culture? Conversely, can 'culture' (in its anthropological, let alone 'Germanic' senses) be at all attained and made sense of through (mere) technology? Such debates have found echo since the early 1980s in the growing literature, including the title, and occasionally the pages of the revue *Techniques & Culture.* The mirror notion of 'Techniques & Nature', by the way, seems to make increasing sense, just as the expression 'material nature', set in a diptych with 'material culture', might find its takers (see Ingold 2000) to highlight the intangible, skilled and lived-in dimensions of both nature and culture in the making.

208   *Nathan Schlanger*

Upon this, it is interesting to observe, historically, that mentions of 'material culture' actually occur quite frequently in Leroi-Gourhan's early writings (1964, 1965, 1993), though they will become much scarcer later on, and effectively vanish from *Le Geste et la parole*. These mentions rather refer back to a 'classic' conception of culture, implying the acquisition and the mastery of knowledge. The peoples whose specific tools or techniques are discussed, for example in *L'homme et la matière* and *Milieu et techniques*, are said to have a well-mastered or a poorly-developed 'material culture', alongside their 'spiritual culture' (Leroi-Gourhan 1936, 1943, 1945; Schlanger (2021); and see Soulier's (2018) definitive biography of Leroi-Gourhan). To be sure, these are above all the key notions of technology, techniques and technicity that predominate in Leroi-Gourhan's publications, spanning as they do from ethnographic experimentation through Bergsonian philosophy to paleontological emulation. Within this broad framework, Leroi-Gourhan developed highly relevant formulations – formulations that are generally relevant for an international readership, and more specifically to our MaP preoccupations here – regarding, for example, the notions of organ projection or exudates, exteriorisation from the body, incorporation within it, rhythmicity and sequence in both effective movements, and semiotic patterns, and the like. Last but not the least, the same relevance can be found in the notion of *chaîne opératoire* (operational chain). Besides its specifically descriptive, methodological use as a means to anchor material observations in time and space (as Douny and Mohan indicate in their introductory chapter), the *chaîne opératoire* as developed by Leroi-Gourhan and his anthropological and archaeological successors draws attention to the processes of transformation from naturally occurring raw materials through to culturally approved, used, and consumed products (amidst the growing literature, see Bouillon et al. eds. 2017, Coupaye and Douny 2009, Lemonnier 1992, Naji and Douny 2009, as well as the recent issue of *Techniques & Culture* dedicated to 'technographies', cf. Buob, Chevalier and Gosselain eds. 2019).

With further theoretical investments, a wider space can be opened here for considering together objects, behavior, body, perceptions and intentions. Recalling Mauss' insight that there are 'techniques of the body' with instruments as well as without, we can also appreciate Leroi-Gourhan's parallel observation whereby 'the tool really exists only within the gesture that renders it technically efficient' (Leroi-Gourhan 1965: 35). Such expectations have been expressed before (notably by A. Van Gennep, and by Mauss himself), and in Leroi-Gourhan's case they partly originated in a (self-addressed) critique of the illusory ambitions of the museum, pretending to exhaustively encompass the 'material culture' it holds (through the erstwhile *fiche d'objet* and nowadays its on-line multimedia database variants). Be it is as it may – and this is precisely what we can seek to obtain through a historical understanding of our disciplinary past and present, as I have briefly attempted to show in this Afterword – we can now seize upon and expand the idea that technical efficiency, recognised from the onset to be also cultural, social and symbolic, can be thoroughly constitutive of the subject-in-becoming.

References

Anonymous, (1931), *Instructions sommaires pour les collecteurs d'objets ethnographiques*, Musée d'ethnographie (Muséum national d'histoire naturelle) et mission Dakar-Djibouti, Paris: Palais du Trocadéro.

Bénéton, P. (1975), *Histoire de mots: Culture et civilisation*, Paris: Presses de la Fondation nationale des sciences politiques.

Bert, J. -F. (2009), 'Marcel Mauss et la notion de "civilisation"', *Cahiers de recherche sociologique*, 47: 123–142.

Bert, J. -F. (2012), *"Les techniques du corps" de Marcel Mauss. Dossier critique*, Paris: Publications de la Sorbonne.

Bidney, D. (1944), 'On the Concept of Culture and Some Cultural Fallacies', *American Anthropology*, 46: 30–44.

Bouillon D., A. Guillerme, M. Mille and G. Piernas, eds. (2017), *Gestes techniques, techniques du geste*, Paris: Septentrion.

Bourgeois L., D. Alexandre-Bidon, L. Feller, P. Mane, C. Verna and M. Wilmart, eds. (2018), *La culture matérielle: Un objet en question. Anthropologie, archéologie et histoire*, Caen: Publications du CRAHAM – Presses universitaire de Caen.

Braudel, F. (1979), *Civilisation matérielle, économie et capitalisme, XV-XVIII siècle. Tome 1. Les structures du quotidien: le possible et l'impossible*, Paris: Armand Colin.

Buchli, V., ed. (2002), *The Material Culture Reader*, Oxford: Berg.

Buob, B., D. Chevalier and O. Gosselain, eds. (2019), *Technographies, Techniques & Culture*, 71. https://journals.openedition.org/tc/10930, last accessed 3 September 2019.

Coupaye, L. and L, Douny (2009), 'Dans la trajectoire des choses. Comparaison des approches francophones et anglophones contemporaines en anthropologie des techniques', *Techniques & Culture*, 52–53: 12–39.

Cresswell, R. (1996), *Prométhée ou Pandore? Propos de technologie culturelle*, Paris: Kimé.

Digard, J. -P. (1979), 'La technologie en anthropologie: fin de parcours ou nouveau souffle?', *L'Homme*, 19 (1): 73–104.

Fowles, S. (2016), 'The Perfect Subject (Postcolonial Object Studies)', *Journal of Material Culture*, 21: 9–27.

Haraway, D. J. (1989), *Primate Visions. Gender, Race and Nature in the World of Modern Science*, London: Routledge.

Harris, M. (1968), *The Rise of Anthropological Theory: A History of Theories of Culture*, New York: Cromwell.

Haudricourt, A. -G. (1987), *La technologie science humaine. Recherches d'histoire et d'ethnologie des techniques*, Paris: Editions de la Maison des sciences de l'Homme.

Haudricourt, A. -G. (2010), *Des gestes aux techniques. Essai sur les techniques dans les sociétés pré-machinistes*, Paris: MESH Editions/Quæ.

Hicks, D. and M. Beaudry, eds. (2010), *The Oxford Handbook of Material Culture Studies*, Oxford: Oxford University Press.

Hinsley, C. M. (1981), *Savages and Scientists: The Smithsonian Institution and the Development of American Anthropology, 1846–1910*, Washington: Smithsonian Institution Press.

210 *Nathan Schlanger*

Hobhouse, L. T., G. C. Wheeler and M. Ginsberg, (1915), *The Material Culture and Social Institutions of the Simpler Peoples – An Essay in Correlation*, London: Chapman and Hall.

Ingold, T. (2000), *The Perception of the Environment. Essays in Livehood, Dwelling and Skill*, London and New York: Routledge.

Kroeber, A. L. (1948), *Anthropology. Race, Language, Culture, Psychology, Prehistory*, New York: Harcourt, Brace and Co.

Kubler, G. (1962), *The Shape of Time. Remarks on the History of Things*, New Haven: Yale University Press.

Lemonnier, P. (1992), *Elements for an Anthropology of Technology*, Anthropological Papers Museum of Anthropology, University of Michigan, No. 88, Ann Arbour: Michigan.

Leroi-Gourhan, A. (1936), 'L'homme et la nature', in *Encyclopédie française. VII L'espèce humaine*, Paris: Comité de l'Encyclopédie française édition.

Leroi-Gourhan, A. (1943), *Evolution et techniques. I, L'Homme et la matière*, Paris: Albin Michel.

Leroi-Gourhan, A. (1945), *Evolution et techniques. II, Milieu et techniques*, Paris: Albin Michel.

Leroi-Gourhan, A. (1964), *Le geste et la parole. 1, Technique et langage*, Paris: Albin Michel.

Leroi-Gourhan, A. (1965), *Le geste et la parole. 2, La mémoire et les rythmes*, Paris: Albin Michel.

Leroi-Gourhan, A. (1993), *Gesture and Speech* (translated by Anna Bostock Berger), Cambridge: MIT Press.

Loeve, S. and T. Deldicque (2018), 'Les malentendus de la technologie', *Artefact*, 8: 215–254.

McGrew, W. C. (1992), *Chimpanzee Material Culture. Implications for Human Evolution*, Cambridge: Cambridge University Press.

Mauss, M. (1930 [2006]), 'Les civilisations. Eléments et formes', in Fondation pour la Science – Centre international de synthèse (eds.), *Civilisation. Le mot et l'idée*, 1re Semaine internationale de synthèse, fasc. 2, 81–108, Paris: La Renaissance du Livre. Translated by J. R. Redding and reproduced in Mauss, M. *Techniques, Technology and Civilisation* (edited and introduced by N. Schlanger), 57–73, Oxford: Berghahn books.

Mauss, M. (1936 [2006]), 'Les techniques du corps', *Journal de psychologie*, 32: 271–93. Translated by B. Brewster and reproduced in M. Mauss, *Techniques, Technology and Civilisation* (edited and introduced by N. Schlanger), 77–95, Oxford: Berghahn books.

Mauss, M. (2006), *Techniques, Technology and Civilisation* (edited and introduced by N. Schlanger), Oxford: Berghahn books.

Mauss, M. (2012), *Techniques, technologie et civilisation* (édition et présentation de N. Schlanger), Paris: Presses Universitaires de France.

Métraux, A. (1928), *La civilisation matérielle des tribus tupi-guarani*, Paris: Geuthner.

Miller, D. (1987), *Material Culture and Mass Consumption*, Oxford: Blackwell.

Miller, P. (2017), *History and Its Objects. Antiquarianism and Material Culture since 1500*, Ithaca: Cornell University Press.

Naji, M. and L. Douny (2009), 'Introduction: "Making" and "Doing" the Material World', *Journal of Material Culture Studies*, 14: 411–432.

Pesez, J. -M. (1978), 'Histoire de la culture matérielle', in J. Le Goff (ed.), *La nouvelle histoire*, 98–130, Paris: Retz.

Pfaffenberger, B. (1992), 'Social Anthropology of Technology', *Annual Review of Anthropology*, 21: 491–516.

Pitt-Rivers (Lane Fox), A. H. (1874 [1906]), 'On the Principles of Classification Adopted in the Arrangement of his Anthropological Collection, Now Exhibited in the Bethnal Green Museum', *Jr. Anth. Inst.* 4, reproduced in *The Evolution of Culture and Other Essays*, 1–19, Oxford: Clarendon Press.

Rivet, P. (1929), 'L'étude des civilisations matérielles: ethnographie, archéologie, préhistoire', *Documents. Archéologie, Beaux-Arts, Ethnographie, Variétés*, 1: 130 –134.

Roche, D. (1997), *Histoire des choses banales. Naissance de la consommation, XVIIème-XIXème siècle*, Paris: Fayard.

Schatzberg, E. (2018), 'Why is There No Discipline of Technology in the Social Sciences?' *Artefact*, 8: 193–213.

Schlanger, N. (1999), 'De la rédemption à la sauvegarde: Contenu et contexte de la technologie du Bureau of American Ethnology', in J. -L., Jamard, A. Montigny and F. -R. Picon (eds.), *Dans le sillage des techniques. Hommage à Robert Cresswell*, 483–512, Paris: l'Harmattan.

Schlanger, N. (2012), 'Une technologie engagée: Marcel Mauss et l'étude des techniques dans les sciences sociales', in M. Mauss, *Techniques, technologie et civilisation*, 17–134, Paris: Presses Universitaires de France.

Schlanger, N. (2019), 'Marcel Mauss (1972–1950): Socializing the Body Through Techniques', *History of the Humanities* (Theme: Classics of the Humanities), 4/2.

Schlanger, N. (2021), *André Leroi-Gourhan on Technology. Material Civilization, Operational Behavior and the Evolution of Technicity*, New York: Bard Graduate Center.

Schlereth, T. J. (1985), 'Material Culture and Cultural Research', in T. J. Schlereth (ed.), *Material Culture, A Research Guide*, 1–34, Lawrence, KS: University Press of Kansas.

Segalen M. and C. Bromberger, eds. (1996), 'Culture matérielle et modernité', *Ethnologie Française*, 26.

Sigaut, F. (1987), 'Préface. Haudricourt et la technologie', in A. -G. Haudricourt (ed.), *La technologie science humaine. Recherches d'histoire et d'ethnologie des techniques*, 9–34, Paris: Editions MSH.

Sigaut, F. (1994), 'Technology', in T. Ingold (ed.), *Companion Encyclopaedia to Anthropology*, London: Routledge, 420–459.

Sigaut, F. (2013), *Comment homo devint faber. Comment l'outil fit l'homme*, Paris: CNRS Éditions.

Soulier, P. (2018), *André Leroi-Gourhan. Une vie (1911–1986)*, Paris: CNRS Editions.

Stocking, G. W. (1995), *After Tylor. British Social Anthropology 1888–1951*, London: Athlone Press.

Vatin, F. (2004), 'Mauss et la technologie', *Revue du MAUSS*, 23, 418–433.

Index

Italicized pages refer to figures and page numbers followed by "n" refer to notes.

absorption/absorb 87, 88, 113, 143, 147; *see also* appropriation
academic knowledge: practical *vs.* 169, 180; vocational *vs.* 170–172
actions: action of matter 51, 52, 56; actions-on-objects 77, 84; bodies-in-action 83; bodily actions 48–49, 98; catalogue of actions 35; continuous 12; daily 17; doing action 17; dynamics 171; efficacious xix, 3, 22, 111, 152; embodied 82–83, 108; human 21, 153; interaction 6, 8, 15, 17, 19, 22, 39, 83, 137, 170, 172, 174, 178, 180; logics 179; of making do 39–40; materiality of 70; on materials 90; moral 148; motor 17; network of 20, 34, 37, 42, 43, 62–63, 67–72, 83; networks on others actions 42–43, 67, 68–69; objects-in-actions 6, 34, 77, 82, 84; performed actions 36; power of 95, 98, 100, 101, 102; as practice 95; reciprocal 13, 21, 50, 98, 102, 142, 146; science of 17; sequence 8; social 95; socialised 71; on the subjects 99; technical actions 50, 57; traditional 152; upon action 62–63, 67, 85; upon materials 21; value 153; *see also* Mauss
actor 172; human *vs.* non-human 11; *pace* Lemonnier *vs.* Latour 10
Actor Network Theory 11
adaptability 39–40
ad interim workers 35, 38, 39, 43
adolescence 61, 70
adults 1, 62, 68, 109; grown-ups 200

aesthetics: bathing 157–158; built surfaces in Paiwan 192; deity images and 153; female beauty in Iran 116; of gestures 53; Hindu devotion 154, 155, 160; Marka-Dafing image 96; of *Musée du Quai Branly* 88–89; of Paiwan 194; pattern-making 160–162; perception of 204–205; of *priyayi* 126; of *shifu* 190; sheen as value 98; as taste 54; of weaving 194, 206; of workers' art 57; *see also* agency; art
Africa 18; Burkina-Faso 20, 93; Cameroon 13, 15, 20–21, 108–110, 113, 117; Morocco 21, 49, 137; territorialisation in 109–114
African artefacts *81*
African undocumented strikers 87
age/aging: chronological 65; gender and 65–67, *66*, 70–71; as objective matter 65–67; psychophysiological 65
agency: action on self and others 107, 109; agentive interfaces 10; Didi-Huberman and 86; disjointing of subject from 131; empowerment and 12; Gell's concept of 6, 10, 18, 21, 85, 153, 164; Hindu devotion and 21, 153, 163, 164; Latourian actor 11; praxic value and 14, 18, 116; wild silk wrappers and 94–98, 101–102
Algeria 138
alienation 51
altar: cleaning on *ekadasi* 157; devotion on home 151–163; dressers of 199; ISKCON devotee and 163; Snehalata's 156–158
Amazon 9

214   *Index*

anatomo-physiological dimension 14
ancestors: knowledge 94–96, Kota
Gede Cemetery 125; Māori 80, 85;
and power of sacred king 109–110
anglophone scholarship 7; Anglo-
American/Anglo-Saxon tradition,
theoretical anthropology 204
animals: *fama* of chameleons, snakes,
leopards 111; sheep 137, 142–144, 148;
silkworms 20, 95, 98–101, 102
Anlo-Ewe approach 16
Annales school 204
anthropology 19; cultural 115, 203;
heterogenic field of 170; history of 6;
of knowledge and techniques 21–22;
of knowledge transmission 169–181;
MaP's 4; phenomenology in 9, 16, 18,
114; of religion 152; social 6, 7, 115;
theoretical 204
*Anthropology and the Cognitive
Challenge* (Bloch) 169
Anthropology of Remains (Debary) 87
apprenticeship 15, 22, 44, 67, 169,
171, 172–174, 181, 199; as method
187–188
appropriation 113; of objects 17; *see also*
absorption/absorb
architecture: *astta,* loom and house
139; and control, panopticon, Jeremy
Bentham 12; Paiwan houses 188–189;
of *Palais de la Porte Dorée* 84; reversal 87; transformations 47–57
Argenti, N. 6, 118
aristocracy 122, 123, 125, 126, 129
art: conventionalized 201; deity image
and 153; Didi-Huberman on 86–87;
Gell's concept of agency and 85, 153,
164n6; Javanese martial 124; Paiwan
artist 192–193; primitive 80, 88; Quai
Branly, ethnographic collection as
primitivism 88–89; revitalisation
of crafts 193; universality of 87–88;
whitewashing with 83; workers 57;
working site as 34; *see also* aesthetics;
artefact
Art Deco heritage 84
artefact 77; African *81*; animal 142–145;
astta as house-spirit-artefact 139–140,
143; destruction of 191; ethnographic
80; as French heritage 90; importance of 171, 177; living 142–145;
made by *pulima* persons 191; Mauss
views on 83; reshaping materiality of

84–85; transmission vectors 177–178;
use of 8, 174; watchmaker's 'mechanical sense' and 175
artist/artisans: external 140; internal
140; Paiwan 193; rehabilitation of 33
asceticism 21, 123, 124–125; defined
132n3; practice of 129; subjectivation
by 123–125, 131
Asia: India 21, 122, 151–152, 154, 155,
158, 159; Indonesia 12, 21; Taiwan 22,
185–186, 190, 192–193, 185
'aspects moyens' of material civilisations 205
assignation 70
astta 138; as animal-artefact 142–145;
as artefact-as-emerging 138–139;
end of 143; fear about 142, 144–145;
jnûn and 139–140, *141*; 'killing' of
143, 144; life course of 140–142, 145;
origin of 147; power and behaviour
142; ram-victim and 144; as sacred
house-spirit-artefact 139–140; as the
term 138–139; term *tazettat* and 140;
as a *zawit* (saint shrine) 140; *see also*
Sirwa weavers
Austronesian languages 191, 192
Austronesian populations 190
autonomy 21, 52, 54, 175, 177
avant-garde artistic movements 205

bagalbandhi (a shirt that ties on the
side) 161
Balacescu, A. 117
Balandier, G. xviii, 7
Barthes, R. xvii, 61
bas matérialisme 205
Bataille, G. 87, 205
Bateson, G. 15, 62, 115
Baudrillard, J. 3
Bayart, J. -F. xx, 6, 7, 57, 78, 108,
115–117, 170
Bell, Q. 61
Bengali Vaishnavism 152–153, 154
Bentham, J. 12
Bertrand, R. 21, 206
Bessin, M. 71
Bhagavad Gita 154
Blidon, M. 71
Bloch, M. 169, 187
Boasian tradition 115
bodily-and-material xix, xx, 6–8, 15, 16,
19, 21, 77, 114, 118, 152, 162
bodily engagement 50, 51, 53, 56

Index 215

body/bodies xviii–xx, 4–5, 7–21, 43, 48, 62, 63, 68, 70, 84, 95–97, 101, 107, 109–110, 113–118, 129, 139–140, 144, 145, 146, 148, 152, 158, 162, 169–170, 178, 186, 206, 208
body hacking 9
Bourdieu, P. 3, 5, 8, 61, 67, 69, 71, 114
boy 65–69
Braudel, F. xvii, 204
bricolage 33, 38, 40–41, 42, 49, 57, 57n2
Buchmann, C. 64, 72n7
Burawoy, M. 71
Bureau of American Ethnology 202
bushfalling process 113–114, *114*

Cabanis, P. -J. -G. 65
Cameroon People's Democratic Movement (CPDM) 108
catachresis 33, 39
categorisations 63–64, 153, 169, 170
chaîne opératoire 17, 23n19, 187, 208
child/childhood 62, 65, 124, 128, 155, 159, 163, 192
Chinese tradition lacquering 17
chronological age 65
City of Tucson's Urban Sanitation Service (*Garbage* program) 47–48
civilisation 47, 49, 62, 192, 204–206
civilisation matérielle 204
Clifford, J. 195
clothes/clothing *64*; according to social situation 68–69; advice about 69–70; age group 63; aim of 61; categorisation of the self 64; of children 20, 62; general sociology of 61–63; gifts of 69–70; at the heart of technologies of self 67–69; lending 67; materiality of 61–62; Mauss' concept in 62; moral dimension of 71; morality of 68–69; and techniques of self 63–64; as a tool of self-knowledge 62–64
cognitive gap 15, 116
cognitive neurosciences 9, 15
colonial 77–90, 117, 121, 128, 130; and French imperialism 87
commodities 131
compliance/compelling: political 13; religious 15
compulsory cropping system period (1830–1870) 130
conflict 126–128
connectivity 18, 21, 162
conscious/unconscious 10
consumption xvii, 3, 5, 19, 48, 53, 61, 77, 94, 115–116, 118, 130, 155, 202, 206, 207

containers (as vessels and envelopes) 11, 13, 109–110, 140, 145
Cook, D. 61
CorAge ANR project 62
Corcuff, P. 71
cotton fibre kapok *(Bombax ceiba)* 97
Coupaye, L. 17, 137
coupling/decoupling: *couplage/ découplage* 8; relationship to objects 8–9; *see also* incorporation/ disincorporation
craft 6, 19, 22, 79, 93, 171–172, 177–178, 180, 185–187, 190–193; craftsmen 6, 169; craftspeople 171, 172, 174; crafts-person 186, 188, 199; indigenous 193; knowledge 172; politics of 186
creativity: agency and 11–12, 18; in break rooms 52, 54; craft and 79, 93, 171–172, 174; devotion and 158–162; knowledge and 49–50, 178, 187; in Paiwan 195; *pulima* and *shifu* 190, 192
cultural diversity 80, 89, 90
culture mortice (motor culture) 14

Damasio, A. 186–187
daoula of wild silk 20, 95, 98–102
Darmakoesoema, 124
Debary, O. 48, 87, 89
De Boeck, F. 113
de Certeau, M. 3, 33, 40, 56
Dejaiffe, B. 68, 72n7
Delbos, G. 173, 180
descriptive knowledge 17
détournement des objets (misappropriation of objects) 3
dichotomy 16, 171, 175–180
Didi-Huberman, G. 86
disincorporation 5–6; bodies 8–9; of material culture dynamics 13; of object dynamics 4
disposability 39–40
disposable men 34
diversity 7, 80, 89, 90, 108, 199–201
djanjoba (big event) 95, 99, *100*
doka tree *(Isoberlinia doka)* 97
Douglas, M. 48–49
Douny, L. xi, 4–5, 9, 20, 23n20, 108
Downey, G. 186
dynamic sociology 7

education 70, 147, 177, 178, 181n1
efficacy: André Leroi-Gourhan on gestures and tools 3; 'efficacious

216   *Index*

intimacy' concept 153; Elias, N. 49, 62; Foucault and 'technologies of power' 111; global subject and 115; Kabyle women 142; Mauss on 22n3, 153; non discursivity and 151

embodied actions 78; colonial pride and shame 83–84; objects-in-action as material culture 82–83; reshaping materiality of artefacts 84–85; on tangible things 83; *Toi Moko* 85, *86*

embodiment: Csordas' 7–8, 16; as disincorporation 7–9; dynamic of 7; fleshiness of 12–13; MaP on 8; practicing 8; women's, of silk garment 94; *see also* empowerment

emotion: aesthetic pleasure 89; anxiety 49, 50, 124; appreciation and charisma 98; devotional love 153; dispossessed of desire 129; emotional-cognitive dimension 14; enjoyment 52, 54, 69, 187; enjoyment of influence 129; fear 49, 58n4, 126; *gami* as suffering 99; loss 9, 163; orientalist perception of 114; *see also* feeling

empowerment 12, 124, 131

enchantment/disenchantment: Gell and 86; and magic 98, 124, 129, 141, 143; technical action and 50, 57; weavers and 147

Espinas, A. xix, 17

ethnographers researching practices 163, 187–188

ethnography 13, 175; Bertrand 21; Jeanjean 20; of Marka-Dafing 20; of objectification 19

ethnomotricity 17; *see also* motor, actions

Europe: France 3, 4, 17, 20, 22n1, 33, 34, 48–56, 80, 82, 86–90, 199, 207; Switzerland 169–181, 199

expedition: as fascination with trip 48; and museum collections 77, 82, 200; 1905 Jessup 202; 1931 Dakar-Djibouti 205

family: *astta* and 144; clothing negotiations 64, 69–70, 99; competence of 40; handling deities as 163; heritage of 96; Hindu devotion and 155–158, 162–163; housing of 188; status of 126

father 70, 108

Fatima, M. 147

Fauvelle-Aymar, F. -X. 108

feeling: agency and 86; Anlo-Ewe and 16, 53; and *astta* 144; of autonomy 54; body and 5, 10; Damasio on 187; de Certeau 56, 67; of ownership 188; of spirits 140; and spiritual body 162; *see also* emotion; senses

First World War 206

Fo Angwafo, S.A.N. III 108, 112

Forty, A. 190

Foucault, M. 5, 71, 114, 118, 170; approach of clothing choices 20; archaeology of knowledge 19; definition of power 87; definition of subject 67; *dispositif* 23n13; expression on MaP 49; idea of subject 10; notion of governmentality 12–13, 115, 117; *savoir* (knowledge) *vs. connaissance* (awareness) 72n4; subjectification/subjectivation process 12–13, 121; 'techniques of the self' by 13, 23n16, 62, 63, 67, 68, 83, 148; *technologie du sujet/technologie du soi* 12; technologies of power 111, 114; work on subject, power and body 18

France 20, 199, 207; Chinese immigrants in 17; clothes/clothing choices 61–71; cultural politics 77–90; Jeanjean ethnography in 20; museums 80–82; national heritage 88; OTPF 39–40; political approach 80; precarious employment category 44n9; professional divers in public works 19–20, 33–37, 43; trends in 3, 22n1; waste marginalised in 48; waste workers 49; workshop kitchens 51–54, *53*; workshop storehouses 54–56, *55*, *56*

France's national heritage 88

Frazer, J. G. 34, 108

French civilisation and material culture 204–206

French immigration policy 88

French Ministry of Cultural Affairs 83

French modernity 17

French national museum 89

French theory 6; tradition of ideas 203, 204–206

Freud, S. 10, 49

frontier 109–114

gami 99

Garbage program 47–48

Gaudiya Vaishnavs 152–153
Geertz, C. 126
Gell, A. 6, 10, 18, 85; on agents and agency 10, 18, 85; on personhood 153; on technology 18
gender 3, 6, 42; and age 63, 65–67, *66*, 70–71; clothes 63–64
gestures: André Leroi-Gourhan on 3, 208; *fama* 111; handiwork of hospital carpenters 53; by Sirwa weavers 137–148; as a way of acting 21
Geurts, K. L. 16
Gibson, J. J. 14; theory of affordance 21
Godin, P. 65
Goffman, E. 51
The Golden Bough (Frazer) 34
Goody, J. 169
Gouhier, J. 57n1; founder of *rudologie* 47
governmentality: Foucaldian concept of 13, 71, 117, 118; notion of 12–13; through asceticism 129; Warnier's analysis 13; *see also* sovereign/ sovereignty
Gowlland, G. xi, 22, 23n12, 199, 206

habitus 206; definition of 8, 67, 69, 71; empirical weakness of 71; habituation 8, 12, 13, 195–196; objects of 8, 61, 206
haptic knowledge 50
haram (unclean) 123
Haudricourt, A. -G. 206–207
hegemony 9, 109
Heritage Day in Paris 36; cultural heritage 93, 96, 101
hierarchy 79, 87, 100; as privileges of subjectivation 21, 121
Hindu/Hinduism 151; devotion as a practice of 'efficacious intimacy' 153, 162–163; knowledge of Brahmins and 151; *Shastra* 151–152; spirituality and religiosity of 151–152; *see also* International Society for Krishna Consciousness (ISKCON)
Hindu worship 151–163
Hoarau, F. 36, 116
Hobhouse, L. T. 202
Horton, R. 110
hospital, waste management at 20, 54–55
housekeeping theory 35

Hugo, V. 47
human *vs.* non-human actor 11
Husserl, E. 16

idolatry: Gell on 164n6; Max Müller and 151
incorporation/disincorporation: divers' processes of 14; of *habitus* 61–71; of object dynamics 5–6, *5*, 7–9, 152; of subject's dynamics 12–13, 94; of wild silk's material properties 20, 99–102
India 151–163, 202
indigenous people 185–196; assimilation policies 191; heritage 80–82, 87; indigeneity xi, xiii; indigenous activism xi, 195; rights 87, 89, 185
Indology 151
industry xviii, 42, 114, 171, 174, 185, 187, 190, 193
Ingold, T. 14, 169, 186, 187, 193, 207
Institut d'ethnologie 205
Institut National de Plongée Professionnelle (INPP) 42
Insulinde/Indonesian archipelago 128, 129; formation of state in 122–123
intellectual traditions, MaP 10–11
interchangeability 39–40
International Society for Krishna Consciousness (ISKCON) 21, 151, 152–153; bathing of deities 157–158; *Bhagavad Gita* and 154; case studies 155–162; deities' garments 160–162, *161*; devotional attitudes and behavior 162–163; headquarters 153–154; Prabhupada figure *159*; *pushpa samadhi* 158
interstitial areas 57
ISKCON *see* International Society for Krishna Consciousness
Islam: ethic 130; exegesis 140; practices 124; sacrifice in 144; Sufi influences 123; in Turkey 116

Java: devotional practices 125; industrialisation of 129–130; *parang rusak barong* motif 126, *127*; *priyayi* of 122, 124, 130; techniques of the self 131
Javanese state: aristocratic ideals 130; ascetic exercises 124–125; *batik* 122; compulsory cropping system period (1830–1870) 130; eremitic ideal of *priyayi* 123–125; formation

218   *Index*

of 122–131; history of 122; liberal era (1870–1900) 130; martial arts 124; money *(uang)* 123; moral conflict of *priyayi* 126–129; mysticism 124; right to command 131

Jeanjean, A. xi–xii, 3, 20, 22n6, 38, 43

jihad 148

Jnûn (house-spirits) 139–140, 143

Jorion, P. 170, 172, 173, 180

Jounin, N. 35, 37, 38, 42

Julien, M. -P. xii, 3, 17, 20

Kabyle weavers 138; slipper-wearer 8

Kaufmann, J. -C. 3, 35, 68

kaupina (undergarment) 161

kinesthesia 16; *see also* senses

king: as sacred, as container 13; *see also* sultan

Knappett, C. 187, 188

Knebel, J. 124

knowledge 115; academic *vs.* vocational 170–171; clothes as tool to improve 62–65; dichotomous categorisation of 170; haptic 50; *kanuragan vs. kebatinan* 124; matter of 169–196; occupational 172–174; procedural 152; types in Javanese mysticism, 124; verbalised *vs.* procedural 15–17; weaving 138; in wild-silk production 95–102; *see also* education; knowledge transmission

knowledge transmission 170; case studies of Swiss watchmakers 170–180; dichotomous typology of 170–171; re-mapping typologies of 180–181

Kopytoff, I. xvii, 34, 79, 110

Körperschema 9; *see also* Schilder

Krishna consciousness 151, 163

Kroeber, A. L. 203

Kubler, G. 203

Küchler, S. xv, 7

Kuturkreise protagonists 204

La civilisation matérielle des tribus tupi-guarani (Métraux) 204

'La technologie, science humaine' 206

Latour, B. 10, 11, 178

La transmission des savoirs (Jorion and Delbos) 173

Lave, J. 169

Le geste et la parole 208

Leroi-Gourhan, A. xviii, 3, 47, 207, 208

les indépendances 83

Les statues meurent aussi (film) 77

Lévi-Strauss, C. 57n2, 115, 202

l'homme total 7, 14

lineage: Cameroonian king xviii, 15; Hindu *parampara* 158

loom 21, 98, 137, 138, 140, 141, 145, 147

luxury 122–123, 129, 171

MACUDA (Mankon Cultural Development Association) 113

magic 98, 124, 129, 141, 143; *see also* enchantment/disenchantment

Magritte effect 15, 115

maintenance 35, 36, 51, 52, 84, 145, 180, 194

Malafouris, L. 186

Malraux, A. 83

management: architectural transformations 57; in hospital 54–55; quest to reconquer refuse 47–57

Māori: heritage 80–82; in museums 80–81; *see also Toi Moko*

Marchand, T. 187

Marka-Dafing 93; *Anaphe* and *Epanaphe* 93; concept of *laada* 93–94, 96; *daoula* 98–99; heritage of 94; subjectivation process 95–97

Marxism 3

material culture: among human/non-humans 203; culture and material 202–204; designation of 206; experience of wanting 37–38; expression of 203–204; French civilisation and 204–206; global subjectivation through 114–118; historiographic retroprojections 200–202; 'incremental marker' conception 202–203; Knappett's definition of two scales of analysis of 188; materiality and 9; Mauss about 199–200; Mauss technique of 14; objects-in-action as 82–83; Pitt-Rivers about 201; recycling 37; retrospective attribution of 201–202; Rosselin-Bareille about 200; Roustan about 200; technology and 206–209; turned *inside out* 11–12; Warnier about 200

Material Culture Studies: in France 3–5; at University College London 7, 16, 201–202

material habituations 8

materiality: of closure and aperture 145–147; differential allocation of

121–122; hands-on approach to materiality 17; and material culture 9; *pace* Ingold *vs.* Tilley 10; in (post) colonial contexts 89–90; praxic and procedural value of 16–17; reshaping of artefacts 84–85; of Sirwa weavers 137, 145–147; subject's identification with 13; as a transformative process 16–17; of weaving 21

material religion approach 21; *see also* matter of religion

materials 10; actions on refuse 49–57; cement, concrete, slate, silk, wool, cotton, silk-cotton, neoprene 41; in museum objects 77–79; raw 33, 37; recuperating 39; recycling 37–38; relation between matters and 13; weaving upon woollen 21; wood, plywood, polystyrene, metal, palm oil, camwood powder, alabaster 130

Matière à Penser (MaP) 3–4, *5*, 62, 78; action on refuse matter 51–57; anthropology 4; cloud (of ideas) 4, 17–19; definition of subject 9–10; on embodiment 7–8; Foucauldian subject 11, 13; focus on creativity 196; focus on subject and subjectification process 5–6; fundamental issue 7; Gellian and Latourian view of objects 10; intellectual traditions 10–11; international dimensions 18–19; key idea 19; material culture program 4–5; as multimodality 4–7; phenomenology and 9, 16, 18, 114, 199; political dimension of refuse 48–49; praxeology and 16–19; praxic and procedural value of materiality 16–18; *pulima* and *shifu* 186, 188, 196; representatives 170; research on clothing 62; Sirwa weavers 137–148; subjectivation 11–12, 95; subject-object relationships 19–22; techniques/technologies of subject 13; tool kit 15; view 16

Matière à Travail (matter for work) 33–34

matter of heritage 18, 77–103; silence of 85

matter of knowledge 18, 169–176; anthropology of knowledge transmission 169–181; forms of knowledge 169; Paiwan skilled workers 185–196; vocational knowledge 170–180

matter of politics 18, 107–131; burden of kingship 108–109; Javanese state, formation of 122–131; *Matière à Politique* 107; territorialisation process 109–114

matter of religion 18; around weaving 137–148; Hinduism 151–163; *Matière à Religion* 152; techniques in 152

matter of technology 18

Mauss, M. 3, *5*, 7, 62, 96, 118, 206; about material culture 199–200; about technique and religion 152, 164n4; concept of a 'Whole Person' or *l'homme total* 13, 14, 18, 199; concept of socialisation 62; formula 22n3, 98; material culture as instrumental techniques 14; *On Prayer* 152, 164n4; Prout *vs.* 62; views on gifts 69; views on artefacts 83; views on 'body techniques' 13–14, 18, 62, 83; views on 'total social facts' 83

Mead, M. 6, 15, 62, 115

mechanical sense 175, 177, 178

mental culture 202, 203

methodological materialism 203–204

Métraux, A. 204

Miller, D. 6–8, 23n12, 79, 151, 201

mise-en-objet 8; *see also* objectification

Mohan, U. xii, 21, 43n1, 107–108, 116, 200

money: as ancestral life essence 110; monetarising 129–131; satirical text 128; as sustenance 155; as unclean 123

Morgan, D. 15

mother 64–69, 99, 147, 158

motor: actions *(action motrice)* 17; conducts 13–17, 38, 116

Müller, M. 151, 164n4

Munz, H. A. xii, 21–22, 199

Murphy, C. 47, 50, 87

Musée de la France d'Outre-mer (Museum of French Overseas Territories) 79

Musée de l'Homme (Museum of Man) 79, 80

Musée des Arts d'Afrique et d'Océanie (Museum of African and Oceanic Arts) 79, 80

Musée d'ethnographie 205

Musée du Quai Branly xv, 78, 79, 80, *81*, 84, 87, 88

Musée national de l'histoire et des cultures de l'immigration (National

220 *Index*

Museum of the History and Cultures of Immigration) 79

Musée permanent des colonies (Permanent Museum of the Colonies) 79

museum(s) 77; collections and heritage value 80–82; from colonial palace to immigration museum 79–80; curator/curating 20, 77–78, 83–85, 88, 201; dynamics of heritage making 79; from ethnographic artefacts to primitive art 80; heritage making in 89–90; metamorphosis of 77–78; 1930s–1970s 83–84; 1980s–1990s 84; practices of heritage in 77; trajectories of 79–82; 2000s–2010s 87–89; 2010–2011 87–88

Naji, M. xii–xiii, 4–5, 21

natural appearance 160, 164n5; *astta* 141; body as 206; categories and 61; functions and 49; gender and 42; and heritage 79; material culture as 202; naturalist 81; raw materials and 97, 208; supernatural 97–98, 124; technology as 207

naturalisation/denaturalisation 42, 62, 71

New Zealand 78, 80–82, *86*; indigenous rights and 89

non-human actor 11

norm 70–71, 83, 121, 126, 152, 203

Nouvel, J. 80

Nyamnjoh, F. B. 108, 113

objectification 5–6, 7, 12, 16, 121; ethnography of 19; *pace* Miller *vs.* Baudrillard 10–11; parameters of 131; *see also mise-en-objet*

objects: agency 10; as central transmission vectors 177–180; *corps-à-corps* of 83; Gellian and Latourian view of 10; as objects-in-action 82–83; praxic value of 13–17

ontology: and the Cartesian *cogito* 10; and conflicts about *Toi Moko* 82; and divinity 152; properties of materials 203; surface-depth 151; Warnier on subject/object relationship 146

Organisation du travail à prescription floue (OTPF) 44n7; France 39–40; unpredictability of 40

orientalist: bias 114; and Indology 151

Osgood, C. 203

pace Foucault *vs.* Sartre or Descartes 10

pace Ingold *vs.* Tilley 10

pace Lemonnier *vs.* Latour 10

pace Miller *vs.* Baudrillard 10–11

Paiwan houses 188–192, *189*; with bricks and mortar *191*; 'modern' building forms 190; slate walls for *189*; in vernacular style 189–190

Paiwan/Paiwan people: aesthetics of imported materials 194, *194*; artists and artisans 192–195, *194*; construction work 188–192, *189*, *191*; craft practices, revitalisation of 192–193; creativity *vs.* habituation 195–196; empirical research on 188; enskilment and subjectivity gap 186–188; material culture 192–193; in migrant work 190–191; overview of 185–186; *pulima* and *shifu* as the term 185–186; renewed subjectivities of *pulima* 192–195; skilled practice of the *shifu* 188–192; slate carving *194*; typhoon Morakot at 194–195

Palais de la Porte Dorée 79–80, 87; social biography of 83–84

panopticon 12; and Jeremy Bentham 12

parang rusak barong motif 126, *127*

parent 64, 66, 68–70

Pavavalung, S. 192

peer 70, 72n3

Perrot, C. -H. 108

Pétonnet, C. 47

phenomenology: in anthropology 16; applications of 9, 16, 18, 114, 199

A Phenomenology of Landscape (Tilley) 16

physical displacements 79, 80

Pinney, C. 7, 15

Pitt-Rivers (Lane Fox), A. H. 201

pluralism: action of refuse matter as critical 51–56

politics: burden of kingship 108–109; bushfalling process 113–114, *114*; common notion of political power 108; definition of 107; introduction to 107–108; territorialisation in Africa 109–114, *111*

post-human bodies 9

The Pot-King (Warnier) 11, 20–21, 96–97

power: of action of wild silk 95; as actions 85–87, 98; administrative 128;

Index 221

ancestral 13, 22, 109–110, 192; *astta's* 142; of attraction on women 100; creative 48; desires and 90; devotional 125; dynamics 79; functions 67; hegemonic 9; issues in clothing 62; Javanese concepts 125, 131; luxury and 122–123, 129; mystical imagination of 130; as network of actions 83; pastoral 12; physical 124; physiological 49; political 107–108; subjects in relations of 186–188, 192, 195, 196; subversive 50; technology of 68, 111, 114–116; webs 85

Prabhupada, A. C. 154

practical: knowledge 17, 169, 172–173; magic 124; mastery 175

practices: austerity and mortification 124; balance with bucket 14; bathing deities 157–158; of *bhakti* and *sewa* 153; building houses and tombs 188–190; bushfalling 113; carving 193–194; clothing of children 63–70; divers 34–43; dressing of deities 155–162; dressing of humans (*see* clothes/clothing); driving a car, singing religious songs 16; eating 54, 116, 125; king distributing body contents 109; lacquering wood, wearing high-heeled shoes, making pottery, diving 17; opening and closing 146–147; pattern-making 161; ploughing and harvesting 138; poaching, recycling, bricolage, catachresis 33; of *priyayi* 126, 129; processing wild silk 98; sacrificial ritual at loom 143; singing and dancing, *djandjoba* 99; sport sciences and games 17; spraying raffia wine 13, 110; spraying saliva, *fama* 111; striking by workers 87–88; walking 14, 17, 67, 99, 125; waste work 49–57; watchmaking 21–22, 170–175, 177–180; weaving 138; worship 148, 152–153, 155, 162; of worship, *darshan* 154

praxeological relationship, subject/object 146–147

praxeological value 15

praxeology 7; MaP 18; as science of actions 17–18; Warnier 18, 146–147

prayer: Hindu worship 151–163; Islamic 124, 144; Mauss *On Prayer* 152, 164n4

precarity: and disposability 34; and fieldwork 187; in French employment 44n9; in historic Java 123, 131;

resisting 55; and risk, 38, 101, 139, 140–141, 145

Prentice, R. 187

priyayi of Java 122, 124; eroding classical doctrines of 130; moral conflict of 126–129; subjectivation by asceticism for 131

procedural knowledge, verbalised *vs.* 15–16

process 4, 5, 8–9, 12–13, 17, 21, 23, 35, 43, 44, 62, 72, 77–78, 83–85, 87–88, 90, 93, 95–96, 98, 102, 110, 113, 115–118, 130, 132, 143, 147, 160, 162, 169, 173, 177, 179, 187; of appropriation 112; of bathing 157; of being-in-the-world 16; civilization 62; cross-cultural 6; of cultural recognition 88; decolonisation 77, 83; of (dis)corporation 152; of incorporation 13, 19, 20; of innovation 153; of learning 172, 174, 180; of life 139; living 137, 147; making 148, 187, 196; material 12; micro-processes 5; neuro-physiological 16; political 107; processual 22, 117, 147, 171; production 206; of socialisation 68; subjectivation 12, 20, 56, 78, 94, 95, 96, 102, 116, 121, 196, 200, 202; technical 140, 142, 145; technical processing 48; of territorialisation 110; of transformation 78, 140, 208; of weaving 137, 141, 148

professional qualifications, recycling 40–41

propositional knowledge 175

propping 8

prosthetic 9

Prout, A. 62

psychology: and abuse 101; Anglo-American psychologists on material culture 23n18; Anglo-American theoretical anthropology 204; Californian cult of the self 23n16; Freud 10, 49; and knowledge 50; Lacan 10, 47; Marka-Dafing 96–97; as Maussian 'Whole Person' 14; neuropsychology 186; psychophysiological age 63, 65; society of psychology 206; of workers 50

Public Work Divers 19–20; in building and construction work 35, 42; dealing with waste 35–37; in France 33–37; raw materials, recycling 37–38;

222   *Index*

recuperating objects/materials 39–40; working on leftovers 40–43

pulima workers 22, 185–188, 192–196; creative work of 193–194; reintroduced carved images 194; renewed subjectivities of 192–195; revitalisation efforts of 194

purchase equipment 55

Quai Branly moment, the 88

Radcliffe-Brownian tradition 115
Rancière, J. 121
Rathje, W. 47, 50
raw materials 33, 37, 137, 208
recuperating objects/materials 39
recycling: materials 37; professional qualifications 40–41
reflexivity 13, 18, 67, 71
refuse matter 52; action on 51–56; waste workers acting on 51
religion: of ancestors 13, 109–110; Christianity 65, 151; Hinduism 151; Islam 93, 116, 123, 124, 130, 140; offerings 109, 100, 139, 141, 155; spirits 139
religious culture 202
renunciation 129
repair 51–53, 56, 84; *see also* maintenance
representational value 15
Revue de synthèse 204
Rosini, P. 35, 38, 39, 40
Rosselin-Bareille, C. xiii, 3, 7, 19, 22n6, 50, 199, 200, 204
Roustan, M. xiii, 20, 200, 206
Rowlands, M. xvii, 6, 7, 137
Royalty and Politics. The Story of My Life (Fo Angwafo) 108
Rubbish Theory. The Creation and Destruction of Value (Thompson) 48
rubbish/waste workers: as an object 36; definition of 36–37; in MaP 47; researchers examination of 48
rudologie, defined 47

Samoh, I. 148
Sasana Sunu (Yasadipura II) 126
Saunders, N. 7
savoir-faire 94, 98
scarcity 33, 37–38, 40; questions of 38
Schilder, P. 8, 9, 17, 113

Schlanger, N. xiii, 4, 19, 199–209
Schwartz, O. 54
senses: body and 5, 19; discipline of 129; kinesthesia and 16; of scarcity 37; *see also* feeling
sensori-affective-motor conducts or *conduites sensori-affectivo-motrices* 7, 14, 17
sensori-motor algorithms 115, 116
sensory: Anlo-Ewe model of 16, 34, 95, 98, 153, 154, 159; prosthetics and 9
sexual abstinence 129
The Shape of Time (Kubler) 203
shea butter *(Vitellaria paradoxa)* 97
shifu 22, 185–186; skilled practice of the 188–192
Sigaut, F. 6, 50–51, 173, 187, 206, 207
sign value. *see* representational value
silk-cotton *(Ceiba pentandra)* 97
Simmel, G. 10, 61
Sirwa weavers: activity of weaving 145; *astta* as the term 138–140, *138*; human and non-human parallel life courses 140–142; materiality of 137, 145–147; mortality in 138–139; rituals and gestures by 137–148; terms *razq* and *baraka* 139, 144; theories of MaP and 137; weaving ritual practices 137–138; women's access to education and new technologies 147–148
Sirwa women: access to education and new technologies 147–148; *astta* and 139–145
skill: enskillment in Paiwan 185–189; *priyayi* strategies 126; production of silk 95; Swiss watchmakers 171, 175, 177, 180; terms denoting skilled persons 192–193; weaving 138
social culture 202
socialisation 61–62, 68, 69
social movements 80
sociological knowledge 50
sociology of clothing 61
sovereign/sovereignty: of divine 152; as Foucauldian governmentality 13, 115, 117; mythical founder 125; relationship to *priyayi* 127–128
spa technicians 51–54, *53*
subject: alternative to Latourian 'actor' 11; Cartesian approach 10; definition of 9–10; Foucauldian philosophy of 9; Foucault's definition of 67;

Foucault's idea of 10; and Gellian and Latourian view 10; identification with materiality 13; Lacan and 10; *pace* Foucault *vs.* Sartre or Descartes 10; techniques/technologies of 13; *vs.* notion of the 'self' 10
subjectification: 5–6, 7
subjectivation: conflicts and wars of 121–122; of Javanese nobility 21; MaP approach to 95; of peasantry 126; privileges of 21, 121; processes 12–13; through bodily and material cultures 114–118; Warnier, Jean-Pierre process of 96–97
subjectivation process 12–13; by asceticism 123–125; case studies 116–117; definition of 121; notion of 121; privileges of 121–122
subjectivity of curators 84–85
subject-object relationships 19–22, 146–147
sultan: 123, 125; court of Solo 124, 127
Sultanate of Atjeh (Aceh) 122
Sultanate of Malacca 122
Summary Instructions for the Collectors of Ethnographic Objects 205
Swiss watchmaking 21–22, 170, 180; *see also* Switzerland watchmakers
Switzerland watchmakers: apprenticeship 173; case studies 170–180; initial vocational training at school 173–180, *176*; learning beyond dichotomies 173–174, *174*; mechanical sense 175, 177; mediation of objects in watchmaking education 178–179; re-mapping typologies of knowledge transmission 180–181; Sigaut's critique of 173–174; transmission and appropriation of 170–180
symbolic dimensions 48, 49
symbolic reversibility 87

Taiwan 22
Takivalit, C. 193
tamarind *(Tamarindus indica)* 97
technical bodily engagement 53; gestures 53
techniques: analytical focus on 131; Foucault term 63, 68, 71, 83, 99, 115, 117, 148; in Java 131; in matter of religion 152; Mauss' definition of 152; of the self 12

Techniques of the Body (Mauss) 3
technology and material culture 206–209
technology of power 68
temporal dimension of refuse 48
territorialisation of space 21
territorialisation process: in Africa 109–114, *111*; implications of 110–112; in Indonesian archipelago 122
textiles: batik 122, 126–127; motif *parang rusak barong* 126, *127*; products 122; weaving 21, 98, 137–148
theory of housekeeping 35
Thompson, M. 48
Thorne, B. 71
Tilley, C. 7
Toi Moko 80–82, 85, *86*; with violent memory 89
trade 122
transformation: ancestral life essence 110; in breakrooms 54; Hindu 153, 163; indigenous artist 193; in Javanese mysticism 124; in Maghrebi societies 138; from natural to cultural 208; of Paiwan settlement and Paiwan subject 188–192; as part of identity 17; Swiss vocational education and training system 181n1; of *Toi Moko* 85; watch industry 171; wild silk 98
transmission 22, 69, 70; *see also* knowledge transmission
'Treachery of Images' 115; *see also* Magritte effect
tuntun (wild-silk wrappers) 94, 96, 98
Turner, F. J. 110
typhoon Morakot 194–195

University of Ibadan 108

Vaishnavism 152
value 13–17, 18
varnashram dharma 153
Veblen, T. 61
verbalised knowledge 13, 99, 101, 152, *vs.* procedural knowledge 15–16
vocational knowledge: Swiss watchmakers case studies 170–180

wage claims 42
warehouse worker 9
warfare 9, 18; man-with-weapon 8–9

224 Index

Warnier, J. -P. xiii–xiv, xviii, 3, 7, 8, 11, 13, 18, 20–21, 43n1, 44n3, 49, 57, 132n1, 188, 200, 206
waste archaeology program 47–49
waste workers: acting on refuse matter 51; field studies 49–51
watchmakers 169–181, 199
watchmaking 169–182
weaponry 9
weaving rituals 137–148
Weber, F. 53
Weber, M. 118
Wenger, E. 169
wild silk 93; *daoula* of 98–99, 100; material agency of 95; material expressiveness of 101–102; peculiarities of 97; power of action of 95; production and sheen properties 97–99; sheen of 98; wrappers as material identity *94*, 99–102, *100*
women: 14, 20, 107, 142–144, 116, 163; and domestic spaces 102; Kabyle 142; material shaping of 93–102; weaving knowledge 137–138, 142–148
workers: about complex administrative procedures 54–55; *ad interim* 35, 38, 39; technical activities 54
work organisations: 'woolly prescription' in 39–40, 43, 49
workshops: as free zones 51–52; healthcare facilities 51; kitchen 51–54; for spa technicians 52–53; storehouses 54–56; with tools and store of supplies 55–56

zawit (saint shrine) 140